Man and the Sea

Man and the Sea

From the Ice Age to the Norman Conquest

PHILIP BANBURY

Adlard Coles Limited

Granada Publishing Limited
First published in Great Britain 1975 by Adlard Coles Limited
Frogmore St Albans Hertfordshire AL2 2NF and
3 Upper James Street London W1R 4BP

Copyright © Philip Banbury 1975

ISBN 0 229 11506 3

Printed in Great Britain by
William Clowes & Sons, Limited
London, Beccles and Colchester

To my Father, George Banbury.
He would have helped so much
but he died too soon.

Contents

Illustrations

Acknowledgements

My thanks are due to all who have answered my queries, sent me information, or shown me the material under their care:

Mr Tucker, editor of the *Model Shipwright*; Mrs Tucker who introduced me to the Caister Intaglio, and Mr Martin Henig who discussed it with me. Miss Angela Evans of the British Museum; Dr Arne Emil Christensen jr, of the Viking Ship Museum, Oslo; Dr Ole Crumlin-Pedersen of the Viking Ship Museum, Roskilde; Dr Philipsen of the Central Museum, Utrecht; Dr Helmut Geiblinger of the Schleswig Holstein Museum; Mr Edward Wright who excavated the Ferriby boats; Mr Sean McGrail of the National Maritime Museum; Mr Robin Piercy of the Ship Excavation, Kyrenia, Cyprus; and Mr Wilson Duff of the Provincial Museum, British Columbia.

Mr John Andrew, ship-model maker and student of the Gaelic, for material on Celtic shipping; Mr Donovan Brown for the photograph of the Volga, and Mr Stewart Fairlie for the equally magnificent one of the Tarbert Isthmus; Mr Frank Steer for reading the chapter on navigation; Mr R G Bowden for the maps and Mr Trevor Sharot who tracked down the Aberdeen kayak. And the staffs of the National Maritime Museum, the Science Museum, the City of Hull Museum, the City of Norwich Museum, the London Museum, the Geological Museum and the Royal Air Force Museum.

Finally, my thanks are due to my wife who typed the manuscript and accompanied me to seven countries in search of material; to Miss Phoebe Mason of Adlard Coles Ltd; and to my son who sailed the seas from 'Gottland to the Cape of Finisterre' while the book was being written.

The responsibility for the opinions expressed and all the mistakes is my own.

Ruislip 1974

Preface

If he were completely honest the writer of a book about this period would qualify every statement with 'probably' or 'possibly' for there can be no certainty about anything that happened in those early centuries.

The evidence for a trade route may be no more than a few score beads scattered across Europe; all that is left of a ship a few nail stains in the sand. Greek and Roman writers rarely took a detached view of their subjects and hardly ever quoted sources. When they wrote about wars or trade it was without the help of maps or charts. The Venerable Bede claimed miracles without testing the evidence and the Anglo Saxon Chronicle has many conflicting texts. Large numbers often confused the early chroniclers who in turn have confused us. I have tried to be honest without introducing so much doubt as to make the book unreadable.

For later centuries the chief qualification needed for writing about ships is a knowledge of ships, but for this early period so much else is needed that the job could only be properly tackled by a team which would include a small-boat seaman, naval architect, ship archaeologist, geologist, graduate in half a dozen ancient languages, botanist, demographer, historian, metallurgist, astronomer, navigator and several others. I wish I could say I was qualified in all these subjects. As well as trying to learn from more academic sources, I have worked in the tradition of earlier enthusiasts who went round the creeks and harbours with sketchbooks and measuring tapes, recording surviving smacks, punts, galleys and barges. And I have sat at the feet of men who learned the ancient boat-building skills and plied the ancient longshore trade.

I have watched the tide drain away in the little creeks and waited for it to creep up over the mud. I have waited for a wind while the ebb swept me back the way I had come. I have rowed long and hard, and been afloat in too much wind and sea. A few of the things that happened to Stone Age men have happened to me.

All miles quoted are nautical miles; boat and ship dimensions are in feet and (metres) and pounds and (kilograms). Tons are always Imperial tons of 2240 lbs—the US ton, metric tonne and Imperial ton are so close that the reader can read my figures in his own units.

I Background

All that has been imagined from of old
Is, but more glorious a thousand fold

JOHN MASEFIELD
The Wanderer

With every year the past gets more remote, not only by the passage of twelve months but by the passing of techniques that have endured for thousands of years. Thirty years ago every dinghy was made of the same materials as a Viking ship, joined in the same way; craftsmen of either era could have taken each other's jobs. Today we build boats with a bucket of resin and a brush.

This book is about the seafarers and the boats of northern Europe from the melting of the ice to the end of the Viking era, a span eight times as long as the span of all the seafaring since. Once those sailors left the shore they were alone until they reached the further land. A century ago a polar explorer was just as alone. Today he can speak to his wife every day and if he falls ill some aeroplane will find him and bring him back to safety.

All that remains of pre-Iron Age voyaging, apart from thousands of rock drawings, are a few tools that look almost useless to the passing glance. But by piecing together the remains of such cultures, ancient and existing or recently existing, European, Middle Eastern, Amerindian, circumpolar, Pacific, we get a composite picture of incredible richness, and providing we are careful we can give life to the blunt stones and dry bones in the museums.

Five or six thousand years before the northern seas existed in their modern form man drew and painted animals with almost Renaissance skill deep in the caves of southwest Europe. In Siberia he was wearing Eskimo-type tailored skin clothes and using the harpoon; elsewhere he used the bow.

Before the 4th millennium BC European man was using skis and by the 2nd he loaded his goods onto solid wheel carts and ploughed with a traction plough. Less than a thousand years later he was building spoked wheels, and by the 5th century BC they were as elegant and well engineered as those on the curricle of a Regency whip. Around 100 BC in Denmark a cart was made with roller bearing wheels. Before 2000 BC northern man was making pottery, practising agriculture and using axes and adzes with ground cutting edges. In the 2nd millennium he was fishing in 90 fathoms off the coasts of Norway.

Before the end of the 2nd millennium Danish bronzesmiths could cast the trumpets called lurs, masterpieces of lost-wax casting, 6 ft long made up of three sections with very thin walls. These trumpets were used aboard boats which one might otherwise think were made by primitive people. Central European smiths could fashion elaborate body armour. During this period the Beaker people, originally from Spain, were building in Britain hundreds of star-orientated stone circles, accurately laid out on consistent geometric principles.

The earliest dugout canoe so far found has been dated at 6000 BC, and before 1300 BC there were plank-built boats in northern Europe. Heavy planks sawn out with a two-handed saw were built into graves in south Germany in the 6th century BC. Two-handed bronze saws were used in Crete in 1400 BC. The lathe was in use in northern Europe in the 2nd or 3rd century BC. Sizeable sailing ships with iron anchors and chains date from at least the beginning of the 1st century BC.

Much has been written about the 'myth of the noble savage'. There was something noble in men and women paddling across the open sea in a skin-covered wicker boat with their children and animals 5000 years ago. We can smell that boat now; rancid fat that kept it watertight, human sweat, animal dung and babies' urine. In it we should have found not only axes and bows but children's toys.

Any sensitive modern man will feel shrunken and cowardly as he examines the magnificent exhibition of Stone Age Eskimo culture in the National Museum at Copenhagen.

We have tended to regard everyone who crossed the sea in prehistoric times as an invader, to see every axe found as a battle-axe. Most of the people were migrants: family groups who stepped ashore in almost empty lands no better armed than the inhabitants. They introduced domestic animals and better methods of forest clearance and agriculture.

Wheat and barley were brought across Europe from the homeland of wild wheat and barley in Asia Minor. Sheep and goats came from the same source. Wild pigs were not native in Britain. All these animals were carried to the offshore islands of Europe by boat. Wild cattle roamed everywhere except in Ireland, to which the first domesticated animals had to be shipped.

As the population increased and more advanced peoples from the south or east pressed on the original inhabitants of Europe, the toughest of them moved to the coast, learned to build boats, and paddled across to any land they could see. Looking out from Dover Castle or Cap Gris Nez we may marvel that any family would have been bold enough to do it. But the frailest boats have crossed. In 1911 the Reverend S Swann crossed in a single sculling skiff in 3 hours 50 minutes and one of his sculls is preserved in the Marlipins Museum in Shoreham, Sussex. A university boat-race crew once took an 'eight' across, and a folding canoe went to Dunkirk in 1940. There is an Eskimo kayak in the University of Aberdeen Anthropological Museum which quite possibly arrived there from Greenland or Denmark at the beginning of the 18th century, blown by a northerly or easterly wind; its occupant was still alive (Plate 1). Other kayaks seem to have been blown to the Orkneys and Shetlands. In the heyday of smuggling a couple of longshoremen would row a skiff halfway across the English Channel to pick up contraband.

1 Kayak found off Aberdeen ca AD 1700—the Eskimo in it was still alive. (Courtesy University of Aberdeen)

In due course the sources of Europe's wealth were discovered and trade began. The earliest cargo to cross the sea is thought to have been a load of obsidian carried from Greece to Milos in the 7th or 8th millenium BC. It is not easy to be sure exactly where the prehistoric sources of metals were. The requirements were infinitesimal by modern standards, and tiny deposits now forgotten may have had enormous importance in their day. On the other hand the early peoples, even the Romans, needed rich ores and many deposits would have been impossible for them to work.

The earliest source of all was little pellets of pure metal lying on the surface of the ground.

Small amounts of copper ore occur fairly widely in Europe with the principal ancient mining areas in Spain, Cyprus and Bohemia. Copper by itself is of comparatively little use, though when cast or beaten into thin blades, easily sharpened, it has some advantages over stone. But when alloyed with a small proportion of tin it became the material which finally ousted stone for nearly all purposes.

Tin is very rare, and the Carthaginians imported and traded tin from Spain and Brittany until they heard of the rich Cornish deposits around 600 BC. At about this date they occupied Gades near modern Cadiz and from there traded along the shores of Spain and France probably as far as Brittany. There is no evidence that they ever came to Britain. Cornish tin was also needed wherever bronze was used in the north. It must have been carried via Brittany to the Low Countries, Wales, Ireland and Scotland, and up to Orkney and Shetland, where there was a bronzesmith's foundry by the broch of Clickimin.

Scandinavia was without copper or tin and relied entirely on imports, either from Spain, Brittany, Cornwall and Ireland or from the rich deposits in Bohemia to the south. They probably came from all of them.

Gold was found in Wales, Ireland and east-central Europe, but north Europe obtained most of its gold from Ireland. It quickly became used as currency, even before the introduction of coins, in the form of ingots, torcs and armbands.

Scandinavia paid for its gold, copper and tin with amber, furs and walrus ivory, which flowed back along the trade routes. Amber is found chiefly in Scandinavia and the Jutland peninsula and quickly became prized for its rich colour, its mysterious magnetic qualities, and the curiosity of the insects sometimes found embedded in it. Amber beads have been found in Denmark by the thousand and were a major export to the Mediterranean.

Iron, on the other hand, is found almost everywhere in Europe but was by far the most difficult metal to smelt and work known in early times. Casting was unknown and objects like anchors and fire baskets, using bars up to 5 ft long and 2 in. square, were hammered out of solid billets. Because it was so plentiful there was less need to move the raw iron from country to country. But it was much cheaper than bronze and became used in enormous quantities for utility things, cart tyres, fire irons, boat nails, cooking pots. Quantities of these must have travelled along the trade routes.

The first great period of overseas trade in base metals was there-

fore the Bronze Age, with Spain, Brittany, Cornwall and east-central
Europe as the sources of the small quantities of tin needed for
alloying with the less rare copper. A few sacks full of ingots in each
boat and worth a fortune.

For this purpose no doubt there grew up at favourable points
around the coasts professional sailors, merchant seamen crossing
and re-crossing the narrows with passengers and cargo or taking
them up and down the coast. Others making their living from the
sea would be fishermen using net, long line and lobster pot; there
is a rock carving of people fishing off Sweden in perhaps 2000 BC.
For preserving the fish they would have needed salt; some they
would have made in saltpans near the beaches but they would
also have imported it from deposits like those in Germany and
Austria.

During the Bronze Age man lost his innocence. As his techniques
improved food surpluses were accumulated, wealth created, and
rank established from slaves to princes. Leadership of these larger
and more complex social groups passed into the hands of families
with the necessary ambition and strength of character. They also
had weakness of character, greed, inferiority complexes, vanity
and treachery, which led to raiding on land and piracy at sea. The
High Barbarian Age had begun, led by a warrior aristocracy who
demanded fine weapons and ornaments (about 1500 BC a chieftain
was buried on Salisbury Plain with a sceptre inlaid with bone decorated in the style of Mycenae).

As the northern world moved towards the Iron Age the Mediterranean peoples had got far beyond the stage of tribal squabbles
and were organised into large empires. Their demand for raw
materials was large and increasing and their desire for domination
expanding. Spain produced copper and tin, England tin, Ireland gold,
Scandinavia amber and furs. Southern merchants moved by the
great rivers Rhone, Loire, Garonne, Seine, Moselle and Rhine and
took passage across or along the English Channel by the native
merchant ships. For the first time we find written records.

Perhaps we are wrong to call it civilisation; much of it was ugly,
mean and treacherous. But some men created great architecture
and built palaces with planned sanitation, others studied science
and mathematics and dreamed of universal law. When the standard
bearer of the 10th Legion leapt into the undertow on the beach at
Deal he held high the crest—SPQR: Senatus Populusque Romanus—
and perhaps he thought he was bringing democracy. But at least
the Pax Romana had reached the northern seas and soon cargo
ships moved in relative safety for 400 years. They were large efficient
sailing ships, descendants of those already in the north when

Caesar reached the Channel coast in 56 BC. During the Roman occupation of Gaul and Britain, galleys, transports and storeships sailed regularly from strategically placed dockyards, and interlopers from the north German coast found their way blocked by ships, coastal forts and signal stations.

About AD 407 the Romans left Britain and the Saxons, the Picts and the Irish came in. Why or even how the Saxons came we cannot say for certain. The bolder and more aggressive spirits crossed the sea in a slow trickle, a few boatloads a week every summer during a couple of centuries. Apparently they came in rowing ships in spite of the fact that sail had been known in the north for centuries. Hengist and Horsa and their like, probably mercenaries and raiders of long standing, may well have had sailing ships but the average boatload consisted of farmers and their wives and children. They were the best farmers Britain had yet seen.

These were the Dark Ages—though ill-recorded, or difficult, might be better adjectives. But the light was shining brightly in Ireland from the 6th century AD onwards and the gleams shone out across the seas. Ireland became the home of a Christianity in which the romanticism of the Celt blended strangely with the desire to commune with God in utter isolation. Why anyone should have desired such absolute loneliness when he had only to walk ten miles to be away from every living soul is just another mystery of the human mind. But the great Irish saints, rowing and sailing, sometimes in hide boats and sometimes in wooden, reached the western isles of Scotland, Orkney and Shetland, Norway, the Faroes, Iceland and possibly Greenland. The papae and the vestmaen left their names on the charts of the northern seas.

In the 9th century AD the Viking volcano erupted. Hordes of young men with romantic ideas about fighting, daring sailors in magnificent sailing ships, descended on western Europe from Jutland to Gibraltar, and Scapa Flow became the crossroads of the northern world. Like most pirates they could soon cry off if the opposition was too strong. They seemed to accept baptism as a bargaining point in treaty negotiations and some Vikings received it twenty times and lapsed between. They were Christian longer than they were pagan. Buried with them in their ships were the steelyard of the merchant as well as the sword of the soldier. Latterly, the Viking states became imperial powers sending fleets of 300 ships across the sea, and the unfortunate nation that received them was concerned not with a trickle of immigrants but 7000 or 8000 professional fighting men.

Even allowing for a more equable climate than our own, their achievements were astounding. They settled in Iceland where they founded a long-lasting Christian democratic state with a great literary culture. They pushed the boundaries of the known world to a new limit when they discovered America. They were not hardy primitives but the heirs of 7000 years of sea voyaging.

On the whole the climate was more favourable to voyaging in open boats than it is now. After about 8000 BC the weather got steadily warmer, large trees spread over much of the land and the last glaciers melted away. Between 6000 and 3000 BC the summer average temperature in mid-Britain was probably 65°F and the winter temperature was in the lower 40s.

From 3000 to 500 BC the summers were warmer than now and less windy. This was the age of the Neolithic and Bronze Age migrations and trade; the age when the presence of Irish gold ornaments in Scandinavia indicates considerable voyaging across the North Sea. Professor Manley suggests that during this period the Azores anticyclone was considerably north of its present position and extended far to the northeast. He deduces quiet dry weather with light variable winds lasting until 1500–1300 BC, weather roughly corresponding to that of August 1947, when day followed day of perfect weather.

It seems possible that the Icelandic depression was both further north and less deep due to the smaller amount of ice in Arctic seas. Evidence suggests that trees then grew both further north and at greater elevations than now. From ca 1000 BC onwards it seems that a slow deterioration set in, though there may have been another dry and quiet period corresponding roughly to the later Saxon migrations. In Viking times we read again of trees growing in Scotland where the ground has been bare in more recent times. There were vineyards in England before the Norman Conquest, after which the weather seems to have become wetter and stormier again. In the 13th or 14th centuries AD the Norse settlements in Greenland were abandoned. Recent research in America and New Zealand suggests that the worsening weather not only halted expansion by the Scandinavians but also the peoples of the Pacific.

But let no man think that 'Bronze Age weather' made voyaging easy: it merely made it possible on a scale otherwise out of the question for the vessels of the time. The Neolithic and Bronze Age captains can be placed confidently alongside Leif Eiriksson and Columbus, Anson, Cook and Parry. They showed them all the way.

2 Early Migrations

All the rivers run into the sea
yet the sea is not full

Ecclesiastes 1–7

As the ice retreated in the 10th millennium BC the peoples of Europe travelled far and wide reaching northern Britain, Scandinavia and Siberia. It was once thought they became the ancestors of the Eskimo people, but scholars now agree that Eskimo culture never came west of eastern Siberia. Finds suggest that Proto-Mongoloid people from there crossed the land bridge into southwestern Alaska in 30–20,000 BC, moving south, to people the whole continent while the Bering Sea flooded behind them. During the last cold spell of 11–8000 BC others crossed over, and as the sea rose to its present level in warmer weather, moved right across Arctic Canada reaching northern Greenland at least 3000 years ago. These were the ancestors of the Eskimos.

The typical Eskimo inventions have been widely found or inferred. Umiak* and kayak were probably used in eastern Siberia, Alaska and the Bering Sea from the 6th millennium BC onwards. The boats have not survived but quantities of whalebone too large to have come from occasional strandings are present on the settlement sites, suggesting whale hunting from boats. Harpoon heads of the special type used by modern Eskimos for throwing from the kayak have also been found together with remains of subterranean winter houses, snow goggles and the large sledges used for carrying umiaks across the ice just as 19th century Arctic explorers moved their boats.

To reach the earliest settlements known in Greenland the migrants moved from island to island in the Canadian Arctic. The weather was a little warmer than today and possibly the sea level a little higher. The longest sea crossings were about 50 miles. There were umiak/kayak-using Eskimos in northern Greenland at least from the 1st millennium BC. This is the Thule culture which is named after the settlement where the United States Arctic airbase now stands.

* The umiak is a large skin-covered boat with a driftwood frame. The most shapely examples are built by the Koryak Eskimos of Siberia.

In 1949 an almost complete umiak was found in north Greenland and C_{14}-dated to the 15th century AD. It is now in the National Museum at Copenhagen. After this Eskimos travelled down the whole east coast of Greenland, but by AD 1800 they had passed their peak and the settlements became isolated. From the 10th century AD they also moved down the west coast until they met the Norse settlers. But at this date the Eskimos were still expanding and the sagas show that the people the settlers met in western Greenland were virile and aggressive, and as the struggle continued in worsening weather it was the Europeans that gave up.

Pre-Neolithic Europe was so sparsely inhabited as to be almost empty. The finest soil in the world was hidden by dense forest or impassable swamp. The great rivers followed much the same courses as they do now, but where today a child can safely navigate them in a canoe they were raging torrents or hundreds of square miles of marsh-fringed water. To go up them meant weeks of back-breaking labour for boatmen as skilled as those who haul their sampans up the gorges of the Yangtze. To descend called for an opposite skill and daring. Across the great plains the boatman needed an instinct for choosing the right channel akin to that of an ice pilot indicating a lead from the crow's-nest of a whaler.

The Neolithic revolution is now linked more with the domestication of animals and the beginning of agriculture than the transition to polished and ground stone tools. And only in Asia Minor were there originally the wild ancestors of sheep, goats, wheat and barley. There the skills were learned which spread all over Europe. Wild pigs were native everywhere south of Denmark and the Channel shore, and wild cattle roamed everywhere except in Ireland and Scandinavia, but they were not domesticated until man discovered how to do it in the Middle East (Map 1). Stock rearing and corn growing were practised in Mesopotamia in the 9th millenium BC, in Eastern Europe in the 6th, northern Europe in the 5th, and reached Britain in the middle of the 4th millennium and Ireland about 3000 BC. A thousand years or more later there were Neolithic people in Orkney and Shetland.

In 3000 years men and women carried the revolution throughout Europe by an itinerary and a timetable so complicated that we can only guess at the details. Some moved along the shores of the Mediterranean. Some trekked inland over the high passes to the north. Others moved wherever possible by river. It was perhaps the greatest pioneering movement of man's whole existence and not one single film company has ever had the imagination to attempt to re-create it!

Families would have moved on generation by generation as the

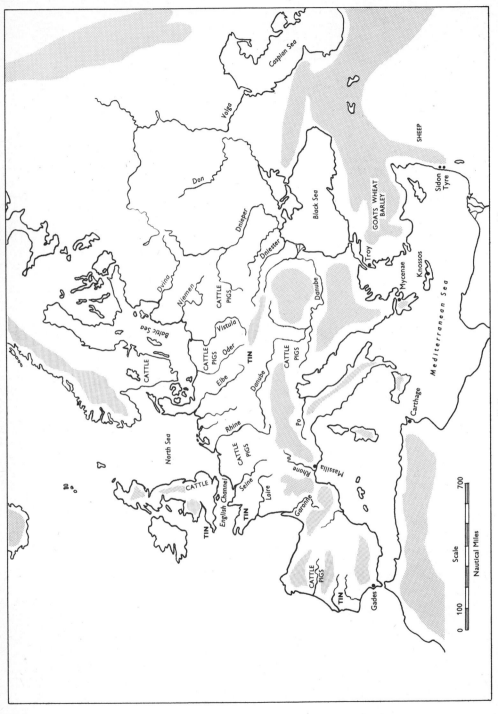

1 *Rivers of Europe*

usable land filled up, like the spread of the pioneers across the American west. Every acre of forest had to be cleared by immense labour, the ground broken with crude tools, the sheep protected from wolves. The early cattle fed on elm leaves, and elms grow to immense size and can be carved into large canoes. Once a holding had been established the group would have stayed there until the soil was exhausted or until a son quarrelled with a father and decided to move on to found his own colony.

Wherever they went the Neolithic people changed the face of the land: Europe was never the same again; not only were animals and plants domesticated, so was nature itself. And behind the moving fringe of pioneers were always more settled people with a slightly higher technique, in contact ultimately with those using first copper and then bronze, and plank-built ships.

The taming of the rivers only began in the 18th century AD, but today there is hardly a natural river left in Europe. To the southern Englishman some faint idea of the ancient rivers can be obtained by looking over Amberley Wild Brooks in winter when the gentle Sussex Arun becomes a waste of water spread over ten square miles, or at the upper Thames in 5 knot spate in February when all the locks are open and flood water flows free. In Europe then there was neither lock, weir, dredged channel nor flood wall: surplus water spread out over the countryside or foamed down in cataracts. Drought dried up the flow and there was no alternative supply.

The Dnieper–Pripet–Niemen route from the Black Sea to the Baltic looks easy enough on a small scale map, but there are 35 miles of rapids on the lower reaches of the Niemen, and the Pripet marshes are famous in history as a maze of lakes and swamp. This route and the routes by the Dvina carried the Neolithic peoples to the eastern shores of the Baltic and later became Viking highways carrying amber or furs to Constantinople. The unfortunate people who had settled by them earlier became the chief source of slaves for the European and Western worlds.

The Dniester–Vistula and Dniester–Oder routes may also have carried early agriculture and stock rearing to Scandinavia.

Finds of pottery and a type of Mediterranean seashell used for ornament suggest that the Danube, Elbe and Rhine were the principal routes across Europe though the Oder and the Vistula were also used.

The Danube, in spite of colossal engineering, is still not wholly tamed and was then so difficult that the early peoples may not have been able to ascend it the whole way. In the delta it used to cut a new channel with each year's floods, and at the Iron Gates it has scoured a channel 26 fathoms deep—deeper than the Strait of Dover. At the Little Iron Gates it narrows to 250 yards with a fierce current. In Hungary it was a wild shallow torrent 3 miles wide in the wet season, and a mass of small channels when low. Through Austria there were rapids, reefs and whirlpools. Flood water created shingle banks and deposited silt to confuse the navigator. Its tributary the Drina, in Yugoslavia, has a fierce current, rapids and waterfalls.

Once over the watersheds of the great mountain masses the Neolithic peoples could move more freely. The rivers could still be dangerous but they were moving in the right direction. The Elbe in its higher reaches was often shallow and difficult in the dry seasons, and although it moved at a leisurely pace over the great low-lying plain of north Germany it was liable to change its course and spread far and wide.

The upper Rhine has an 8 knot current and is now bypassed by an enormous canal with locks every few miles. Until the coming of the fast paddle steamer this part of the river was of little commercial use, and down past the Lorelei the current still surges around the rocks in the narrows. Nearer the sea the river is now prevented by flood walls from over-running the countryside but carries a strong current the whole way. Its final course has changed since ancient times.

Those early farmers who crossed France by river also had immense difficulties. The Rhone is now nearly tamed by twenty locks so deep that their walls soar up like office blocks in a city street. Yet there are still stretches where vicious waves swirl round the 1000-ton motor barges. But it takes a lot to deter a good boatman and modern canoeists have 'done' the Rhone since the days of Rob Roy MacGregor.

The Seine, which brought the Neolithic peoples to their first view of the Channel, introduced them to powerful tides and the tidal bore, the Mascaret, which reaches 13 knots at Caudebec. Rouen, one of the most ancient city-ports of Europe, is 57 miles from the sea and the tide today flows on up another 22 miles. Above this there are now locks, indicating that the river once flowed fast and shallow here. The lower reaches used to flood. The Seine was the highway for Viking fleets to Rouen and Paris, and it requires a considerable effort to picture a hundred or more longships rowing deep into hostile country, only protected from arrows by the wide belt of marsh on either bank.

The Loire is now either too shallow to be of much use or so full that it spreads far outside its banks. However, Neolithic craft were small and this river undoubtedly helped to spread farming, pottery and weaving. But the early peoples had to be just as skilled boatmen on the Loire as on the other rivers for there were long stretches of rapids for many miles below Nevers.

The Garonne flows almost across Europe at its narrowest point, where the Atlantic and the Mediterranean were joined before man appeared. In spite of the strong currents of its lower reaches, which may sweep uprooted trees along at 5 knots, the Garonne soon became one of the greatest of the trade routes, presently connecting the towns of Bordeaux, Toulouse and Narbonne.

The maritime enterprise of northern Europe—Saxon, Frisian, Scandinavian, Gallic—undoubtedly drew on the great reservoir of experience and tradition that existed within the Continent. The farmers who looked out across the northern seas for the first time were often expert boatmen, able to paddle for hours and at home in rough water. In Neolithic times the boats were probably dugout canoes, the almost universal primitive boat where big timber is available. They can be very useful craft, and even today explorers and those in charge of nature reservations on the upper Amazon and its tributaries rarely go to the expense of buying modern boats. They traverse the dangerous rivers in native dugouts driven by outboard motors.

For river use even a tree 2 ft in diameter will provide a useful boat 20 ft long, and if the crew sit low the stability is good. When the wall thickness is pared down to under 1 in., as is done by many native users, the canoe will carry five or six people comfortably. The young man who had quarrelled with his father and decided to move on could have moved himself and his wife, children, dog and a breeding pair of sheep or goats in such a craft. But much larger dugouts than these have been recovered and are described in Chapter 5.

Plate 2 shows a modern boat shooting a rapid in Finland, a country we think of as dead flat. Although crudely built of planks she is probably not unlike a Neolithic migration boat and one could have found scenes like this all over Europe, though not often for the population was too small.

The Neolithic peoples took their techniques right across Europe, diffusing them everywhere from Asia Minor to the Atlantic and the Baltic. It was a one-way traffic. With the metalworking peoples it was different. The first ores to be exploited, copper and tin, were in the region of the Caucasus, and metalworking like agriculture and stock rearing began in Anatolia and Mesopotamia. But the peoples who moved across Europe with knowledge of the new materials found rich new sources of ore in Iberia and Bohemia, and henceforward there were not only emigrants to the west and north but trade back to the point of origin.

South-eastern Spain and the land round the mouth of the river Tagus in Portugal were occupied in the 5th millennium BC by agriculturalists who had almost certainly come by sea. Later immigrants, about 3000 BC, were probably responsible for the spread of chambered tombs made of enormous blocks of stone. The men who left these near-indestructible stones to record their passage are usually regarded as a maritime people because their structures seem to follow the line of the coasts. In fact they cover a broad coastal belt in Spain and Portugal and almost the whole of France except the sandy *etang* country near the coast south of the Gironde.

2 *Primitive style boat in Finland. Early migrations must have presented scenes like this. (Crown copyright Science Museum, London)*

There are few in Holland, which was a waste of marsh unable to support a megalith, but there is a broad band of them across the north German plain. They cover the whole of Denmark and there is a narrow coastal belt in south Sweden and along the rivers and around the lakes a little further north. In Britain they lie all along the western seaboard to the Hebrides and are found in the Orkneys and Shetlands. They occur over the whole of Ireland and in the coastal fringe of northern and eastern Scotland. But while not all the tomb builders travelled by boat, it is almost certain that the main movement was by sea, spreading inland by various means.

The cult is thought to have originated in the Near East. Not only did the people who spread it coast along the Mediterranean shore via Italy and Sicily to Iberia, they also voyaged 40 miles or more offshore to Malta, Corsica, Sardinia and the Balearic Islands. In Sardinia there is a Neolithic pillar carved with the relief of a high-prowed 'ship'. In Malta a Neolithic people built more shrines than the inhabitants could have needed and voyages seem to have been made for spiritual rather than practical reasons: Malta possessed nothing they needed and even the ritual axe blades were of Sicilian stone.

As Stuart Piggott wrote, 'the collective chambered tombs of third and second millennium western Europe are . . . monuments to a lost faith, the adoption or propagation of which must have preceded the construction of the monuments themselves.' Dimly we perceive people of impressive stature and powerful religious beliefs, who journeyed round and across western Europe. Men who 5000 years ago crossed the English Channel and the Irish Sea, paddled their canoes round Scotland and up to the northernmost isles of Britain.

They were followed by the Beaker folk. A previous people from the eastern Mediterranean had introduced copper working into the Iberian Peninsula using closed-mould casting. When they vanished, an indigenous race using an inferior copper technique decided to travel far and wide across Europe for reasons we cannot even guess at. In France, the Low Countries, Germany, central Europe, Britain and Ireland they left their hallmark, the bell beaker, a pottery drinking cup like a shapely plant pot, impressed all over with criss-cross ornament.

Great numbers of these beakers have been found near Lisbon and Corunna, in Brittany, the Netherlands and the Rhineland and across Central Europe—whence the makers seem to have moved back via large find areas in the Rhone valley, around Narbonne and in central and southern Spain. Although various styles and datings are established the cups are generally so similar that rapid move-ment seems certain, a few hundred years around 2000 BC. The finds suggest that the Beaker people moved along the Atlantic and Channel shores of Europe by sea. The evidence is not conclusive and the suggestion on some maps that they voyaged direct from northwest Spain to Brittany across several hundred miles of open sea is unlikely. If they travelled by boat it would have been along the shore, putting in to land every night after the day's voyage of about 30 miles. They could of course have walked the whole way, but once they reached the Netherlands there is little doubt that they followed the courses of the great rivers to central Europe. Later still, as mentioned above, they adventured down the Rhone and would have been then quite capable of coasting along the shore back to Spain. Once again we are dealing not with a single great journey but a series of short journeys probably by successive generations.

They had an enormous capacity for large scale and long sustained organisation. In England they built Stonehenge, in the Hebrides Callanish, and in Orkney Stenness, as well as hundreds of other stone circles over western Britain. In Brittany they reared the colossal stone alignments at Carnac. All were creations of a people who searched the heavens and kept track of time in the 2nd millennium BC. While not all their stones are near the sea, the most spectacular arrangements are. As G R Levy says in *The Gate of Horn*, 'On the wind-tormented point of Finistère and about the shores and islands of the Gulf of Morbihan the gigantic circles and alignments betray the energy born of terrible adventures.'

By now the pattern of water travel around and across Europe was set, and succeeding migrants moved not blindly but along known routes, passing merchants hurrying back towards the Mediterranean with the promise of the north.

There was, however, another series of routes that do not at first seem important to this story, the routes of the wagon peoples whose great covered carts rolled out of the south Russian plain in the 3rd millennium BC. These wagons were built of heavy planks and had solid wheels usually formed of three planks joined edge to edge. On their way across Europe the wagons had to cross river after river and the boat people must have seen them at the crossing places: the idea of the plank boat may have thus been born, as is discussed in Chapter 7.

The peoples who inhabited Europe around 2000 BC must have thought that they had mastered all knowledge. They could grow many grains of corn where one had grown before. They had learned to make animals do their bidding. And because of these two skills they could now settle comfortably in villages until the circumstances they had created caused them to multiply too much and forced them to move on to virgin territory or the lands of less skilled tribes.

But man's discoveries had gone even deeper. He had learned to change animals' behaviour by castration and to set up wooden posts or stones to enable him to tell the seasons by the stars. By the use of fire, fanned or blown to great heat, he could change the nature of clay and make the stones we call gold, silver and copper flow and take new shapes.

Man had passed a climacteric; his numbers would continue to grow, life would change from being self-contained and local to being at least partly dependent on long distance trade that sometimes even reached across the sea. Two forms of transport were needed, the wagon and the plank boat. The former he already had, and he was within a few centuries of the latter.

3 Seascape

Never trust any man unless he has gone
round Portland Bill in something under ten tons

HILAIRE BELLOC
The Cruise of the Nona

Eight or nine thousand years ago the only waters dividing Britain from continental Europe were those of the Thames and the Rhine flowing together up the floor of what is now the North Sea, and the waters of the Somme and the Seine flowing westward along the bed of the future English Channel. The climate was sub-Arctic and, providing they could cross the rivers and lakes in their paths, the inhabitants of northern Europe could walk from Ireland to Denmark and from southern England to the Alps.

There was plenty of shallow calm water in which to try out their first boats, but very few men to do it. The population of southern England at the time has been estimated at between 200 and 2000 people: they would not have required many boats.

According to Professor Grahame Clark, the melting of the ice was swift 'like the thawing of the ice on a summer pond'. There followed a seesaw of land and water. The ice water flooded the hollows and the land, freed of the weight of the ice, rose up and further changed the geographical pattern. By about 6000 BC the distribution of land and water had in general reached its present form, though there were many areas of difference that continued down to late medieval times.

We cannot reconstruct the coasts of northern Europe with certainty for any part of the period covered by this book. There is controversy about what happened in historic times and the pre-historic shorelines are less certain still. Map 2 attempts to show the coast as it was in the first millennium AD.

The river Elbe flows into the sea at the base of the Jutland peninsula. It was a trade route stretching to Bohemia where much of the Bronze and Iron Age technology evolved. Another route ran across the base of the peninsula to the port of Hedeby, and from there one route went across the Baltic to Birka near modern Stockholm and another to harbours on the Russian shore.

From north Denmark to Germany and westward to Holland there seems to have been a chain of islands much as there is today, and a small vessel could have rowed or sailed almost to the Strait of Dover in the shelter of islands or sandbanks. Great stretches of sand dried out behind them and crews could have rested while their ships or boats sat on the seabed at low tide. The tides do not run very fiercely in the southern North Sea, but it is doubtful if any crew would have rowed against a foul stream unless it was absolutely essential. The tidal systems of any locality must have been bewildering to strangers, especially if they were only migrating farmers: they would have had to question local men and hope they spoke the truth.

Between the 4th century BC and around AD 400 the land along the north German coast was slowly sinking. Settlements made on level ground at the early date were slowly built up to escape flooding, century by century, with turf, clay and dung until the resultant *terpen* or settlement mounds were 15 ft high. According to some geologists the mainland was continuous out to the northern shores of the present islands, which were divided from the mainland just before the Saxons came to Britain. But Tacitus tells of a Roman fleet lost among these islands in AD 16.

The Low Countries were then more water than land, a maze of islands, swamps and lakes sheltered by the coastal dunes in the north and clustering round the mouths of the Rhine. Fierce currents scoured the channels and mist and fog rolled over the wet landscape. In medieval times ships could sail inland all the way from the mouth of the Zuider Zee to the Scheldt estuary and this was true in the first millennium AD as well, for no serious land reclamation took place before AD 1200. The Roman fleet mentioned above went this way.

The Rhine was another great trade and migration route, and the Morini who built the ships for Caesar's invasions of Britain lived between the rivers Rhine and Somme and overlooked the Strait of Dover.

In the eastern approaches to the Dover Strait there are now lines of sandbanks parallel to either shore. Off Dunkirk they stretch for nearly thirty miles and off Deal for ten. We cannot say just what they were like 2000 years or more ago, but sandbanks similar to those of today almost certainly existed and at certain states of the tide gave shelter to small vessels creeping along the coasts. To the ships of today a sandbank is a menace, but to the frail craft of yesterday it could be a shelter and a haven. In some periods ships could probably sail from the Scheldt to Gris Nez just inland of the present coastline which was then no more than a chain of islands or sandbanks. Maps in the Royal Museum of Art and History in Brussels show that in the 9th/10th centuries AD the coastline

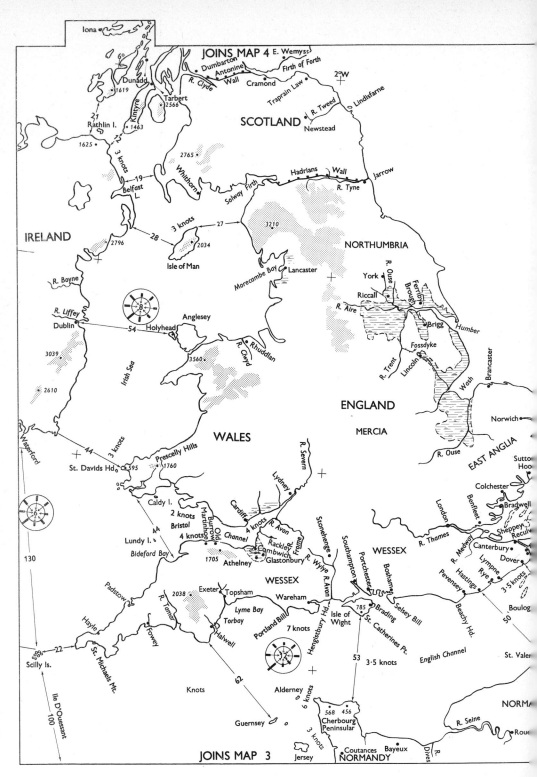

Iona

6°

Dunadd
1619

Kintyre

Tarbert
2566

27
Rathlin I.

1625

12 1463

3 knots

19

Belfast
L

IRELAND

R. Boyne

R. Liffey

Dublin

3039

2610

Irish Sea

E. Wemyss

Dumbarton
Antonine
Wall

R. Clyde

Cramond

Traprain Law

2°W

Firth of Forth

R. Tweed

Lindisfarne

SCOTLAND

Newstead

2765

Whithorn

Solway Firth

Hadrians   Wall   Jarrow

R. Tyne

3210

28

3 knots   27

2796

2034

Isle of Man

Morecambe Bay   Lancaster

NORTHUMBRIA

York   R. Ouse

Riccall

R. Aire

Ferriby
Brough

Brigg   Humber

Fossdyke

R. Trent   Lincoln

Wash

Brancaster

Anglesey

54   Holyhead

R. Chwyd

R. Rhuddlan

3560

WALES

Prescelly Hills

St. Davids Hd   595   1760

44   3 knots

Caldy I.

2 knots

Bristol

Lundy I.   4 knots

Bideford Bay   44

1705

Burrow
Martinhoe   Old
Channel
4 knots
Cardiff

R. Avon

Rackley
Combwich
Athelney   Glastonbury

R. Severn

Lydney

R. Frome

ENGLAND

MERCIA

R. Ouse

Stonehenge

Southampton

WESSEX

Norwich

EAST ANGLIA

Sutton
Hoo

Colchester

Benfleet   Bradwell

London

Sheppey
Recul

R. Thames

Canterbury

R. Medway

Lympne   Dover

Hastings   Rye

3.5 knots

Pevensey   Beachy Hd.

Boulog

50

St. Valer

Padstow

R. Tamar

2038

Exeter   Topsham

Lyme Bay
Torbay

WESSEX

Wareham

R. Wylye R. Avon

Portchester   Bosham

Selsey Bill

Isle of
Wight   785   Brading

St. Catherines Pt.

English Channel

Hayle

St. Michaels Mt.

22

Scilly Is.

Fowey

Halwell

Portland Bill

7 knots

Hengistbury Ph.

53   3.5 knots

130

Waterford

Ile D'Ouessant

100

62

Knots

Guernsey

Alderney

Jersey

3 knots

568   456
Cherbourg
Peninsular

Coutances   Bayeux

NORMANDY

R. Seine

Roue

NORMA

R.
Dives

2 English Channel, North Sea, Irish Sea

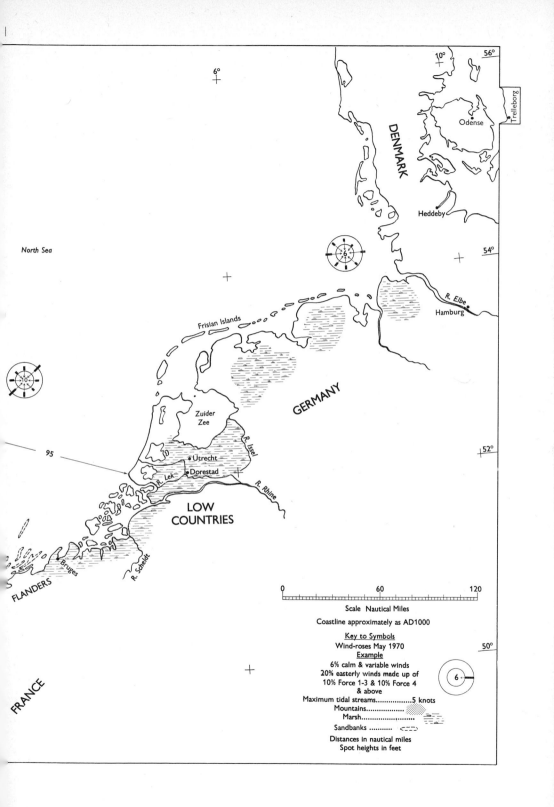

ran almost east–west through Bruges to the Scheldt estuary, while around AD 1200 Bruges was at the southern end of a deep inlet (Map 2). Just how it would have been when Tostig's ships operated from Bruges in 1066 is not certain.

The general depth of the North Sea and the English Channel is 20 to 40 fathoms, but in most of the Dover Strait it is 10 to 30 fathoms causing strong tides in the shortest crossing between Britain and the Continent. The Varne sand and the Ridge between Cap Gris Nez and Folkestone have only 1–2 fathoms over them at mean low water springs today and may have showed above the surface in prehistoric times. Some authorities hold that the tides were stronger still then and that the longer crossing from Cherbourg to the Wight may then have been the safer way, but Map 2 shows that the fiercest tides do not necessarily occur in the most constricted channels.

As we move westwards from Cap Gris Nez towards the Seine and beyond we find that the modern harbours do not represent the ancient scene. This is obviously so at Boulogne which, although the main Roman fleet base and terminus of the crossing to Britain for nearly 400 years, looks a poor harbour if you imagine it without the mile-long moles that now protect it. Quentavic, another great port of entry into Europe in the 9th and 10th centuries AD, was 10 miles south of Boulogne on the little river Canche. This is the modern Etaples, which dries out completely.

The Baie de la Somme, which stretches 7 miles inland and is 3 miles across the mouth, was William the Conqueror's point of embarkation for the invasion of England but nowadays it is all high and dry at low tide. Those ships were largely built or assembled in the little river Dives 15 miles west of the Seine entrance. The modern port is Cabourg and it dries out everywhere to 10 ft above MLWS.

Early ships might end their voyages anywhere over a wide stretch of coast, carried by contrary winds and tides, and an inland settlement was best placed to handle their cargoes. St Omer, Rouen, Canterbury and Winchester are examples.

The coast beyond the Seine is partly sheltered from westerly gales by the Cherbourg peninsula and ships or boats could proceed relatively safely to the second shortest crossing to Britain. The hills behind Cherbourg rise to 568 ft and St Catherine's Point on the southern tip of the Isle of Wight is 785 ft. Not only was this a relatively short crossing of 53 miles, it was almost possible to have the land or at least the 'loom of the land' in sight for the whole way. The remains of the medieval lighthouse at Niton close to St Catherine's Down emphasise the importance of this route.

The sea area bounded on the east by the Cherbourg peninsula, on the south by the French coast, and extending to the west beyond Guernsey, was one of the most dangerous sailed by the ancient inhabitants of Europe. There are at least twenty islands and innumerable dangerous rocks and reefs. In the 7-mile strait between Alderney and the mainland the tide runs at a maximum of 9 knots and the chart is marked 'heavy overfalls' and 'occasionally breaks'. The tidal range is enormous. It was about places like these that the legends of ship-swallowing whirlpools were invented. Almost all vessels voyaging between the Garonne or the Loire, either right up the Channel or across to Britain, must have passed through these dangerous seas or else gone many miles to seaward as the medieval sailing directions instructed them to do.

Westwards and southwards round the Breton peninsula for 300 miles the coast is heavily indented and there are numerous islands with fierce tides (Map 3). Here in the full path of southwest winds lived the Veneti whose fine sailing ships caused the Romans so much trouble in 56 BC. They carried the cargoes that travelled across Europe via the Loire, which formed the southern limit of their territory, and the Garonne. As Caesar wrote, 'The Veneti are much the most powerful tribe on this coast. They have the largest fleet of ships, in which they traffic with Britain; they excel the other tribes in knowledge and experience of navigation.'

Southwards the shore continues past the great islands of Noirmoutier, Yeu, Ré and Oleron to the river Garonne, the western end of the shortest land route to the Mediterranean. This west coast of France was of more than ordinary difficulty for the early peoples who moved by paddle, oar and simple square sail on a keel-less hull. The tidal streams do not run true along the coast for six hours from low to high water: they may run north for two hours, onshore for three hours, and south for one. Between the islands the tides may run at up to 8 knots and exceptional local knowledge is needed.

But sailing ships could have made good use of the pronounced land breeze usual between noon and dusk, and sea breezes between midnight and 8 a.m., if they had been prepared to sail at night on a dangerous coast. Columbus in a ship no more weatherly than those of the Veneti made brilliant use of such winds in the Caribbean on his fourth voyage. From 500 BC onwards there is frequent reference to trade between Britain and Bordeaux. Early ships also went to Lisbon and Cadiz, but there can scarcely have been an important route to the Mediterranean that way. Guarding the Gironde Estuary is now the Cordouan lighthouse, successor to one built by Charlemagne in the 9th century.

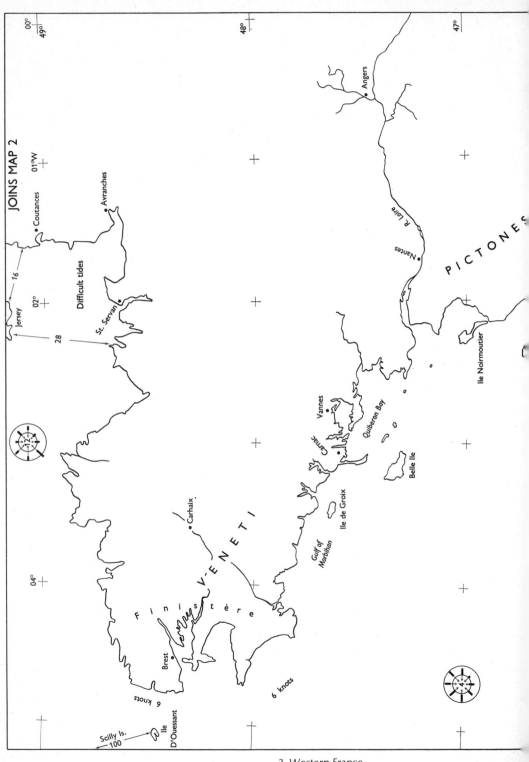

3 Western France

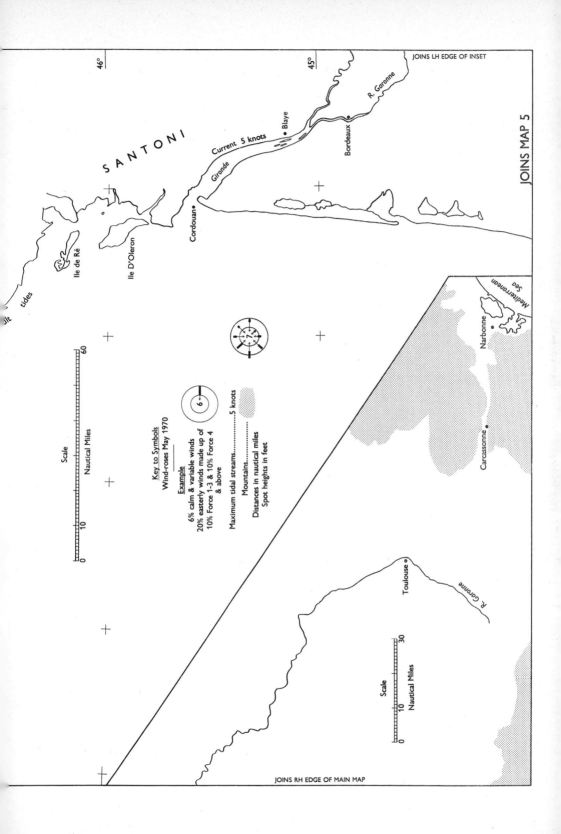

JOINS MAP 5

JOINS LH EDGE OF INSET

46°

45°

SANTONI

Current 5 knots

• Blaye

R. Garonne

Gironde

Bordeaux •

Cordouan •

Ile de Ré

Ile D'Oleron

tides

Mediterranean Sea

Narbonne •

Carcassonne •

Toulouse •

R. Garonne

Scale

60

10

0

Nautical Miles

Scale

30

10

0

Nautical Miles

Key to Symbols
Wind-roses May 1970

Example

6% calm & variable winds
20% easterly winds made up of
10% Force 1-3 & 10% Force 4
& above

Maximum tidal streams..........5 knots
Mountains.........................
Distances in nautical miles
Spot heights in feet

7

6

JOINS RH EDGE OF MAIN MAP

Returning to England, the Channel coast to Lands End from Portland Bill (Map 2) was much the same as today, largely cliff-bound with great natural harbours in the western half on the route to some of the richest tin deposits in Europe. Portland Race runs at up to 7 knots and it seems likely that ships bound for Cornwall from Brittany may have sailed direct to Torbay. The Scilly Isles, 22 miles west of Lands End and rich in megalithic monuments, pose the question whether the Beaker people of ca 2000 BC crossed this way to South Wales, where they are known to have buried their dead in stone tombs.

Behind the shelter of the Wight an important cross-country route wound inland up the Hampshire Avon or from the head of Southampton Water to meet the Bristol Avon and join the sea route to Wales and Ireland, a route known to have existed in the early Bronze Age and even perhaps in Neolithic times.

On the chalk downs between the two rivers the Beaker people and their predecessors built Avebury and Stonehenge, Woodhenge and Silbury Hill and several other constructions, the glories of prehistoric Europe. This trade route became the location of the Wessex culture and presently of the kingdom of Wessex which was to unite all England.

What has happened on the Isle of Wight and the mainland opposite underlines what has been going on round the coasts of Europe for centuries. Until just over a hundred years ago Bembridge was the entrance to a great harbour extending two miles inland to Brading, where an important Roman, perhaps the governor, had his villa and where a Roman boathook is on show today. The little river may even have trickled through to Sandown, making an island of the eastern part of the Wight. Saint Wilfred landed at Brading; Alfred the Great's ships fought the Vikings in Brading Haven. Vespasian's landing craft may have beached here and Harold's fleet waited for William the Conqueror.

Newtown Harbour, west of Cowes, now a bird sanctuary, was once a thriving harbour and even more astonishing so was Lepe, at the entrance to the Beaulieu River opposite. Yarmouth harbour, before the bridge was built, used to enable ships to sail two miles inland at high tide. Lymington River, before it was blocked off by the causeway, was navigable up to Brockenhurst and the current flushed the mud out of Lymington harbour leaving deep-water quays. The remains of Henry V's *Grace Dieu* of 1000 tons lie *above* the bridge at Bursledon showing that the road shut off once navigable reaches of the Hamble River.

Most of Portsmouth Dockyard is built on reclaimed land and in Chichester Harbour Roman ships used to sail up to Fishbourne and Harold sailed from Bosham. The southern tip of Selsey Bill has eroded away and Pagham Harbour is now much smaller than it was, for a channel used to curl round the north of the present village of Selsey reaching the sea again at Medmerry and making Selsey an island, as its name indicates.

Eastwards, the great natural harbour at Pevensey where William the Conqueror landed has been reclaimed. At Rye only a narrow river now joins the ancient town to the sea two miles away. Once there was a great forked creek here that stretched up to the walls of Rye and Winchelsea and their predecessors. Romney Marsh did not exist in the period of this book, and the sea lapped the walls of the Roman fort at Lympne.

Inside the walls of Dover Castle, 260 ft above the sea, the stump of a Roman lighthouse is built into the tower of the church. There was another on the cliffs a mile to the west and the Roman harbour lay between them where the town now stands. A third Roman lighthouse stood at Boulogne and a drawing from 1544 shows it twelve storeys high. Accurate charts were beyond even Roman techniques, but lighthouses (leading lights would be a better term) existed more widely than the scant remains suggest. That from the 13th century AD near St Catherines Point and the Carolingian one off the Gironde Estuary have already been mentioned and there was probably a Viking beacon at Birka in Sweden. From the 4th century AD there seems to have been a lighthouse at Corunna in northwest Spain. In the Verulamium Museum at St Albans there is a pottery lamp chimney in the form of a six-storey lighthouse which suggests that such structures were known about even in inland towns.

East of Dover the Wantsum channel ran north-northwest from Sandwich to Reculver on the north Kent coast. Bede described it as three furlongs across and fordable in only two places. East of the Wantsum the sea wall now presents a solid barrier, but the discovery of the Graveney boat half a mile inland gives a clear indication of what this flat pastureland was like in the 9th century AD. This safe short-cut is now grazing land and the Isle of Thanet is now part of the mainland. Another short-cut from the Thames to the Medway River ran across where the Isle of Grain oil refinery stands. The present coast of Sussex and Kent bears little relation to the pre-medieval coast, and where it was once rich in great harbours and refuges there are now nearly continuous beaches broken only by a few narrow rivers.

In Roman times the tide in the Thames only reached to London Bridge and many parts of riverside London like Putney, Chelsea, Battersea and Westminster (Thorney) were eyots or islands. At high tide the waters of the estuary lapped the higher ground at Woolwich, Purfleet and Cliffe.

The deep creeks of the Essex coast were havens for the Saxon immigrants. From the Thames Estuary to the Suffolk coast is a maze of sands many of which dry out at low water, treacherous and difficult to penetrate today and much more so for the early inter-lopers without charts, tide tables, buoys and leading lights. But a Bronze Age boat only drew about a foot, a Saxon one three feet, and the largest Roman or Viking ship not more than eight.

The area of the Norfolk Broads was then a many-armed tidal inlet 20 miles from north to south and extending inland for nearly 15 miles from the sea, which entered where Great Yarmouth now stands. The Roman Saxon Shore fortress of Burgh Castle, now inland, then stood on a tidal river and denied the use of this great stretch of sheltered water to the Saxons. Before the Norman Conquest herring were caught near Norwich.

The Fens stretched right up to the Wash and included part of Lincolnshire in an area nearly as large as Norfolk, of lakes, rivers, estuary, marshes and saltings which extended southward as far as Cambridge. Remains of whales and dolphins stranded in pre-historic times have been found in the Fens, which were all but impassable and formed the boundary between Saxon Mercia and East Anglia. Mercia was reached by sea via the Humber; like Burgh Castle, the Roman fort of Brancaster overlooked a great natural harbour and closed it against invasion.

Today the Humber is constrained by embankments; then it flooded over great areas of fenland like the true Fens further south. Five hundred square miles of island-studded water and marsh that could only be penetrated by boat.

The Wash is a meeting point of two tidal systems; to the north the tide runs out in one direction and to the south in the other. Tidal movements are complex and in the days before tide tables they had to be memorized for long stretches of coast. Each succeed-ing voyager discovered more as he slipped along on a favourable tide or sweated against a foul one, ran aground or was thrust far out of his way to spend hours lost upon the open sea. What he learned went into the folk memory of his people. Finally, the Vikings sailed all these seas and many more, drawing on a vast store of hard-gained knowledge.

In the eastern English Channel the tidal streams divide about a line sometimes nearly straight and sometimes bent like a bow; a line that moves in the course of one tide, from between South Foreland and Gris Nez to between Beachy Head and Arromanches west of the Seine. The movement is difficult to follow even on hourly charts. The Romans recruited local Gauls and Germans into their fleets, but although these officers may have known their local tides they were not always loyal. Similar tidal phenomena occur off the north coast of Holland, the Moray Firth, near the Isle of Skye and in the Irish Sea.

A hundred miles out to sea from the Yorkshire coast is the Dogger Bank, 40 miles by 10 with 9 fathoms over it at mean low water springs. In very early times after the melting of the ice the Bank was above water, as shown by the peat which has been dredged up from it. Perhaps it was a precarious haven for some early sailor blown off course.

Northwards from the Humber there have been few startling changes until we reach the Firth of Forth (Map 4) which, even in historical times, extended almost halfway across to Loch Lomond, proved by the remains of a whale stranded twelve miles west of Stirling. And the hard east coast of Scotland is much as it was when Stone Age men standing at John o'Groats looked across the 9 miles of Pentland Firth to Orkney. At the height of the flood tide they could have seen a 9 knot current swirling and cresting in the Firth. If they had come up by way of the Western Isles and been storm-bound on the north Scottish coast they might have seen stones thrown up 100 ft by the waves breaking on Dunnet Head. Such is the Pentland Firth, yet they dared to cross it!

To us the Orkney Mainland looks a treeless waste, but it probably seemed a paradise of sheep pasture with ample room for their tiny crops, and building stone on every hand. There were all the fish they needed in the 20 square miles of Scapa Flow with shellfish on the rocks and beaches. There was peat and seaweed for fuel and heather for bedding, though peat was less widespread in the warmer drier climate before 500 BC.

Bones of sheep and cattle have been found in the Neolithic village of Skara Brae on the Orkney mainland and Beaker pottery at Rinyo on Rousay. Immigrants or traders brought them across the Pentland Firth around 1500 BC.

There are fourteen principal Orkney islands and Atlantic gales drive great seas against the western coasts. Wind speeds reach 120 knots in winter and spray is thrown up to 200 ft and driven across the narrow places into the opposite sea. The normal maximum height of waves in the North Sea and the other sheltered seas round Britain is 10 ft, though a freak vertical-sided wave 40 ft high overwhelmed a lifeboat off northeast Scotland not long ago. Atlantic waves sometimes reach 50 ft.

North Ronaldshay is reached northwards from the Orkney Mainland by several sea crossings of up to 4 miles through

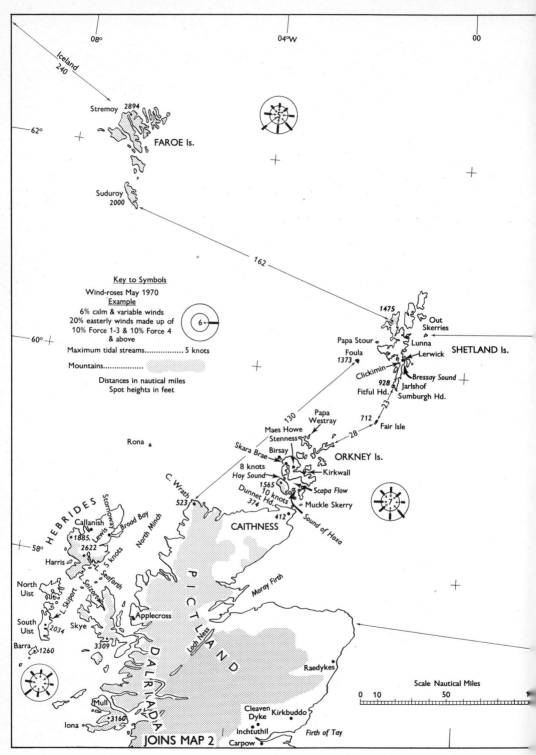

Iceland
240

Stremoy 2894

FAROE Is.

62°

Suduroy
2000

162

1475

Out
Skerries

Papa Stour
Lunna

Foula
1373

Clickimin

Lerwick

SHETLAND Is.

Bressay Sound

928
Fitful Hd.

Jarlshof

Sumburgh Hd.

60°

712
28

Fair Isle

130

Papa
Westray

Maes Howe
Stenness

Rona

Skara Brae

Birsay

ORKNEY Is.

Kirkwall

8 knots
Hoy Sound

Scapa Flow

1565
C. Wrath
523

10 knots
Dunnet Hd.
374

412

Muckle Skerry

Sound of Hoxa

HEBRIDES

Stornoway

CAITHNESS

Callanish

Lewis

Broad Bay

1885

2622

North Minch

Harris

5 knots

Seaforth

PICTLAND

North
Uist

L. Skiport

Snizort

Moray Firth

South
Uist

Applecross

2034

Skye

Barra 1260

3309

Loch Ness

DALRIADA

Raedykes

Mull

Cleaven
Dyke

Kirkbuddo

3160

Iona

Inchtuthil

Firth of Tay

Carpow

JOINS MAP 2

Scale Nautical Miles
0 10   50

4 *Scotland, the Northern Isles and Norway*

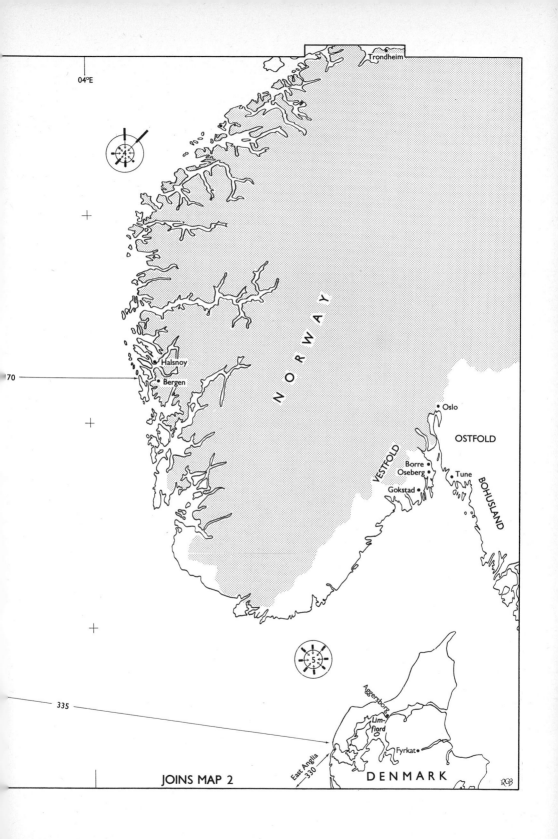

04°E

Trondheim

N O R W A Y

Halsnoy
Bergen

70

Oslo

OSTFOLD

VESTFOLD
Borre
Oseberg
Gokstad
Tune

BOHUSLAND

5

Aggersborg
335

Lim-
fjord

Fyrkat

East Anglia
330

JOINS MAP 2

DENMARK

RGB

dangerous tide races, and from there the voyager can see Fair Isle 20 miles away, its northern slope 712 ft above sea level. Perhaps in the clear northern atmosphere he could even see Fitful Head on Shetland, 928 ft, 50 miles from Ronaldshay.

Even this passage across the full Atlantic swell was dared by Stone and Bronze Age man, and in Orkney and Shetland he left more traces per square mile than now exist anywhere else in Britain. Remains of sheep and oxen of around 1500 BC were found at the earliest settlement at Jarlshof, which lies under Sumburgh Head. Shetland is another archipelago that, like Orkney, covers the area of an English county. The land rises up steeply from the sea to heights of 1000 ft of treeless, peat-covered moorland littered with stone outcrops. Sea lochs penetrate deeply between the hills, safe havens for the mariner if he can reach them. The weather is warmer than might be expected, the winter mean being about the same as London.

For the Stone and Bronze Age peoples Shetland was the Ultima Thule, but four Roman coins of the 3rd century AD discovered in Iceland suggest that somebody preceded the Irish missionaries who settled there before the Vikings. And as far as we know it was not the Romans.

Returning to the south, there is one part of the Bristol Channel which is of special interest; the rest we will leave to chapter 6, which tells of the transport of the bluestones to Stonehenge.

Between the Mendips and the Quantock Hills, between the steamboat pier at Weston-super-Mare and the nuclear power station on Hinkley Point, is the land of ancient legend and ancient fact: of Arthur, Alfred, and Joseph of Arimathea; Avalon, Camelot, Athelney and Glastonbury. We may think it unlikely that Joseph of Arimathea came to convert Britain in AD 63 (we are certainly sceptical that he and his companions sailed across on their cloaks), and King Arthur is far too shadowy a figure to be included, but this is a very ancient part of England's maritime history.

The little rivers Parret, Brue and Axe meandered through 200 square miles of swamp and sea marsh running southwest of the Bristol Channel coast for 15 miles. Near the inland border of this fenland were the villages of Glastonbury and Meare, built either around 50 BC by refugees from Brittany or possibly in 150 BC by colonists from the Devon peninsula. In either case they came by sea and found navigable channels penetrating inland. The former would have come in 50 ft sailing ships and the latter almost certainly in planked boats with sail.

The two villages of about a hundred large huts each were solidly built on piles like little Amsterdams, with causeways leading to breakwaters and landing stages. The standard of carpentry was in keeping with the powerful Breton ships described by Julius Caesar, though the only boat found was a 20 ft dugout canoe probably used for local fishing with net and spear.

Even allowing for the accidents of preservation these villages were important trade centres importing iron, copper, tin and lead and exporting their manufactures, including enamelled work and glass, to Brittany, Wales and Ireland. These are the only examples in Britain of seaports of this date.

Irish missionaries came in the 6th century or earlier, in curraghs or more substantial vessels, and in AD 940 under Saint Dunstan Glastonbury became one of the largest monasteries in England. In between Alfred sought shelter at Athelney, relying on his boatmen's loyalty. Others have been less compelling, and renegade pilots have brought the enemy to the secret rendezvous.

The maritime history of southwestern England has been almost but not quite lost. Rackley on the river Axe 8 miles inland from the Somerset coast was the port for Glastonbury in the mid-12th century and ships traded there from south Wales, Dartmouth and Brittany. Combwich was a small Roman port at the mouth of the Parret, Exeter was a Roman city, and Topsham a Roman port; Halwell on the Dart was a Saxon one. Early travellers often preferred to cross the peninsula rather than go round Lands End. This they did by the valleys of the Exe, or Torridge and Tamar; or from Padstow to Fowey by the Camel and Fowey rivers. Saint Breoca led an Irish party from Hayle to St Michaels Mount, a route where several churches were dedicated to them.

The Irish Sea is a small sheltered sea with southwest winds predominating. In Cardigan Bay there has been a considerable buildup of sand and shingle across what were open havens in the centuries of the Irish and Viking raids. When Harlech Castle was built in AD 1286 ships could sail in to a harbour below its walls; today a 3 mile spit of sand and shingle shuts off the castle from the sea half a mile away.

On the other shore the Boyne and Liffey were important routes into the interior of Ireland. In AD 836 sixty Viking ships sailed or rowed up each of the two rivers to plunder all Meath.

Opposing tidal systems meet between the islands of Anglesey and Man and the tidal stream runs between Dublin and the Lancashire coast, a distance of 120 miles and a passage that might have taken 20 to 30 hours even in a Viking ship, with several fair and foul tides during the voyage. The Lancashire coastland is one of the great soft areas of England. Travel by land along it was difficult and the importance of shipping in the area enhanced.

At the southern entrance to the Irish Sea it is 44 miles from St David's Head to the nearest point of Ireland. In the north it is 19 miles from the Mull of Galloway to the Ards Peninsula. Further north still the southern tip of Kintyre, 1463 ft, reaches down to within 12 miles of the Irish coast with heights up to 1625 ft. This explains the ease with which the Irish and the Scots intermingled so that the Scots who originally came from Ireland gave their name to Scotland. It was a short route but not always a safe one, for it was just off Rathlin Island that Breccan and fifty curraghs were said to have been lost in the tide race. But it is much more likely to have been Corrie-vrekan, 'Breccan's cauldron', 50 miles northeast near the Scottish coast, the worst tide race round the coasts of Britain.

The North Channel was one of the most used crossing places in early Britain. Standing high on the Mull, the southwest tip of the Kintyre peninsula, 'you seem to be surrounded by all the oceans of the world'* and there is nothing to the west until America is reached. Not only can Ireland be seen from here, it can also be seen from only a few feet above sea level in both Arran and Islay.

The whole Kintyre peninsula is wonderfully fertile between the sea and its mountain spine, and thickly wooded. Ancient duns sometimes one per mile up the 60 miles of each coast show that few ships passed unnoticed. Nor could their crews have sneaked ashore easily in the dark for the sandy beaches are strewn with rocks, except in Machrihanish Bay where summer waves can build up to 8 ft (to the delight of surfers) and in the extreme south where Saint Columba's 'footprints' are preserved. Kilkerran Loch (Campbeltown) is the only harbour until Tarbert is reached.

Tradition says King Harald Barefoot of Norway 'steered' his longship across the land from Tarbert Harbour to West Loch Tarbert to show that Kintyre was part of his domain as King of the Isles. The distance is about one mile (Plate 3). Viking ships were also said to have been dragged between Crinan and Loch Gilp; not along the line of the present canal but up the winding river Add from Crinan to about a mile from the head of Loch Gilp, then a couple of miles further inland. From here and from Tarbert (where medieval Scottish fleets used to lie) ships could make their way by sheltered waters to the capital of Strathclyde in the shadow of Dumbarton Rock. Upstream, before the 'improvements' of 1775, the Clyde was a shallow trout triver studded with islands but navigable by the craft of the day.

When monkish chroniclers wrote of monsters among the Western Isles they probably told the truth. The habits of fish and

3 Portage route across the Mull of Kintyre, Scotland; Tarbert in the foreground and West Loch Tarbert in the distance. (Courtesy Oban Times)

* Said by a lady who had just come down from that very place.

sea mammals vary from century to century, but 40 ft basking sharks are common today and whales nearly twice as long are sometimes seen.

The trading and raiding routes between Ireland and Norway went up the west coast through the Little Minch and the Minch. The Hebrides, Skye and the west coast of the Highlands show us today what prehistoric Britain was like. Take away the roads, the airfields and the steamer piers and you are back in Stone Age times.

Going north the islands of Uist are to port, a mosaic of lochs and islands now joined by causeways; flat land mainly, which for all its bleakness offered early man grazing, building stone and fuel, birds and fish to supplement his diet. From Beinn Mhor, 2034 ft, to Eaval, 1138 ft, a distance of 14 miles, there is little above sea level to break the force of the Atlantic winds. Thereafter, except for the Sound of Harris, there is shelter all the way from westerly gales, and deep sea lochs to shelter a boat with a crew who were tired and cold.

The wide sandy beaches are on the Atlantic side. The shores of the Minches are no place to beach a boat for the edges of the sea lochs are strewn with heavy boulders, painful to walk on. The colours are magnificent, russet seaweed, with black rock above and then yellow lichen. Beyond is green grass and purple heather. But it is not a nice place for a skin covered boat: perhaps the boat-men here turned early to wooden boats and laid down moorings.

The modern Glasgow family with small children contemplating those stony beaches might say, like Captain Scott at the South Pole, 'God this is an awful place', but the Stone Age mother, lifting the children out of the boat while her husband urged the sheep over the gunwale, would have said 'This is a nice sheltered spot, we'll be happy here.' Vessels creeping up the coast would not have gone unseen for the men of the brochs and duns and the people before them would have kept a wary eye to seaward for friend or foe.

But there are some wide, sheltered, sandy beaches where fleets could be careened after a stormy passage or prepared in winter for summer raiding or trading. One is at the northern end of Barra, the beach where the aeroplanes land. Another is on the west side of Loch Indaal, Islay. A third, much less sheltered, is Kiloran Bay on the west side of Colonsay where Mesolithic remains have been found.

From Cape Wrath on the northwest tip of the Scottish mainland some Neolithic crews seem to have sailed straight to Shetland leaving Sule Skerry, a tiny island 40 miles north of Scotland, to port and passing successively the Orkney islands of Hoy, 1565 ft,

Mainland, 881 ft, Rousay, 821 ft, and Westray, 557 ft, to starboard. Then they would pick out Fair Isle, 712 ft, and heave a sigh of relief as they ran to final shelter in slack water under Sumburgh Head. At spring tides Sumburgh Race runs at 7 knots.

The peoples who sailed the seas in the early days had no instinctive ability to foretell weather. Twentieth century man alone can do this, relying on radio for instant reports of wind speeds and pressure changes over an area thousands of miles in extent. The men and women who paddled or rowed through these seas only did so when they could see no bad weather anywhere on a clear day. If they were going 30 miles they might be at sea for ten hours, and anyone who has sailed round the coasts of Britain and Ireland knows how quickly the weather can change. Fishermen, daring professionals in handy buoyant boats, might have taken greater risks and relied on their skill and hardihood if caught out, but the migrating peoples in long, low canoes would have played for safety. Probably they were all very young and that is why they risked it at all.

From the sheltered anchorage of Bressay Sound in Shetland to the southern coast of Norway is 190 miles. Some authorities think that this crossing was made by Bronze Age traders. It was certainly one of the main routes followed by the Norwegian Vikings. The tidal stream flows east to west and west to east here, right across the North Sea. On a fast passage they might have had two fair and two foul tides; on a slow one four each way.

The coast of Norway is a narrow archipelago 800 miles long. Ships can sail up and down the coast and be sheltered all the way. Whether the Viking ship was first developed in Norway, Sweden or Denmark is not known. Perhaps the Atlantic coast of Norway provided just those conditions described by Toynbee in his *Study of History* as essential for progress: conditions hard enough to stimulate and challenge but not so hard that they stultify growth.

4 Pictures and Models

Ships, dim discovered, dropping from the clouds
JAMES THOMSON

Deep in the caves of southwest France and northeast Spain are the rock drawings and paintings of ancient land-roving hunters; from Jutland to the White Sea, open to the sky, are the rock carvings of peoples who followed the sea (Plate 4, Map 5). Fig. 1, Nos. 1–34 show many variations of these petrographs but they cannot illustrate all the differences in shape and constructional detail or all the objects associated with the ships. There are thousands of ships, men, carts, animals and weapons, but ships form a high proportion and often a whole rock face is covered with them (No. 9).

Our impression that the ship was the cultural focus of the northern peoples is enhanced by the way in which many of the ships are linked with sacred sun discs and carry trumpet players. Many ships are richly decorated, and the ship is even pictured on man's most personal belonging, his razor.

Herbert Kuhn in *The Rock Pictures of Europe* says, 'Many of the ships show individual characteristics. There are sun symbols; other ships carry sacred trees; great axes figure on many ships. The symbols indicate that we are in the presence of no ordinary ships but of cult ships, magic ships. On many rocks there are men jumping over vessels. Sometimes divine figures hold these ships in their hands.'

Nos. 1–4 represent a group of about fifty petrographs mostly from north Norway, with very simple outlines, sometimes shown with seal, whale or walrus. No. 1, although it is probably fully decked except for the hunter's cockpit, looks much more like an umiak than a kayak. The lip at the bow is typical. No. 2 is one of several boats that look so much like umiaks that they are often accepted as ancient versions of them. Many Eskimo drawings are strikingly similar to ancient rock carvings and some of the petrograph ships have equally spaced vertical lines along the hull and look just like umiaks with well-greased skins transparent in the sunlight of a spring voyage. No. 3 has something like a mast but it is probably a

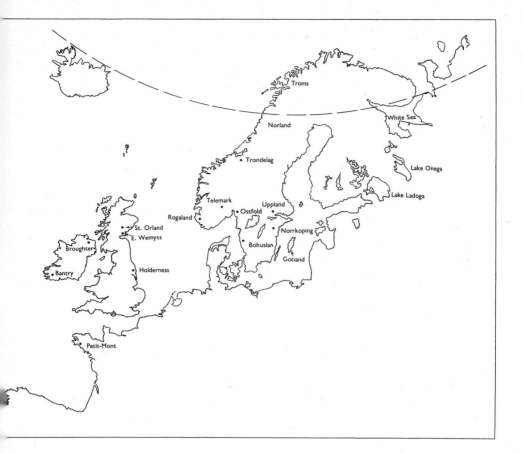

5 Locations of rock carvings and models

man, and No. 4 is the only rock drawing of the whole series to show water. These drawings are Neolithic but may show an Eskimo type hunting culture which had flourished since the waning of the last Ice Age. But as mentioned in chapter 2 scholars now limit the true Eskimo culture to eastern Siberia, Canada and Greenland. If so the skin boats represented in the carvings must have been independently developed.

Nos. 6, 7, 10, 11, 19, 20, 21, 23, 25 and 26 seem to represent vessels of considerable size which are believed by many Scandinavian scholars to be skin covered on wicker frames. They do not look like any known umiaks, but the bifid bow is reminiscent of the bows of two- and three-man kayaks from Alaska, and no satisfactory explanation of it has ever been given.

Whether the stalks above the gunwales represent men or are just the ends of the ribs is a major question. In No. 6 there are 47 'stalks', and if these represent men and there were two rows of

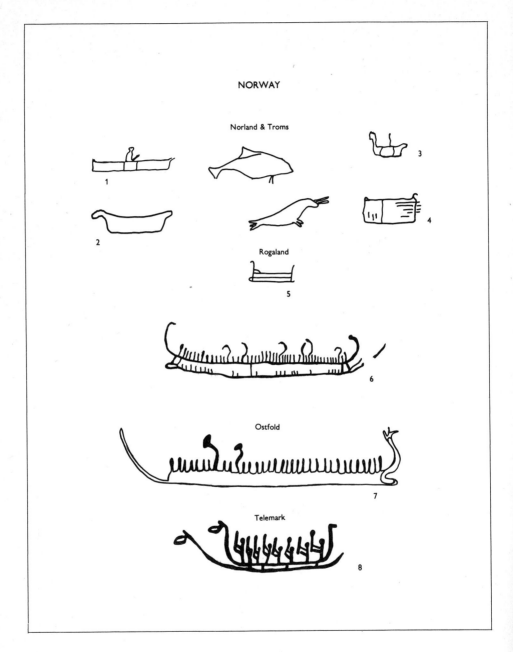

NORWAY

Norland & Troms

1

2

3

4

Rogaland

5

6

Ostfold

7

Telemark

8

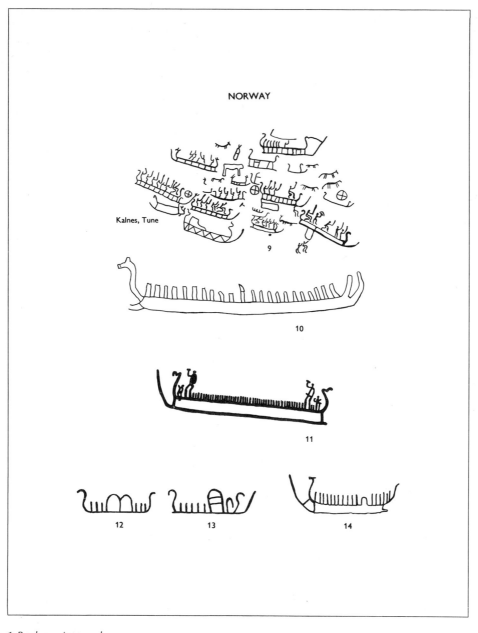

1 *Rock carvings and pictures of boats, 2nd–1st millennium BC*

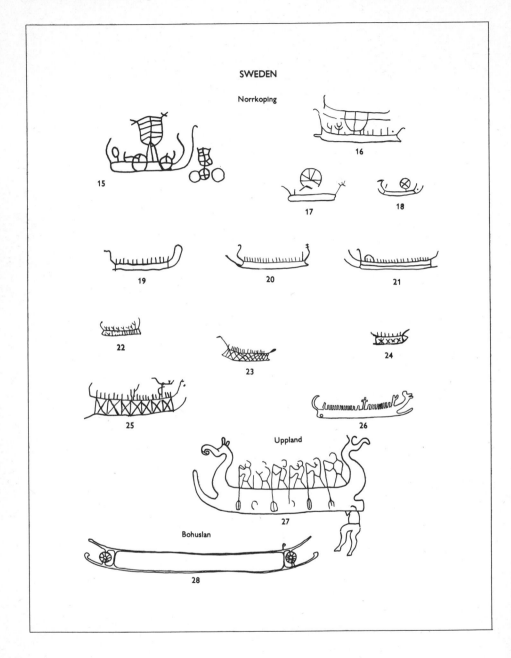

SWEDEN

Norrkoping

15

16

17

18

19

20

21

22

23

24

25

26

Uppland

27

Bohuslan

28

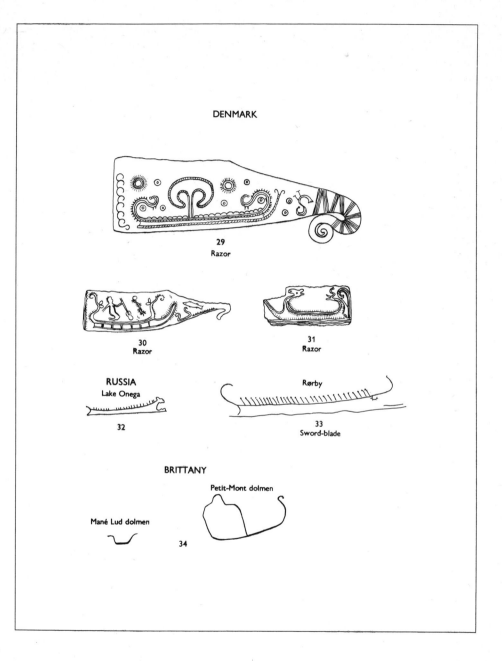

DENMARK

29
Razor

30
Razor

31
Razor

RUSSIA
Lake Onega

Rørby

32

33
Sword-blade

BRITTANY

Petit-Mont dolmen

Mané Lud dolmen

34

them the total crew would have been 94 and the boat would have
been nearly 150 ft (46 m) long, which is out of the question whatever
she was made of. No. 7 has 34 'stalks' and two of them are prolonged
upwards into the shape of lurs, the great bell-mouthed serpentine
bronze trumpets whose deep pure notes boom out at noon in the
National Museum at Copenhagen. Their range and power is such
that to have heard a ship like this ghosting across a fiord with lurs
playing would have been as unforgettable as hearing the 'sunset
call' from a British warship. No. 6 also has lur players, and here they
seem to be swaying and turning like jazz trumpet players.

4 Bronze Age petrograph in National Museum, Copenhagen. (Author)

On this evidence then the 'spikes' are probably men, and the
description 'spikes' suggests that no crew would ever have
tolerated such projections along the gunwale. Whether the boats
carried ten men or fifty, were dugouts or covered with bark or skins,
the crew must have had to jump over the sides at every landing to
save them from damage and haul them up the beaches. They
would never have put up with a boat like a mantrap. If the framework was wicker the ends of the verticals would have been turned
over and woven back into the framework just like a basket.

In many drawings the ribs do not show above the gunwales. In

Nos. 23, 24 and 25 the framework is either diagonal or the rib lines represent nothing more than external decoration. Some boats have pure decoration based on no possible rib pattern at all.

The average length of the ship drawings is 20 in. though some are nearly 7 ft. Some point to the left and some to the right, but it is not always easy to say which is the bow. The pictures are usually described as stylised but they are drawn in fair proportion and do not seem to be distorted. Most date from at least the 2nd millennium BC. Lurs like those in Nos. 6 and 7 date from 1100–400 BC; most were found in Denmark and a few in north Germany.

The sun discs or sail-like symbols in Nos. 15, 16, 17 and 18 are very similar to the one on the Bronze Age sun cart model in the National Museum at Copenhagen. No. 15 shows clearly that the structure is not a sail, and is closely associated with a cart carrying a sun symbol outside the boat. In Bronze Age times the sun was conceived as a fiery disc on a cart or ship which slowly crossed the heavens from sunrise to sunset.

No. 6 from Ostfold appears to be facing to the right and the loop at the stern is thought to represent a drift rudder, a small fin sometimes lashed to a kayak to hold it straight as it blows downwind towards walrus or seal. This is the oldest illustration of a rudder, though it is really only a skeg like that on a modern racing shell.

No. 7 faces left. We should not be sure if it did not show such a remarkable resemblance to No. 8, in which the paddlers do not leave much room for doubt. The bells of the lurs face forward ahead of the man playing, as was usual. The single upturned 'sledge runner' at the bow is similar to recent primitive canoes from Africa (Plate 5).

Nos. 8 and 9 are representative of carvings which show the crews waving their paddles either in salute, threat or sheer joy of living. The men are well drawn and their attitudes are simplified and stylised in No. 22. Nos. 23 and 24, also from Norrkoping, suggest that the simplification may have gone much further and that the 'stalks' are indeed men, not ribs.

No. 11 from Ostfold complicates the matter still further. Eight stalks out of nearly fifty have become the legs of two men or giants and two 'children'. In Nos. 10, 11, 12, 13 and 14 the stalks are so large that it seems they must represent men. But immediately another difficulty arises, and in Nos. 12, 13, 14 and 21 some stalks are looped together. Sverre Marstrander has likened these domes to the simple arched shelters of bamboo and matting found on the boats of India and further east. It seems reasonable enough to think of a chief sitting under cover while his crew of fifty paddlers drove his canoe along at 7 knots just as the princes of Indo-China sat in

their state canoes in the 19th century. In No. 21 the 'cabin' is in the bow. This boat is from Sweden and indicates that whatever the humps were, they were used over much of Scandinavia. The London Science Museum model of a 16th century AD Irish skin boat shows just such an awning (Plate 6). Those who hold that the spikes were ribs will be quick to suggest that in these cases the stalks do represent ribs and have been left long and arched over to form a shelter. Anyone who has been afloat in a small vessel in wind and sea knows what a relief it can be to go below out of sight and sound of the waves. Even those who have rowed across oceans admit the comfort even of a tarpaulin. There would have been plenty of people on migration, perhaps sick, pregnant, children or aged, who would have benefited.

No. 26, which shares a rock with petrographs of a plough, domestic animals, smaller boats and a bow and arrow, shows a vessel with 22 projections above the gunwale which cannot all be rib ends. The one amidships is a cross not much smaller than the sort of mast we would expect to find aboard a narrow boat like this. But Herr Kuhn explains that even at this date the cross, the crossed wheel and the swastika were religious symbols in the north. Right forward is a taller figure paddling or poling as in No. 22. Right aft is a figure slightly taller than the others who might be the helmsman. In the heel of the boat there is a circle like the attachment hole of an amulet.

All the long slim boats like Nos. 6, 7, 10 and 11 must have been canoes 30, 40 or even 50 ft long. Their decorated bows and sterns suggest that they were in permanent use, not mere migration

5 Sese canoe on Lake Victoria, with sewn joints and keel extension. (Crown copyright Science Museum, London)

boats to be abandoned at the end of the voyage. Were they dug-outs, birchbark canoes, skin-covered wicker, or plank-built boats?

Some of the boats like No. 28 resemble the Als boat from Denmark so closely as to leave no doubt that they are accurate drawings by artists who had seen such boats (Plate 7). The date of the Als

6 Model of Irish wicker boat, based on Captain Phillip's drawing of 1685. (Crown copyright Science Museum, London)

boat itself is only a few hundred years BC but the drawings suggest that the type was in use much earlier. Dugout canoes have been found as far north as Latvia so some of the drawings could have been based on log canoes with figureheads.

The Norwegian archaeologist Sverre Marstrander, who has made a deep study of the rock drawings, is convinced that the majority of the boats were skin-covered, some on wicker and some on an open framework like modern umiaks.

A clue to the nature of many of the boats is given by the rock carvings of Karelia; No. 32 comes from the eastern shore of Lake Onega and is based on carvings which also include reindeer and men. Since the reindeer face to the right it is likely that the boats face that way too. The Soviet archaeologist A L Mongait gives the date of these petrographs as about 1500 BC, Neolithic in this area. The reindeer suggest that the boats were built adjacent to an open tundra area with no more than small conifers, too slim to provide the enormous planks used on the Als boat or the hull of a dugout. This was a land of nomadic hunters and the boats were almost certainly covered with skins on a framework of small branches or wicker, for the trees would have been too small to provide any worthwhile area of bark.

They seem to have been more elaborate than umiaks which never normally have figureheads, external runners, or chafing strips. The ships or boats shown in Nos. 19, 20, 21 etc. all have the 'sledge runner' projecting forward, and if they were skin-covered this must have continued underneath the boat since it is unlikely that any internal stringer could have been made to pierce the skin in a watertight manner. It may have been necessary for dragging the hulls over land or ice, and one carving shows two horses harnessed to a boat. No. 19 shows the runner looped up and back to join the upper member in a way reminiscent of the framework of some sledges.

The vessel at the top of No. 9 is very like the carving on the Petit Mont dolmen in Brittany (No. 34) also ca 1500 BC. Herbert Kuhn describes the Breton carving as a ship with a cabin, quoting the

7 Model of boat from Als, Denmark ca 400 BC. (National Maritime Museum, Greenwich)

French specialist Le Rouzic, who likens it to Egyptian ship engravings from the Atlantic Sahara. The simple shapes on the Mané-Lud dolmen close by are paralleled almost exactly by carvings not only on Scandinavian rocks but also at the Neolithic temple of Tarxien in Malta.

None of the Scandinavian petrographs indicate that the oar, steering oar or quarter rudder was in use. There are only two pieces of pictorial evidence for oars in northern Europe in pre-Iron Age

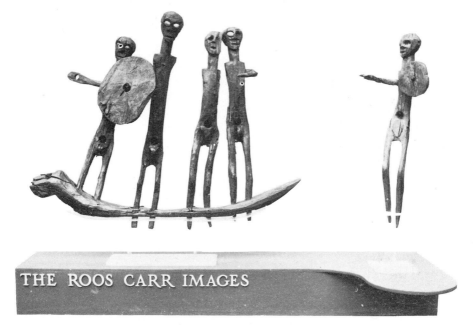

THE ROOS CARR IMAGES

8 Roos Carr model, 6th/7th century BC. (Hull Museums)

times: one of these is the vessel on the bronze sword from Rorby, Denmark (No. 33). Here the 30 starboard rowers lean aft as if on the recovery stroke and the ship moves forward with a 'bone in her teeth', the oculus searching ahead. She looks remarkably like a Mediterranean warship with her eye and hint of a ram. Unless something similar turns up it is best to assume that the man who made the engraving had seen a southern ship or heard about one.

One perhaps detects a tendency for Scandinavian archaeologists to deny all possibility of southern influence in the ships while at the same time conceding Mediterranean influence in the spoke-wheel carts shown on the same rocks.

There is one rock carving outside Scandinavia which may show oars and this is in a cave at East Wemyss, Fife, Scotland. The other drawings in the cave are Bronze Age but some authorities think that this one is Pictish, and this seems the safer view (Fig. 11, chapter 14).

The Caergwrle bowl in the National Museum of Wales, possibly ca 1000 BC, also shows what have been loosely termed oars as well as 'shields along the gunwale'. The image is formed of gold leaf on the curved wood and like most drawings on pots and vases is highly stylised. The 22 'oars' (presumably there were 44 altogether) are shown tossed vertical as if in salute and the row of round shields is above the blades; below, the sea zig-zags along the waterline. There is an oculus at the prow. It is possible that the oars work through ports below the gunwale though they could not have been readily raised to the vertical if they were. Scandinavian evidence suggests that oarports did not supersede thole crutches until about AD 700. This bowl might be important evidence if it could be interpreted correctly.

Pre-Christian ship models are rare. There are some Bronze Age ones of beaten gold in the National Museum in Copenhagen. These are about the size of pea husks and only illustrate the canoe-like proportions of the craft. The Roos Carr model from Holderness, Yorkshire (Plate 8) is usually dated 6th or 7th century BC, and shows a considerable standard of woodcarving. It is obviously far from complete as evidenced by the hole in the 'figurehead' and the fact that the legs of the crew pierce the 'boat', suggesting that there was once another member below. They carry round shields and this is early evidence for a boat raiding party. The model is too small for carbon-14 dating.

Ship or boat engravings on Bronze Age razors are common and have usually been found in Denmark. The giants shown holding ships in the Scandinavian petrographs have their virility emphasised as though virility and ships went together. Man uses a razor to trim the evidence of his maleness, his beard. Whether this forms a reason for decorating his razor with ships is a matter of conjecture.

The razor ships have the same general form as many of the others illustrated, but Nos. 29, 30 and 31 all have the curious 'centipede' shading and No. 29 also has a loop pattern along the gunwale, and hachuring emphasises the lines. The head of the boy in No. 30 also has the spiky decoration and in this case it represents hair. The hairs on the curled-up ends of No. 29 suggest fangs which with the eye symbols give them a dragon's head appearance. The figurehead of No. 31 is a horse's head while the ship in No. 30 seems to be accompanied by a small boat. No. 31 is afloat. There are two suns above No. 29 which makes one wonder whether the 'sail' is a sun disc variant, or a tree of life. A boat carving from Bohuslan, Sweden has a 'tree' at each end, but as there is little possibility of a two-masted ship of this date these are not sails.

None of these things is easily explained or perhaps can ever be clear at all except to somebody with exceptional insight into the Bronze Age mind and an encyclopaedic knowledge of the symbolism, art and religion of the period.

We can only attempt the barest summing up. The petrographs extend from north Russia, through Finland, Norway and Sweden to Denmark. As far as is known there are none like these in the British Isles, across the north German plain or in the Netherlands, which were lacking in rock faces for the sculptors to work on. There are a few carvings or scratchings in Brittany where suitable surfaces were available and these resemble some of the simpler Scandinavian ones, and have a possible tenuous affinity with drawings in the central Mediterranean and North Africa. The Holderness model has considerable resemblance to the Scandinavian petrographs.

The sun, the ship, the horse and the reindeer are featured in great profusion together with giant male figures signifying magic or fertility. Some of the carvings are decorated with dimples around the designs which may be libation cups.

Some drawings seem to show very large ships and while some are obviously wooden like the Als boat, many seem to be skin-covered on a wicker or open framework. Many have horse figureheads, and a large number have the mysterious 'sledge runner' keels. Only paddles are shown and there is no certain example of a sail.

After the most careful study we retire baffled by the profusion and variety of the drawings. We can be sure that the men who drew them were artistic, poetic and with more than a strain of mysticism. We are of the same race, we can recognise from their remains the same physical types, but we can go no further and the study of modern primitives like the Australian aborigines or the South African bushmen does not enable us to penetrate their minds.

5 Dugouts, Skin Boats and Bark Canoes

To the man whoe'er he be
who first cut paddle from a tree

Canoeist's toast

The Neolithic peoples who crossed Europe by the great rivers, paddled through a country of dense forests. Primitive boats in forest regions have usually been dugouts or bark canoes according to the trees available. The dugout is used on the Congo, the Niger and the Amazon; the birchbark canoe was used on the rivers of New England and Canada. Large skin-covered boats are rarely found far inland and are normally made by the inhabitants of the tundra or treeless regions of the circumpolar world. In the Ice Age this came as far south as the English Channel, and even after the ice retreated the tradition of building skin-covered seagoing boats probably persisted in this area.

The birchbark canoes of the North American Indians were magnificent boats, and the one in the Greenwich National Maritime Museum is 30 ft (9 m) long with a 5 ft (1.5 m) beam. Her hull form could hardly be bettered and she is an example of the 'big canoe' used by trappers to bring their furs to the trading posts in the 18th and 19th centuries. She would have suited the Neolithic peoples of Europe admirably.

But the only bark boat found in Europe is a small one from Vestergotland in Sweden. Although the chances of bark boats surviving from the 2nd or 3rd millennium BC seem very small, there are many other bark remains, including coverings of roofs, walls and hearths (sic); there are also containers of many sorts in the museums. If birchbark canoes were widely used we should therefore expect to have found more of them, but chance plays such an important part in the preservation of soft substances that no firm statement can be made.

Suffice it to say that the best bark canoes are superior to both dugouts and skin boats for most purposes. Even where suitable bark was not available it would have been worthwhile to import it from more favoured regions, and not very difficult to do so: whether anyone did is unknown. The birch tree can grow to as much as 4 ft diameter and was once widely available in Europe, and some of this size are to be found in Spain today. A few North American canoes were covered with elm bark and the Australian aborigines used some other variety.

The oldest boat in Europe is a 10 ft dugout canoe of 6400 BC from Pesse in north Holland and there is a paddle of 7400 BC from Star Carr in Yorkshire. The climatic changes must have been dramatic indeed, for even at this early date the dugout was hollowed out of a tree 2 ft in diameter with the rough flaked tools of the Mesolithic period. Once he had discovered how to grind the edges of his axes and adzes man could shape the largest trees and hollow them out to fine limits, cutting away unnecessary timber. With his felling axe and his whetstone Neolithic man could confidently search out the largest trees that grew in the warm dry climate of the time. With the techniques he later used for hauling great blocks of stone, he could have transported the raw trunks or finished boats to water.

The dugout canoe was used throughout Europe from the Ice Age to the end of the 19th century, and one enormous pine canoe was still in use in Norway in 1912. They have been found in France, Switzerland, Germany, Denmark, Norway, Sweden, Russia, Finland, England, Scotland and Wales, and more come to light each month.

Most of the dugouts that have survived from Neolithic Europe are now so rotted, cracked and distorted as to give a totally false idea of their original scope. Most of them are very small canoes of primitive shape, used on rivers and lakes as ferries or fishing boats. A seaman would dismiss them as hardly seaworthy enough to cross a pond.

But a few large dugouts have been found which enable us to reconstruct the type of boat which the early agriculturalists and stockbreeders used to bring their sheep and grain down the great rivers. A very large boat was discovered at Brigg in Lincolnshire when excavating for a new gasholder in 1886 (Plate 9). She was destroyed by a bomb in 1942 and the information used for Fig. 2 was obtained from the *Transactions* of the East Riding Antiquarian Society, 1910.

The Brigg boat was never dated by modern methods and might have been built earlier or later than the Ferriby boats discovered nearby, the earliest of which has a C_{14} date of 1400 BC. Similar dugouts in the area have been C_{14} dated to 800 BC. But since the Brigg boat had two patches fastened in the same way as the bottom planks of the Ferriby craft (Fig. 6), and since the Brigg boat was little more than a dugout, there is no doubt that boats like her were in use long before planked craft of the Ferriby type came into general service.

The Brigg boat, or canoe, was hollowed out of a single gigantic oak tree. The whole length of the trunk was used, the stern of the boat showing the swelling of the bole near the roots and the bow having the great knot holes where the lower limbs branched out. When found she was 48 ft 8 in. (14.83 m) long and 5 ft (1.52 m) in beam. Obviously the builders only selected such an enormous tree and wasted so little of it because no smaller craft would suit their needs. The *Transactions* suggest that even larger oaks grew in Yorkshire in the 18th century.

9 *Brigg boat* ca *1000 BC. (Hull Museums)*

The trunk was probably rotten in the heart when felled and a 'transom' made up of two 2 in. (5 cm) thick boards was fitted in grooves in the sides and bottom to close the after end of the hull. The bottom of the boat was finished to about 4 in. (10 cm) thick and the sides to about 3 in. (8 cm): the knot holes in the bow were plugged. The beam was 4 ft 3 in. (1.30 m) forward and 4 ft 6 in. (1.37 m) aft. She was about 5 ft 5 in. (1.65 m) wide amidships and there was a beam wedged between the gunwales when the boat was found, suggesting that the sides had been slightly spread. None of the measurements is exact owing to shrinkage, distortion and cracking.

The displacement at 1 ft 3 in. (38 cm) draft was 11,600 lbs (5262 kg) or 5.16 tons and the hull weight 5850 lbs (2653 kg) or 2.61 tons. She could have carried thirty men and women, their children and a few animals. The gunwales were pierced for the attachment of washstrakes to increase the freeboard. Another dugout, with part of a washstrake pegged to her topsides, was found at Giggleswick, Yorkshire in 1863.

There is no mention of thwarts for the paddlers in the *Transactions* and the photograph of the boat (Plate 9) does not show any. The paddlers knelt in North American Indian canoes and stood in some of the long boats of southeast Asia. Even around our coasts and in the Mediterranean fishermen sometimes row standing.

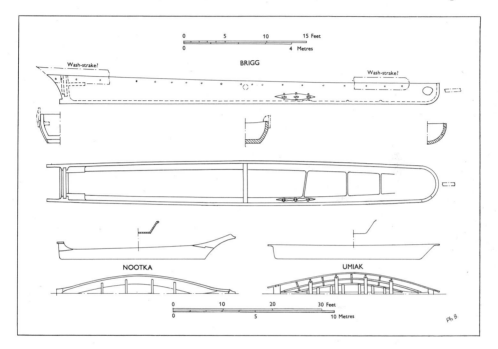

2 *Brigg boat ca 1000 BC*
Nootka dugout, British Columbia (modern)
Alaska umiak (modern)

The Brigg boat was found close beside the river Ancholme and may have been used only for voyaging on the Lincolnshire, Fenland and Yorkshire rivers, the short steep seas of the Humber being her greatest test of seaworthiness. Other dugouts with Brigg type sterns were found at Glasgow in 1847, at Sunderland in 1885, and two 30 ft examples were excavated at Cliften on the river Trent in 1951.

Although this part of Britain has produced the richest prehistoric boat finds in northern Europe it seems unlikely that boatbuilding in this area was superior to that on the European mainland. We can safely assume that boats as large as the Brigg boat and just as efficient voyaged down the rivers of Europe to the Baltic, the North Sea and the Channel shore.

The Brigg boat herself was too heavy and blunt-ended to make a good sea boat, but there are many examples of refined dugouts that were magnificent on salt water in spite of confident denials by A W Brogger in *The Viking Ships*.

The canoes of the Nootka Indians of British Columbia were

probably the best dugouts ever built and in their shape, dimensions, detail and decoration show remarkable resemblance to the skin-covered umiaks or migration boats of the Eskimos to the north of them. They not only tell us a lot about dugouts: they lead us on to an appraisal of skin-covered boats in general and to the links that seem to exist between these two methods of boatbuilding.

The Nootka canoe makers had such magnificent trees to work from they could build cargo dugouts more than 50 feet (15.24 m) long and 6 feet (1.83 m) deep from flat bottom to gunwale.

Their best canoes were used for whale hunting and were 30–35 ft (9–10.7 m) long and 6 ft (1.8 m) beam, carved from a single tree. In Fig. 2 these are compared to the umiaks of the Bering Strait Eskimos.

In every line the umiak and the dugout seem to correspond, as if one was copied from the other. The flat bottom, the flare of the sides, the tiny lip at the stern, and the harpoon rest in the bow are all shared. The dugouts, however, had fine high animal figureheads joined to the hull by a long scarph. There are remarkable detail similarities such as the outward roll of the side just below the gunwale and the horizontal grooves inside the dugouts which seem to imitate the lashings of the umiak's cover.

Both boats were used for offshore whaling and the dugouts went to sea with a crew of eight, the harpooner standing abaft the upswept stem with a foot on each gunwale. Until they were within range the harpoon rested in the groove in the top of the figurehead. The line was flaked out behind the harpooner with a great bladder tied to it to mark the whale's position after it had dived. When a whale is harpooned it swims away towing the boat at a dangerously high speed and this goes on until the whale is exhausted, straining boat and crew to the limit. Nothing could have better tested the strength and seaworthiness of the Nootka dugouts.

When Capt Voss was looking for a boat with news value in 1901 he came across an old Nootka dugout on Vancouver Island and bought her for a bottle of whisky. He put in ribs to stop her splitting, decked her over, gave her a coachroof, rigged her as a three-masted schooner and sailed her round the world!

The dugouts of the Haida Indians of the Queen Charlotte Islands were the largest of all, reaching 60 ft (18 m) long and carrying a hundred men each on tribal raids. The insides were hollowed out with fire and finished very thin with diorite axes. The hull was then wetted and the sides forced apart with stretchers.

The similarity between the Nootka dugouts and the Alaskan umiaks is discussed by Wilson Duff, Curator of Anthropology, Provincial Museum of British Columbia, in its report for 1964.

Similarities between dugouts and bark canoes are also mentioned by James Hornell in *Water Transport*. In some localities there are dugouts and bark canoes of the same shape and the dugouts incorporate ribs carved integral with the hull, useless because of the wrong flow of the grain and apparently only there in imitation of the bark canoe frames.

James Hornell claims to have noticed this not only in the canoes of Australasia and the Pacific but in the dugouts discovered in Britain. The Brigg boat has three ribs as shown in Fig. 2 but they are not imitations of umiak frames; if they had been they would have been spaced along the boat and not grouped near the bow. Furthermore, one is obliquely across the bottom and must have been deliberately carved so.

The only worthwhile suggestion is that they were put there for the crew to brace their feet against when poling the canoe in shallow water. Even the oblique one could possibly be explained away as giving purchase to a man pushing the bow out from the bank. But you can quant or punt a boat without any foot-bracers at all.

It seems very likely that when the European river dugouts reached the sea their crews came into contact with fishermen using light, seaworthy skin-covered boats and were only too glad to learn from these expert sailors whose huts stood along the seashore on great mounds of shells. What sort of craft did they see?

In 1971 Mr Paul Johnstone and Professor Marstrander had a skin-covered boat built to the latter's interpretation of the Ostfold rock carvings (Fig. 3). The hull was 17.7 ft (5.38 m) long, 4.3 ft (1.32 m) wide and 1.74 ft (0.53 m) deep. The 'horns' at the bow and the small stern extension brought the overall length up to 21.9 ft (6.68 m). The shape was like an umiak with a flat bottom, straight keel and hard chines. The nine frames, gunwales, chines, keelson and stringers were all made from newly cut saplings trimmed with axe or knife and lashed together.

Eight cowskins were sewn up into a cover, slipped over the framework, and the upper edge was turned over the gunwales and lashed down to the top stringers. The keel with its upcurving forward extension was then put on *outside* the skin and fastened through it to the keelson.

The boat handled well with a crew of six and 1320 lbs (600 kg) of sand. The hull weighed 396 lbs (180 kg) and the total displacement was 2702 lbs (1226 kg). Freeboard was 1.05 ft (0.32 m). Continuous paddling speed in fair weather was 2.8 knots and a leafy alder branch 5.0 ft (1.5 m) by 3.3 ft (1.0 m) as a sail gave a speed of 1 knot

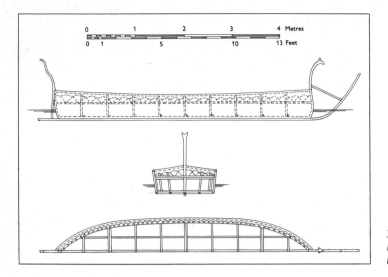

3 Johnstone/
Marstrander skin
boat reconstruction

with a light load. There is no doubt that this boat represents one solution of the vessels shown in the rock carvings.

There are two basic types of skin-covered boat. One has straight frames and a hard chine like an umiak, which is built in a treeless land from driftwood which does not bend. The other is like a modern curragh, a round-bilge boat with frames of pliant branches or osiers. Whether Johnstone and Marstrander were correct in choosing the 'driftwood' form will only be known when really accurate knowledge is available of the contemporary flora on all the northern rock carving sites.

A round bilge reconstruction of the rock carving boats can be seen in the ship museum at Elsinore, Denmark. It represents an immense canoe, skin-covered on a close-woven wicker body which is given longitudinal strength by a plank about 2 ft (0.6 m) deep running on edge *below* the bottom of the boat and joined to it by short struts; the fore-end of the plank is upturned ahead of the bow and carries a figurehead. Forty-four paddlers sit in two rows.

We accept the Bronze Age and the Stone Age but we forget the Wicker Age. For thousands of years wicker was used for houses and even churches, cattle pens, carts and chariots, crates and baskets, furniture, horse collars, fish traps, shields, cradles, perambulators and even statues. There were many types of wicker boats, although whether the Scandinavian rock carvings portray them is another matter. The balloonist, floating like an early mariner at the mercy of the wind and not sure where he will land, travels in a basket of wicker, the strongest and most resilient of all the simple materials.

Figure 4 suggests how the river dugout may have evolved when the migrating peoples applied the shape of a wicker boat to the largest trees available. It is assumed they dubbed down the bottom and sides to 1.5 in. (4 cm) thick and spread the hull amidships after softening it with hot water or hot wet sand, as used to be common practice among dugout makers and was done until recently in Finland. Spreading the gunwales would have rockered the bottom and slightly improved manoeuvrability and seaworthiness. Thwarts are assumed to enable the crew to paddle hard and safely in rough water.

4 Impression of migration dugout

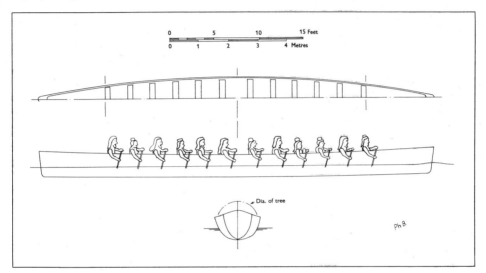

The empty weight of the boat would have been 2000 lbs (907 kg) and the full load displacement 7200 lbs (3266 kg) on 1 ft 3 in. (0.38 m) draft. Twenty-four paddlers, men and women, would have weighed 3600 lbs (1633 kg) and there is 1600 lbs (726 kg) buoyancy left for children and animals, water soakage, bilge water etc.

Time and again we shall be considering how much horsepower was available to drive boats and how fast we can expect them to have gone. In 1960 D R Wilkie read a paper before the Royal Aeronautical Society entitled 'Man as an Aero Engine' and produced the first accurate data on the power of the human body. A modern racing oarsman can exert 0.5 h.p. for over an hour. Paddling is much less efficient as the legs are not used to the same extent. Also, we shall generally be considering mixed crews of ordinary people, not trained athletes but men and women, some very young, some very old; crews a bit ragged in their striking and having to paddle hour after hour in conditions much worse than the university boat race crews experience. So 0.2 h.p. per paddler for long periods seems a safe figure.

With 24 paddlers this conjectural seagoing dugout would have had 4.8 h.p. to drive 3.2 tons. But it would be safer to assume that some of the crew were always resting, feeding the children or looking after the animals and only 4 h.p. was available: 1.24 h.p. per ton.

The liners *Caronia* and *Orcades* described in the *Transactions* of the Institution of Naval Architects of 1953 were designed for 22 knots on a power of 1 h.p. per ton. Their waterline lengths were 685 and 697 ft (209 and 212 m) so that their speed/length ratio* was $0.84\sqrt{LWL}$. This ratio applied to the seagoing dugout gives $0.84\sqrt{45} = 5.6$ knots. We cannot claim that the Neolithic hulls would have had such a low resistance as the scientifically designed, tank-tested hulls of the two liners. But we can suggest 5 knots as a continuous cruising speed with fair certainty. Thus the peoples who brought sheep, goats and cereals to these islands could have crossed the Dover Strait in 5 hours and made the passage from Cherbourg to the Wight in 11 hours.†

Such a long dugout would not have been very seaworthy because of her low freeboard. She would have been the devil to turn, and if caught across any sort of sea would have been easily swamped and rolled over. But 24 people can bail at a terrific rate and the canoe herself would just have floated full of water. But they could not all have bailed *and* paddled, and would only have set out in calm, settled weather. If the crew were caught out in a bad sea they would probably have reversed in their seats and paddled the other way rather than turn the boat, just as Polynesian proas reverse direction instead of tacking. No figurehead is shown because migration canoes were probably plain and simple. A dugout with a figurehead was found in Scotland and may have been a raiding canoe. Canoes like this would have been very heavy to paddle if they had been allowed to soak up too much water and would have split badly if they had been left under the hot sun too long. They were probably kept ashore in boathouses between voyages like the canoes of the Pacific.

Early sailors must have gambled on fine weather. Probably for weeks on end, watchers by the seashore would never see a boat and then on the first fine day there would have been dozens in sight upon the sea. If there were preserved for us some epic poem of that time which told of a great storm that swamped a fleet of boats and

* This formula only applies when the LWL is expressed in feet.
† All speeds suggested for early craft would have been in zero wind and a calm sea.

drowned their crews, it would probably have meant a force 5 wind.

On the coasts of America and India seagoing dugouts were built of two or three logs pegged together and hollowed out. In India they were taken apart after use for drying out, and the Chesapeake Bay log canoes of North America were once greatly sought after by wealthy American yachtsmen for regattas. Multi-tree dugouts have been found in Europe but they are mostly inland craft of medieval or recent date.

The people who crossed the seas in dugout canoes, umiaks or wicker boats were like us in intelligence and physique but different in their outlook and experience of life. They lived more dangerously and were more ready to accept risk. Unfettered evolution had left fewer weaklings among them, and they were happy in what to us is acute discomfort. Today only a few can sleep happily in a puddle like Gino Watkins and his Greenland explorers, but prehistoric peoples accepted it as commonplace. And they were conditioned to paddling hour after hour, just as the Bushmen hunters described by Laurens van der Post chased the giraffe for hour after hour.

The early sailors paid little heed to time or schedule. They would wait patiently for weeks for fine weather, conserving their energy, and then on the tide, at any hour of the day or night, they would set out without complaint to face an indefinite period of backbreak and strain.

We can leave the crews of these conjectural dugouts and skin-boats out on the open sea, some paddling, some asleep in the bilge, a few seasick. The children playing between the rows of their paddling parents, the babies in wicker cots. Nearly all the women would have been nursing mothers and they would have fed whichever hungry child was nearest. Only the sheep, trussed and damp, would have been unhappy.

The task of chopping down a hardwood tree of over 4 ft (1.22 m) diameter with a stone axe looks as if it would require weeks of patient work. But tests in Denmark with Neolithic axes from the National Museum showed them to be nearly as good as steel axes once the technique of using them was mastered. These axes were not even re-ground after being taken from the museum, but the European Neolithic axe-man like his recent counterpart in New Guinea would always have had his whetstone with him, and like any other good craftsman would never have worked with a blunt tool. The trees cut down in Denmark were only about 6 in. (15 cm) in diameter, but there is ample photographic evidence in the British Museum to prove that modern primitives could cut down trees of dugout size with both stone axe and adze.

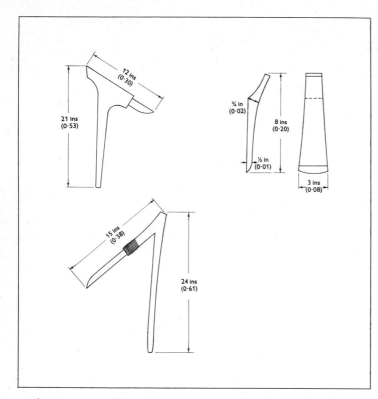

5 Stone tools used
for canoe building

The invention of the adze presupposes that the means of cutting down large trees was already available since the whole reason for making the adze, with its cutting edge at right angles to the direction of use, is to dub down or hollow out broad areas of timber. The adze was the prime tool of the wooden shipwright and until the introduction of the saw was almost his only method of shaping wood.

Those illustrated (Fig. 5) from Samoa, the Solomon Islands and New Guinea are all in the British Museum and the first two were used for hollowing canoes. The one from New Guinea is similar to that used to cut down 3 ft (1 m) diameter trees. There were still such tools and men able to use them in 1964. These adzes were made from stone obtained by trade from a considerable distance and the tools were specialised as the blade taper does not always go the same way.

There were other tools which achieved results comparable to metal tools. Haddon and Hornell in *Canoes of Oceania* tell of a Polynesian canoe builder who preferred his shell-tipped drill to a steel one. No doubt his tool was not as good, but it was adequate and he was used to it.

6   The Voyage of the Bluestones

And we must take the current when it serves
Or lose our ventures

WILLIAM SHAKESPEARE

In 1700–1600 BC the Beaker people transported over 80 stones of up to 5 tons weight from Pembroke to Wiltshire. Professor Atkinson, author of *Stonehenge and Avebury*, says there is little doubt that they moved them largely by sea and, when we look at the problem from our maritime viewpoint, we reach the same conclusion. The journey and voyage from the Prescelly Hills to Stonehenge was along what became one of the most important trade routes of northern Europe. It was already a migration route taking people who had reached Britain, probably by the Cherbourg–Wight crossing, onwards to Ireland.

The early voyagers approaching St Catherine's Point would, according to wind and tide, either have rounded the Island westabout or eastabout. If they knew where they were going from some information that had trickled back along the route, two ways were open to them and they could probably have taken their boats all the way from the coast of Europe to Ireland if any of them had made the whole journey in one operation. Traders probably did so, but in other people's boats, each section of the route being in the hands of local boatmen who knew the run of every tidal eddy or how far they could float a boat along every river and stream.

If the voyager had gone eastwards round the Isle of Wight he would have continued to the head of Southampton Water and then by the river Test to a few miles north of Romsey where he would have picked up a little stream that took him to Salisbury. Today the water table is continually dropping: rivers and streams get smaller and smaller and sometimes dry up altogether. But there are records all over the country of insignificant streams being used for transport even a century ago. In the days before land drainage there was ample water in most summers and, even where the water was low, temporary dams were built to create a 'pond' for the passing of a laden boat.

Had the voyager gone westabout past the Needles—the Hurst channel leading into the Solent from the west was probably not formed until the 1st millenium BC—he would have crossed to Christchurch Harbour and paddled, poled or bow-hauled up the Hampshire Avon to join the easterly route at Salisbury. From here, the river Wylye to Warminster, then portage to the river Frome, would have brought him to the Somerset Avon and the Bristol Channel. He had passed through the homeland of the Wessex culture and what later became the Kingdom of Wessex, both based on the trade passing through the region. No doubt he now crossed over to the northern shore and proceeded on his way to Ireland.

However, he might have voyaged from the Cherbourg peninsula to Lyme Bay and crossed Devonshire by the valleys of the Exe and Taw. From Bideford Bay to St Govan's Head on the Pembrokeshire coast is 44 miles; Lundy Island lies to the west as a refuge in bad weather and cuts down the open sea crossing to 27 miles. The island bears traces of Stone Age occupation and has sheltered landing beaches on the east side. Five-knot tide races form off Surf Point in the south and the North-West Point.

The Bristol Channel has changed little geographically since those times, but the enormous 19th century industrial development of the South Wales coast has disguised the coastline that early travellers would have seen. Around the mouths of the Usk, the Rhymney and the Taff rivers where Newport and Cardiff now stand, there were wide areas of marsh and saltings; in fact it is doubtful if there was much land that did not smell of the sea between Cardiff and Chepstow. Westwards from Barry the coast is more rugged and the stretch to the Gower Peninsula is open to the southwest wind, a reason perhaps why the original harbour at Barry was called The Refuge. Once around the Gower there is plenty of shelter with creeks running deep inland through fertile valleys between high hills.

From Caldey Island to St David's Head the coast is heavily in-dented not only by the 30 miles of creeks behind Milford Haven but by innumerable deep bays. There are half a dozen large islands offshore and shelter here for thousands of early traders and raiders, but there was probably so much shelter and so few craft that in Neolithic, Bronze, Roman and Viking times you could have searched for days and never found a ship. The gold of the Wicklow Hills was reached by this seaway and carried back along it to the continent of Europe.

St David's Head to Carnsore Point, 44 miles of sea, has all the hallmarks of an ancient crossing with high land on both sides, 595 ft at St David's Head and up to 2610 ft on the Irish side which although 26 miles inland would often have produced a noble cloud to lead the voyager westward. The slant of the land behind each point is such that ships approaching in freshening wind can run for shelter to one side or the other where there are ample havens. Just to the north of Carnsore Point is the river Slaney which penetrates deep into the Wicklow Hills.

Across this stretch of water went Neolithic migration boats and Beaker traders. Across it also came the curraghs of Niall of the Nine Hostages, and later still the Viking ships. In the early 12th century Norman knights established themselves in the Pembroke peninsula, and in 1169 Robert Fitz Stephen took the age-old route with 30 knights and 400 men-at-arms and archers, ten shiploads perhaps, and landed at Bannow, one of the several havens on the south side of Carnsore Point.

By 2700 BC Neolithic peoples had moved across from the English to the Bristol Channel. They left causewayed camps on the Wiltshire Downs and built tombs of rough-hewn stones on both sides of the Bristol Channel as far as the Irish Sea and the Prescelly Hills. Before 2000 BC they built Woodhenge close to where Stonehenge was to be. Then the Beaker folk arrived with the fervour and organisation to build circles of great stones to the glory of whatever gods they worshipped and perhaps to help them 'search the stars, the times and triumphs mark'.

They transported the bluestones 210 miles to Stonehenge, a site that was both on the trade route and at the meeting point of the ridgeways of southern Britain. The bluestones are not the great trilithons which weigh up to 50 tons, but smaller stones weighing between 1 and 5 tons and up to 16 ft long by 3 ft square. Nearly all of· them came from the Prescelly Hills; the remainder including the 'altar' stone, the largest of all, came from the shores of Milford Haven.

This must have been the greatest feat of sea transport in the northern world at that time and gives a new dimension to the organising and seafaring ability of the early peoples. Moving the stones by land would have been even more difficult than floating them along on the tide.

The beginning and end of the journey had to be overland, and the part from the Prescelly Mountains to the head of the river which runs into Milford Haven would have been enough for those in charge to evolve an adequate technique and to decide whether it was the best method for the whole journey. No doubt if time, enthusiasm and political conditions allowed, they could have done it that way. But that initial journey may have been so difficult and slow as to set them looking for an easier way even if they had not had water transport in mind at the beginning.

Heavy wooden disc wheels from 2000 BC have been discovered

in Holland and four-wheeled wagons of similar date in central Europe. A corduroy road from about this time has been discovered in Somerset. In general, however, wheeled transport was confined to the great plains, and in hilly districts until comparatively recent times the pack pony and the sledge were used instead. The horse was not then domesticated in Britain, and it is unlikely that oxen were known in Wales though they could have been taken there for the occasion. But it is most likely that the only means available was by man-hauled sledge or over tree-trunk rollers.

The climate was warm and the whole South Wales coastal plain was thickly wooded between the swamps around the river estuaries. They would have had to prepare every yard of the way by immense labour after as big a survey as Brunel or Robert Stephenson ever undertook. It would have been very similar to planning a railway.

Over each section of route a ride would have had to be cut through the trees and the stumps removed. Tree felling was fairly easy for them; grubbing out stumps a much more tedious job. A firm hard road was essential and they would have had to prepare well over 100 miles in South Wales alone, much of it reinforced with timber.

Since nothing like this had ever been done before the work would have had to be planned by intelligent amateurs. Taking the road over marshy ground would have required enormous quantities of brushwood filling as used by George Stephenson to carry the railway over Chat Moss. Movement in undrained country is almost impossible except by a few narrow tracks and much of South Wales was then very like the west of Ireland today, where you can sink up to your waist on the flat and squelch on the tops of the hills. The organisation required would have been enormous: every section of the route would have had to be agreed with local chiefs; hauliers and overseers would have had to be fed and housed by the local people. They would have outstayed their welcome every inch of the way.

To build the Stonehenge we know today, the builders moved stones weighing 50 tons, so the people who built the earlier Stonehenge could almost certainly have moved 5 ton stones by land all the way. But if they had, carving roads in the hillsides, laying down corduroy, filling in the boggy places, surely there would have been some trace left today?

The sea and river operation would have been carried out by professional seamen expert at carrying awkward cargoes, and the crews of the 80 or so convoys would have been objects of wonder as they stopped briefly in sheltered havens to wait for the next tide.

Two of the migration dugouts like Fig. 4 could have carried the largest stone but it would have been much better done with three. The stone could then have been placed across two canoes widely spaced and then the third canoe introduced between them and adjusted fore and aft and athwartships to give the resultant equi-hulled trimaran perfect trim.

The big stone of 5 tons would have left 4400 lbs (1996 kg) buoyancy available for 30 paddlers, who could produce about 6 h.p. to propel a total displacement of 10 tons, quite a reasonable ratio. In fact the whole craft, providing the hulls were satisfactorily braced and tied together (something other Stone Age peoples achieved in the Pacific), would have been buoyant and handy, quite different from the rafts usually suggested for the job. We can quite confidently expect them to have made 2 knots through the water plus tidal drift. We can ignore windage as they would only have chosen dead calm days.

The flood runs between $\frac{1}{4}$ and $1\frac{1}{2}$ knots at the entrance to the Bristol Channel and they might have been able to make 16 miles on the first day's tide. But it is more likely that they would have spent their first night in the shelter of St Govan's Head and the second off Caldy Island, a total of 21 miles made good. They would only have moved on the daylight tides.

On the third day they would have slipped across Carmarthen Bay 14 miles to Burry Holms and on the fourth to the eastern tip of the Gower Peninsula, 13 miles. The fifth day would have taken them 13 miles across Swansea Bay and the sixth day to Barry Refuge, 20 miles; the going is easier now for the tide runs at up to $4\frac{1}{4}$ knots at the eastern end of the Bristol Channel. On the seventh day the stone might have reached Avonmouth, another 20 mile voyage, partly on a 4 knot current that would have taken it close to Flat Holme 3 miles off the Welsh coast. The whole sea voyage might have been done in seven days of 'Dunkirk weather'.

The greatest difficulty would have been the terrific tides which would have forced them to moor in deep water. If they had actually gone into Barry Refuge on the top of the flood they would never have got out of it on an eastgoing tide. For 6 hours at least, and 18 if the light did not serve, they would have had to lie out with the full Severn tide sweeping under them. It is doubtful if their anchors of spiked branches weighted with stones would have held. Perhaps they had previously laid down moorings well offshore; if so somewhere on the route there should still be a block of stone with a hole in it.

The seamen would have had to take the bluestone up through the Avon Gorge since the 40-ft tides here are scarcely a landsman's job, and somewhere near the site of Bristol they would have handed over to some tribe whose custom it was to carry goods across Britain by way of the little rivers already described.

How many seamen were involved and for how long? It has been suggested that each 'trimaran' had 30 paddlers, and we ought to include a couple of boys in each hull to bail. Perhaps dugouts were trimmed slightly down by the stern to carry the water aft. And each trimaran would probably have been attended by a couple of big canoes with tow ropes ready if they got into difficulties and to take off the crews in emergency.

This adds up to five hulls and nearly 80 men to each stone. Estimates of trade volume in this era suggest that it was very small. If it was 100 tons a year in an easterly direction, it would have amounted to 50 boatloads. Trading dugouts would have travelled 35 miles on a tide and traversed the whole Bristol Channel both ways in a week, weather permitting. The number of long distance boat crews could probably have been counted on the fingers of both hands and it begins to look as though they took about 20 years to transport those stones.

The booklet *Stonehenge* published by HM Stationery Office and written by Professor Atkinson is a brilliant account of the monument and on the methods of erecting the stones, but it carries a fearsome picture of a stone on a raft in a breaking sea, the tattered sail blown out by a force 7 wind. The stones never travelled in a wind and sea like this unless someone made a bad mistake. A raft would have had to be 50 by 20 by 2 ft (15 by 6 by 0.6 m) of solid timber to support the big stone with reasonable freeboard. Its total weight of nearly 45 tons and its awkward shape would have made it almost impossible to paddle, and to the best of our knowledge the sail was unknown at this period.

There is one other possibility: there were over 80 stones and if they had a failure rate of just over 1 per cent they lost one stone which should still be lying somewhere between Milford Haven and Avonmouth. What a chance for underwater archaeologists!

Mr G A Kellaway writing in *Nature* of 3 September 1971 suggests that the bluestones were deposited on Salisbury Plain by very early glacial action. The seaborne theory is supported by the booklet published by the Geological Museum in London and many other works, but readers may like to read Mr Kellaway's paper.

7   The Dawn of Boatbuilding

That's not bent that's shaped

SID LAMBKIN
Sussex boatbuilder, 1960

Around 1500 BC, perhaps before, all the elements were present that would lead the peoples of northern Europe to build boats from separate planks. From the rock carvings of Scandinavia we can imagine that skin boats had become so large that they had outgrown the strength of their material and set the builders searching for something stronger than ox or walrus hides.

At the same time the peoples who had crossed Europe by river were probably finding that even the largest dugout canoe was too small for their maximum needs. As agriculture and stock-rearing progressed, the populations of both humans and animals outstripped the boats available. And as their dugouts split or rotted their crews learned to sew on tingles and caulk the seams, as was done on the Brigg boat.

Coming down the great rivers they must have passed ferries or fords where the wagon peoples crossed over. Their wagons, like the prairie schooners of North America, were built of heavy planks, split from the trunk and hewn to shape by axe and adze. Their wheel track was 6 feet and they were drawn by oxen or horses. Many wagon graves have been opened to reveal a burial cult akin to the Viking ship burials of 3000 years later. On well-worn wagon routes there may have been crossing places where rafts or flat boats were kept for ferry purposes and where the dugout men passing by would have seen examples of carpentry suitable for boatbuilding. The wagon pioneers may have learned to caulk the floors of their wagons and build up the sides and ends to make square-ended boats. Or they may have wrapped the wagon body in a 'tarpaulin' of skins sewn together. The wheels were detachable.

But the people with the greatest boatbuilding potential were probably those at the mouths of the Tagus and Guadalquiver in Portugal and southern Spain, where there were towns with bastioned brick walls and craftsmen with exceptional skill in casting copper before 2000 BC. Their ancestors had almost certainly come from the eastern Mediterranean where plank-built ships were already known.

Nevertheless the only extensive remains of early wooden boat-building come from Ferriby on the north bank of the Humber estuary and Brigg a few miles to the south. This part of England was then an enormous area of fenland cutting off the northern part of the country from the south. If ever there was a need for boats it was here (Map 2).

South of the Humber the finds include the Brigg 'raft', another from Yaddlethorpe, and the Brigg dugout. From Ferriby come the remains of three large vessels of which No. 2 was C_{14} dated to 1400 BC and No. 3 to 1200 BC. The Star Carr paddle, 7400 BC, and the model boat from Holderness (Plate 8) came from not far away. Other dugouts with stern boards like the Brigg boat have been found at Hylton in Sunderland (1885) and Glasgow (1847). There is also a record of an 18 ft (5.5 m) boat 'built of several pieces of oak without ribs' found on the north bank of the Clyde at Glasgow in 1825. Others were found on the south bank.

All three of the Ferriby boats are of similar construction. The most complete is No. 1, dated to 1000 BC (Plate 10, Fig. 6). It must have been the outcome of centuries of development, unless there was a sudden infusion of boatbuilding technique from elsewhere.

10 Models of parts found from the Ferriby boats. Top, Boat No. 3 ca 1000 BC; middle, Boat No. 2 ca 1400 BC; bottom, Boat No. 1 ca 1000 BC. (Hull Museums)

The flat bottom, which just possibly suggests an umiak ancestry, was made of four planks, though there are more than four pieces of wood because of splits skilfully repaired. The central member consists of two very heavy planks step-jointed end to end, each one being 26 ft (8 m) long, slightly over 2 ft (0.6 m) wide and 6 in (15 cm) thick. They were carved from enormous baulks of timber, for two lugs 4 in. (10 cm) high were left on the inner face and the bow and stern ends are curved up, being adzed not bent to shape; the original thickness of timber was at least 16 in. (40 cm). V-shaped grooves were carved along the edges of the centre planks to receive thinner planks to port and starboard. These are 35 ft (10.7 m) long, 2 ft (0.6 m) wide and 3 in. (8 cm) thick.

These bottom planks were fastened together by cross rods passing through lugs on the inner faces and by lashings approximately every 13 in. (33 cm) from bow to stern. These lashings were inset from the bottom face of the thick centre planks so that they were protected when the boat grounded. Moss caulking was held in place by battens lashed on the inside of the seams.

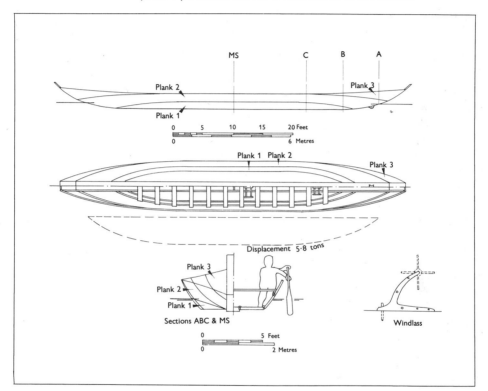

6 *Ferriby boat (author's reconstruction)*

Only one piece of side plank was found, 8 ft (2.44 m) long and 14 in. (36 cm) maximum width. A rebate and lashing holes on its upper edge show that the boat had at least one other side plank. The sides are flared out at about 29° from the vertical. As every piece of plank was adzed from the solid this restricted the steepness of the curves, for every piece of wood had to be within the limits of the tree's dimensions.

At first sight the remains suggest an unwieldy boat, difficult to paddle and very slow, but Fig. 6 shows that she was probably quite graceful. In the reconstruction the length and beam given in the 1965 *Proceedings* of the Prehistoric Society have been used, the chief assumption being that there were only two planks a side. The calculations of displacement and hull weight, and the diagram of the man paddling, all support this.

She was a canoe 51.7 ft (15.84 m) long, 8.55 ft (2.60 m) beam and about 2.2 ft (0.67 m) deep amidships inside. With a displacement of 5.8 tons and a hull weight of 3.5 tons she could only accommodate 24 paddlers and 0.69 tons of children and animals. She was therefore slower than the dugout in Fig. 4. In spite of the thickness of the planks she was probably no heavier than many recent work boats. There are old botters in Holland with 5 in. by 5 in. (13 cm by 13 cm) timbers at 12 in. (30 cm) centres and 4 in. (10 cm) thick planking.

The fact that these three boats were together, with other remains only a few miles away, suggests that this was a permanent boating site—a colony of ferrymen or traders, or perhaps the base of a fleet of raiding canoes.

E V Wright, who excavated the boats, has noted their resemblance to the heavy mahadalparu fishing boats of Ceylon, built of sewn planks, and also to the flat-bottomed fishing boats of Portugal.

The power/weight ratio of Ferriby No. 1 was 0.83 h.p./ton. Taking the hull form into consideration this would have given a speed/length ratio of about $0.7\sqrt{WL}$ or 4.9 knots.

There is no indication of any ribs but some cross-members would have been essential. Used as a migration boat she would have needed all the thwarts shown, but as a ferry boat across the Humber a few would have sufficed for strength and the crew could have paddled standing.

Ferriby No. 1 has a cleat on the underside of the upturn of the centre plank which may have been used for mooring by passing a rope through between two stakes as there is no sign of wear in a forward direction. This suggests constant use from a fixed point, a ferry rather than a far-voyaging boat. A grown oak fork was found nearby which may have been one half of a horizontal windlass.

The so-called rafts found at Brigg on the river Ancholme about ten miles south of Ferriby and at Yaddlethorpe are almost certainly the bottoms of broad river ferry boats. The Brigg 'raft' is 40 ft (12 m) long by 10 ft (3 m) wide, tapering at each end. There are five planks joined by ten battens passing through cleats as in the Ferriby boats. The planks are also sewn together, the seams being protected by battens inside. These rafts have never been properly excavated but almost certainly had built-up sides, as a raft of heavy timber has very little load capacity. There is some doubt whether the seams were caulked, but H E Dudley in *The History and Antiquities of the Scunthorpe and Frodingham District*, 1931, says that they were caulked with moss. This is almost proved by the seam battens.

*11 Ferriby boats:
provisional recon-
struction. Compare
with Fig. 6. (Hull
Museums)*

There is little point in caulking a raft and this further suggests that
these were boats.

It is not possible to fit these various boat remains, models and
pictures into any satisfactory evolutionary pattern. The shape of
the Brigg dugouts is based on the trunk of a tree; the midsection of
the Ferriby boats is very like that of an umiak. The Johnstone/
Marstrander reconstruction of the rock carving pictures was also
based on the umiak. But the Als boat (Plate 7) found in a bog in
Denmark in 1921, which looks exactly like some of the rock
pictures, is round bilged. Once again we have a canoe 44.7 ft
(13.60 m) by 6.6 ft (2.05 m) and 2.3 ft (0.70 m) deep, the overall length

over the horns being 62.3 ft (19.0 m). The mid-section is a spread semicircle like that of a modern sailing dinghy, so her ancestors were probably round bilged, either dugouts, bark canoes or wicker boats.

Plate 7 shows how the parts were made and joined together, and how the keel plank and gunwales were extended to form the two horns which seem to imitate the protecting 'runners' of the skin boats. The side planks are not carried forward to the stem and sternpost but are sewn to end pieces V-shaped in plan and carved from the solid, which sit over the tapered ends of the bottom plank and are sewn to it. These may be wooden imitations of the end sections of skin or bark coverings, which are wrapped round the stem and sternposts and joined to the rest of the covering by vertical seams just where the wooden end-pieces of the Als boat join the side planks.

As in the Ferriby boats cleats were left standing when the planks were hewn out, but in the Als boat they are in groups of five on each plank and enable the planks to be lashed to the ten ribs which were bent timbers continuous from gunwale to gunwale. There were thwarts at each rib position giving the boat a complement of 20 paddlers plus a helmsman who used a steering paddle. The plank edges were slightly chamfered and overlapped to give a sort of sewn clinker construction. The planking, thwarts and runners were lime and the ribs were hazel.

The Als boat was built between 500 and 300 BC but a few of the rock carvings (e.g. Fig. 1, No. 28) portray very similar vessels, which suggests that they were in use around 1000 BC. She was buried as a sacrifice and contained a great collection of iron weapons and armour.

A few fragments of an older boat were discovered in Norway in 1824. This is the Valderhaug boat which is now in the Bergen museum. A W Brogger considers that the remains date from the Bronze Age. There are several fragments of pine planking 4 in. (10 cm) thick (probably shrunken) and two of them have their edges shaped like those of the Als boat and are sewn together and caulked with wool soaked in resin or tar. The seam was also fastened with treenails and is the oldest example of this fastening in northern Europe, apart from the pegs fastening the washboards on the dugout from Yorkshire. All the fragments of plank have lashing holes.

There are canoes in existence today with many of the features of the Als boat. Those from Botel Tobago near Formosa have planks with standing lugs pierced for frame lashings, and the bow and stern are separate pieces V-shaped and cut from the bole of the tree. These are lashed to the bottom and side planks. All that is missing are the 'horns' at bow and stern.

In the British Museum there is a Mon type canoe from the Solomon Islands which, although it has a normal stem and stern-post, has the same arrangement of lugs and rib lashings. Indeed the Als boat and those from Botel Tobago and the Solomons are so similar that some authorities have postulated a connection between them in the distant past. The canoes used by the Sese tribe on Lake Victoria, Uganda (Plate 5) share the heavy chine and plank con-struction of the Ferriby boats and the horns of the Als boat.

Sometimes one comes across detail design in primitive boats so good that one feels that if the builder could somehow be placed in an aircraft design office he would look around for half an hour and then take up his pencil. The T-section upper horn of the Als boat and the strength ribs that run along inside the planks of the Solomon Islands canoes are examples.

Since one reason for changing from skin-covered boats and dugouts was to obtain greater size, we should imagine an Als type boat of the maximum size possible without midship joins in the side planks, and having no part that could not have been carved from a tree as large as that used for the Brigg dugout. She would be 60 ft (18.3 m) long by 6 ft (1.8 m) beam with a plank thickness of $1\frac{1}{2}$ in. (4 cm); a working crew of 34, full load displacement of 6.17 tons and 6.8 h.p. continuous power. This is a little better than that of the conjectural dugout in Fig. 4, and since she is slightly longer her cruising speed would be higher, perhaps $0.85\sqrt{60} = 6.6$ knots. Even if we assume only 6 knots it is still a very useful speed.

Travellers in the Solomon Islands around the year 1900 spoke of large plank-built raiding canoes making 9 knots under paddles but the speeds were never accurately measured. It is obvious, how-ever, that the observers thought they were going much faster than the fine-lined gigs and whaleboats of the day.

There are losses as well as gains in evolution. When he changed from the dugout to the plank boat the sailor gave up a watertight craft that required little maintenance for one that was a mass of potentially leaking seams needing constant work to keep it sea-worthy. Or he discarded a skin-covered vessel that was light to carry and simply built of small timbers for one that was much heavier to launch and drag up the beach.

But there was no turning back. The skin boat was limited in size, strength and shape but there were no inherent limitations in the wooden boat. For centuries the two types existed side by side but the skin boat was obsolescent. Even though the dugout builders may have copied umiak features, they did not change to umiaks.

Today we build aeroplanes with stressed metal skins and although we admire the older types with doped canvas on a wooden framework, we know they are inferior and we shall not go back.

We now have some idea of the boats used by Bronze Age sailors and we can try to fit them into the pattern of life and trade as we think it existed. Copper, tin, stone for tools, livestock, furs, amber and jewellery were carried over long distances, though each sea voyage may have been only a short one.

All these boats, dugout, skin covered or plank built, were big canoes with crews of 20 to 50 and could only carry a ton or so of cargo. They were unhandy and neither very seaworthy nor robust. It is unlikely that they worked from open beaches if they could help it. More probably they used sheltered havens close to the short sea crossings. The volume of trade was so small that only a few boats would have shared the same creek, but the crews were so large that even a village with only three boats might have housed over 100 seamen who with their wives and families would have formed a community of 500 or more. Skin boats could probably have been built by their crews, but such skill and time was needed to build wooden boats that there must have been a professional boatbuilder in each village.

The amount of metal carried across the sea was infinitessimal. Mr Lucas, author of *Ancient Egyptian Metals*, estimated that the total consumption of copper in the ancient world between 2800 and 1300 BC was 10,000 tons, under 7 tons per year on average. We can guess that around 1000 BC, when Troy had just fallen and Athens, Carthage and Rome were not yet known, perhaps a million families in the whole Mediterranean area used bronze, with 10 lbs each—knives, axes, cooking pots—or 5000 tons plus 1000 tons for arms and armour, statues and sheet bronze on temple doors. Like the Inca gold, this was the accumulation of centuries. Ten per cent of that bronze was tin, or 600 tons. But bronze has an enormously long life and was constantly being melted down and re-formed. The yearly requirement for tin was probably under a tenth; 60 tons from all sources—Spain, Brittany, the British Isles, Bohemia and Anatolia.

Leslie Aitcheson in *A History of Metals* gives the European sources of copper and tin. The eastern Mediterranean had its own supplies of copper but was also importing copper, gold and silver from Iberia between 2400 and 2000 BC. Gold was exported from Bohemia in the 3rd millennium and copper production started there about 2200 BC. No important amount of copper was exported from Britain in antiquity and what little was used there before 2000

BC was probably brought in by immigrants from Central Europe.

The alloying of copper with smelted tin took place in Bohemia about 1500 BC. Until 500 BC the principal suppliers of bronze were Bohemia and Spain and on a lesser scale Brittany. Cornish tin was not exported in any quantity until the 1st millennium BC. Jutland and Scandinavia had no copper or tin and when they began to use it around 1500 BC they may have imported a little from Britain or Ireland, but most of it must have come down the rivers from Bohemia or along the coast from Brittany.

In trying to work out the amount of trade in the Bronze Age we must therefore discount all ideas of the shipping of metal by more than a sackful at a time. But the bronzesmith was also a merchant who travelled with his metal, which was so valuable that he probably took both bearers and guard dogs with him. The yearly shipments of copper, tin and gold from Britain to northern Europe cannot have been more than 100 tons, or about 50 cargoes between May and September.

Sheep and cows must have been carried from Neolithic times with their hooves lashed, on beds of seaweed, just as they are carried in curraghs to the Aran Islands today. It was suggested in *Antiquity* in September, 1969 that for a long time cows were brought back for service as was done until recently on the West of Ireland, but sooner or later some daring crew must have taken the bulls to the cows. It hardly bears thinking about, though you see bulls carried across Bressay Sound (Shetland) in old naval pinnaces today.

Horses are better tempered but easily frightened and they prefer to travel standing, as they did in the old cavalry troopships. In 1967 five horses were carried in a replica of the Ladby Viking ship to prove that it could be done. The domestic horse and the spoked wheel chariot were introduced into Britain about 700 BC and from then on there must have been a small trade in expensive horse-flesh. Perhaps also a few chariots crossed, and new types of ploughs for oxen to pull.

The day of low price bulk cargoes had not yet arrived and grain, wine, hides, wool, timber or cloth were not yet shipped in quantity.

As the boats only sailed in settled weather in the summer there would have been days and weeks when they did not put to sea. 'Stand out and face it' may be good advice for a yachtsman with a boat with self-draining cockpit and tight hatches, but not for a 50 ft (15 m) open canoe with a freeboard of 18 in. (46 cm). Passengers and cargo would have had to stay in the village, which would have had some sort of inn, animal pens and a roof to shelter the merchandise.

The captains must have been able to bargain with princes and handle every type of passenger and animal: a princess with her servants on the way to a dynastic marriage; swaggering soldiers of fortune; slave traders and slaves; travelling bronzesmiths; stud mares or a pack of hunting dogs; and the man we read about in the sagas—the man who had killed and was fleeing overseas.

The moment the weather cleared they would have called their crews in from the fields they tended in their spare time, loaded passengers and cargo, and set course. Bronze Age boats could have made any of the short crossings in a day and some of them both ways between sunrise and sunset.

Captains could rarely have told their passengers exactly where they would land and never have been certain of bringing their vessels straight back to the native haven. The sailor with a wife in every port may date from this era: he would have been a frequent visitor to a dozen little havens where he knew the waterfront girls. Born to long hours at the paddle he would have been strong and virile, and if he had been given to worrying about the future he would never have gone to sea. Often when the wind was foul or the sea rough he would have had time to waste ashore and some sort of money in his pouch.

8 Oar, Sail and Trade

Holding out high and aloft
Skins that arrayed her,
Called she the god of the winds
That he should aid her

RUDYARD KIPLING

At some time between 1000 BC and 56 BC, when Caesar described large sailing ships on the Breton coast, the oar and sail were invented or adopted in the north. It is the worst 'documented' period in the whole history of boats and ships.

The need for ships too large to be propelled by paddles alone could only have been caused by migration or invasion on a much larger scale than hitherto, or a great increase in trade. Migration was no doubt continuous year after year, but there is no reason at present to suppose any increase in the numbers on the move at any time in the 1st millennium BC sufficient to require vessels two or three times the earlier size. Nor was the northern world yet able to launch a military invasion requiring large transports.

The most likely reason for bigger ships is a manifold increase in trade following the change from bronze to iron in the 7th century BC. Soft iron is no better than bronze, but because iron ore occurs in almost every country it is much cheaper, and was soon used on a scale that must have seemed sheer waste to a man brought up with bronze. Firedogs 4 ft long made of wrought iron bars 2 in. by 1 in. are an example of the free use of iron in the 1st century BC.

Iron probably occurred too widely to have been carried across the sea as ore or ingots, but there may have developed a considerable trade in simple articles like cooking pots and nails. Every family needed a cooking pot, or several, and the number of enormous nails used in the timber revetted earthworks of the time ran into hundreds of thousands. The estimated weight of nails in the fort at Manching in Bavaria is 300 tons. If such a fort was built near the Channel shore, smiths for miles around would have been forging nails for months and they might even have been imported.

Since there was little that the barbaric north could supply in any great quantity to the civilised south other than furs and slaves, it is probable that it was the growth of the northern population itself that produced most of the bulk cargoes that needed the larger ships. In the ancient world these cargoes consisted of grain, wine, salt, hides, furs, cattle, sheep and slaves. Slave chains found in Britain date from 200–100 BC.

As agriculture improved some areas would produce surpluses, but the cultivated plants would be more subject to destruction by pestilence, drought and storm, creating a pattern favourable to large scale transportation of grain across the English Channel, as took place in Caesar's time and was probably beginning around 500 BC. In 600 BC we see the first movement of wine from the Mediterranean world to central Europe and it cannot have been much later that wine was being shipped to the Celtic princes of Britain. By the 1st century BC Italian wine production is estimated to have reached 3,000,000 tons per year, which gives some idea of the shipping capacity required. The measurement of a ship's size came to be based on 'tuns' of wine, though we do not get pictures of wine being shipped in cask until later Roman times.

By 500 BC there was both a need for larger ships, which could only be propelled by oar and sail, and increasing contact with the southern civilisation where they had been used for thousands of years. Whether the northern sailors invented the oar and sail independently we cannot say, but some rumours of the two devices must have reached them, for the first Mediterranean ships sailed into northern waters around 500 BC.

Every hull change to increase carrying capacity for a given length, or to increase stability to carry sail, or to increase lateral resistance for the same end, makes a boat more difficult to paddle. Chesterton wrote of the wheel as the great paradox, 'always going backward to go forward'. The oar is like the wheel: by facing away from where you are going you get there quicker. Many years ago the author helped to test a sailing canoe on the local millpond. The auxiliary power was a pair of single paddles. In the course of the 'voyage' the shroud plates were used as fulcrums, turning the paddles into oars. The increase in power was astonishing, and when Bronze Age man discovered the oar he must have thought he had unleashed enormous force.

The change from paddle to oar does not, of course, increase the power of the human engine, but within certain limits it enables more of it to be used by bringing extra muscles into play. We estimated 0.2 h.p. per person from a crew of men and women paddling. With oars the same crew, bracing their legs against stretchers, might well produce 0.3 h.p. each for long periods.

By the use of oar ports a ship can be built with higher sides and the crew sit lower, sheltered from wind and spray. And a variable gearing is introduced into the propulsive system: by means of long oars with a great length of loom inboard of the fulcrum a very heavy vessel can be rowed slowly, whereas by paddles it could not be moved at all; 50-ton Thames lighters used to be manoeuvred on the tide by one man with a pair of gigantic sweeps. With a 5 ft canoe paddle he would have achieved nothing though the power output of his body was the same. And in certain circumstances an oar can be pulled by more than one man. The adoption of the oar would have permitted a 50 per cent increase in power, which would almost certainly have been used to propel vessels of considerably greater displacement at the same or a slightly lower speed.

The direct evidence for the early use of the oar in northern waters is extremely small. The few fragments of a boat found at Halsnoy in Norway in 1896 include a section of gunwale plank with an oar crotch lashed to it. Since her planks were sewn together she seems to date between the Als boat of 400–500 BC which was paddled and the Nydam ship of AD 300 which had riveted planks and was rowed.

The boat engraved on the sword blade from Rorby in Denmark (Fig. 1, No. 33) is dated mid-2nd millennium BC and seems to show a large single-banked galley of thirty pairs of oars with an oculus at the prow. She looks so like a Mediterranean galley at speed that one is tempted to dismiss it as based on a traveller's tale, but we have very little knowledge even of southern galleys of this period.

There are contemporary Cretan and Egyptian drawings which show men rowing, but in differently shaped ships. The painting of the eye was customary in the Mediterranean but does not appear on the Scandinavian rock pictures. If this is southern influence it is remarkably early, and could show that someone used oars in the north a thousand years before the date normally supposed. This evidence is best left alone until confirmation appears: the study of early boats is full of anomalies. Tacitus, writing in the 1st century AD, says that a certain German tribe used paddles 'held loose and not constrained like oars'.

A third use of oars in very early times is suggested by the rock drawing from Jonathan's Cave at East Wemyss in Fife, Scotland (Fig. 11). This is discussed in chapter 14 where the Bronze Age date is rejected in favour of a Pictish origin.

The development of the small motor has ruined the age-old craft of rowing and concealed its potential from the present generation. Not only do very few people now learn to row or scull properly, but their very equipment is no longer suitable. Sculls are rarely matched to the boat, and if it is a rubber dinghy half the drive is absorbed by the inflated thwart on which the rower sits while desperately trying not to fall over backwards. Instead of the potential 0.3 h.p. only about 0.15 h.p. is utilised, and rowing becomes backbreaking hard work that gets you nowhere. Such refinements as the little hinged flap that professional boatmen used to put on the thwarts to keep the rain off their seats are totally forgotten. These were the men who rowed on hour after hour without apparent fatigue.

A canoe has very little room for bulk cargo, and so as the amount to be carried increased the extra displacement was probably obtained by greater beam, producing a hull shape that would not only stand up to a useful sail, but needed a sail to move it. The change of proportion from a ratio of eight beams to the length to four or even three was obviously gradual, and greater fullness waited on the improvements in the sails.

To set a sail so that a boat will blow downwind is so obvious that an enormous number of people must have thought of it. A small bush carried forward or a man standing near the bow will show the effect of the wind. When Anson's *Centurion* (a 64-gun ship) was in irons off the Horn in a strong wind the crew manned the after shrouds to form a human sail which forced her head round.

A sail looks simple. It can be made of matting, bark cloth, leather, wool, cotton or flax, but it differs from other things made of these materials in requiring great strength in all directions to keep its shape under high stress. The earliest textiles known in Europe are linens from Swiss lake villages of 2940 BC. There is no evidence of matting or bark sails in Europe, though there is little chance that they would have survived, and there is no tradition or evidence that either material was used at all for tents, curtains or anything else. The only literary mention of leather sails is by Julius Caesar in 56 BC. Cotton was not grown in northern Europe until it was introduced into Spain by the Moors.

Flax is the traditional sailcloth material, stronger and more stretch-resistant than wool. But the material by itself will not take the strain, and a fully developed sail is made up of narrow cloths with interleaved and overlapping seams to increase the strength. A rope is sewn on all around the edge of the sail with slightly over a yard of cloth to a yard of rope to put the strain on the rope and not the cloth. Eyelets or cringles are sewn into the rope to take the controlling sheets and braces. Until something like this degree of strength is achieved a sail can only be used in light winds, when it is probably quicker to row.

All the knots, bends, splices and whippings required had probably been invented long before for other purposes. And if the sail was independently developed by the northern peoples they would first have set a very small one on a portable unstayed mast and only used it running downwind in a smart breeze. As they set more canvas they may have learned to reef it by gathering in or tying a knot in one corner. No doubt many generations passed before they dared to carry enough sail for general use, and learned to swing the yard diagonally and bowse down the fore lower corner of the sail to enable the ship to proceed at right angles to the wind. Only when they reached this stage could they do without such a large, expensive, space-filling, hungry crew, and so the merchant ship was born.

The sort of sail necessary to maintain a course with the wind at right angles to the boat has to be bent to a yard which is hoisted and lowered by one rope (halyard) and held against the mast either by an encircling rope or a curved fitting something like a cow's horn, which was often used. At least two ropes (sheets) are needed to control the lower corners of the sail. This is the absolute minimum; many more ropes can be used with advantage. We may wonder whether the northern seamen reached the solution independently. Unless the area of the sail can be varied it must either be made too small to be of any use in light airs or too large to be safe in strong winds. Viking longships carried 25 sq. ft (2.3 m²) of sail per ton, which is far too little by modern yachting standards, even though the Vikings undoubtedly had some system of reefing.

The Ferriby boats of 1000 BC were about 6 tons fully laden, and if boats had doubled in displacement by 500 BC when we have supposed the sail was introduced, they would have carried less still, perhaps 200 sq. ft (18 m²) on a length of 50 ft (15 m) and a beam of 6–10 ft (1.8–3 m). A square sail of this area needs a mast at least 20 ft (6 m) high and a yard 16 ft (5 m) long. A modern 14 ft dinghy has a mainsail of 90 sq. ft (8.4 m²) and this can be frightening enough to a beginner in a strong wind, when the sail cannot be controlled without a purchase on the mainsheet to increase the helmsman's power.

Modern yachts sail within 45° of the wind, the result of 150 years' development with little regard for expense and load-carrying capacity. The best fore-and-aft rigged working boats, smacks, luggers and spritsail barges could not sail closer than 50° to the wind; 19th century coastal traders with single square sails, like the Humber keels and Yorkshire billyboys, could not get closer than 70°. This is easy to accomplish; it is the other 15°–30° that is so difficult.

Doubtless, for a long time the Bronze and Iron Age seamen did not sail nearer than 90° to the wind, and this was sufficient for most of their crossings. It would have involved long waits for the wind to change and occasional backbreaking passages under paddle or oar alone. But the wind-roses on the maps show that one does not have to wait forever.

To push a heavy boat across the English Channel in a south-westerly wind demands that the sail works with the wind at right angles to the hull. The pressure of the wind on the sail, which in the sort of boats we are talking about would have been a square sail with the yard hauled diagonally across the boat, would tend both to upset the boat and push it sideways through the water. At this stage in development the Pacific islanders built a narrow deep hull and added a balancing float or outrigger to windward. The mariners of the west and northwest never tried this easy solution: instead, they built wider, deeper boats which became the ancestors of the true sailing ship.

Stability increases rapidly with size, and a vessel 40 or 50 ft (12 or 15 m) long with a length/beam ratio of 6:1 will stand up to a useful sail area. The Norfolk and Suffolk beach yawls of the last century, 50 ft (15 m) long and 10 ft (3 m) beam, carried a tremendous press of sail (Plate 12). The Deal galleys of the same era, 30 ft by 5 ft (9 m by 1.5 m), were also heavily canvassed. Once the Bronze Age

12 Nineteenth century AD Norfolk beach yawl. The model demonstrates that adequate sailing performance is possible without a pronounced keel. (Crown copyright Science Museum, London)

sailors increased the beam of their boats to 6 ft (1.8 m) they could have stood up to winds strong enough to move them usefully.

Much has been written about changes in the hull form of ancient sailing ships, to give them a grip on the water and decrease the tendency to slide to leeward. But for sailing across the wind comparatively little change is needed. The Suffolk beach yawls and Deal galleys had nothing beyond some 18 in. (46 cm) draft of hull and a keel of no more than 4 in. (10 cm) depth. The Norfolk wherry, which had a very good windward performance indeed, had a detachable iron bar keel less than 1 ft (0.3 m) deep for a very short portion amidships.

A modern racing dinghy in search of maximum ability to windward has an enormous centreplate, but this is because she has a very large sail area for her size and her keel is rockered fore and aft, only just touching the water at stem and transom. The old general purpose dinghies had small triangular plates which dropped a couple of feet (0.6 m) at the after end and nothing forward. Victorian yachtsmen such as E F Knight bolted a false keel 6 in. (15 cm) deep onto a ship's boat and sailed away. The *James Caird* (in the National Maritime Museum), the 18 ft (5.5 m) ship's lifeboat in which Sir Ernest Shackleton and his crew sailed from Elephant Island to South Georgia, has no special keel. The Nootka Indian canoe *Tilikum* which Captain Voss sailed round the world in 1901 had an 8 in. (20 cm) keel bolted to her flat bottom.

A sailing ship with a very small crew relies on her anchor to maintain position when the tide turns against her in light airs, and to keep from being driven on a lee shore. The ships of the Veneti of 56 BC had iron anchors and chain cables probably superior to those of the Romans. This argues a very long development independent of southern influence, since Roman anchors were usually made of wood and weighted with lead.

Pliny mentions production of sailcloth by the Morini of the Calais coast, who built Caesar's ships for the invasion of Britain, and by the Cadurci inland on the river Garonne and the Bituriges on the Loire. Yet another centre was at Narbonne, not far from the Mediterranean coast. Sailcloth weaving on this scale implies centuries of development, and the location of the weaving centres suggests the introduction of the sail from the Mediterranean and its use throughout the rivers and coasts of Gaul, from whence it must have spread to Britain. There can be little doubt that several hundred years BC full-bodied cargo-carrying sailing ships with auxiliary oars were voyaging all along the Atlantic and Channel coasts of Europe from Gibraltar to the Rhine. East of the Rhine sail may not have been used on any scale until the 7th or 8th centuries, when the Vikings suddenly appeared with sailing ships that were probably superior to anything else in Europe.

Until the invention of Watt's steam engine the sail was the only large-scale source of power. Watermills and windmills for all their bulk only develop a few horsepower; treadmills only convert the power of a few men or animals: but the sail of a Viking ship provided 50 h.p. and that of a big Roman merchantman perhaps 500. When Bronze or Iron Age man first saw a ship moved by wind and sail instead of thirty paddlers he must indeed have thought that she was being moved by the god of the winds, and it would have been quite reasonable for him to pray to this enormous and sometimes destructive power.

9 Mediterranean Contrast

Contemplating...this divine sea
one still longs for the real sea

ANDRE SIEGFRIED
The Mediterranean

Some peoples to the east of the Mediterranean were cold-working copper when the ice sheets were still over southern Britain and before the northern seas were formed, and their technology and cultures were immensely more advanced than those of northern and central Europe.

In the papyrus swamps of the Nile Delta there was a boatbuilding material to hand and in pre-dynastic times bundles of reeds were lashed together into boat-shaped rafts of the type made familiar by Thor Heyerdal's ocean crossing. The only native boatbuilding wood was the acacia tree, small and twisted, from which only planks of irregular shape can be cut. The Egyptians learned to join these edge to edge into a ribless shell with tenons set in the mating faces. There is also evidence that at a very early period good long timber, cedar of Lebanon, was imported for shipbuilding.

In the eastern desert there are rock carvings of ships, some of which seem to have a cabin and to have been propelled by oars, not paddles. Other drawings show boats of a crescent shape, like the reed boats; these also carry a cabin. From the very early dynastic period there is a drawing of a boat with a square sail at one end. In the 3rd millennium BC Egypt possessed warships and merchant ships in the eastern Mediterranean and the Red Sea, and river ships on the Nile. The very early civilisations arose in Egypt and Meso-potamia because conditions were especially favourable. The Nile itself encouraged the development of large ships; it has a strong north-flowing current to carry ships down and a predictable and steady northerly wind to blow them back under simple square sails. Obelisk barges of over 1000 tons, possibly several thousands of tons, were later towed along the Nile by fleets of galleys. The hulls were strengthened transversely by three tiers of beams projecting through the sides.

The seagoing merchantmen, not having a rigid framework, were strengthened by hogging trusses from bow to stern. Some had bipod masts, possibly developed originally to distribute the stresses over papyrus bundle hulls. Some early sails were bent to two yards, the lower supported by a fan of rope lifts from the masthead to keep its weight off the weak sailcloth.

The early Egyptians did not bury their dead in boats, but they buried boats with them in separate brick boat-shaped graves. These were solar boats to carry the king on his celestial voyage. The largest of the grave boats, buried in a dismantled state of thirteen layers containing 1274 separate pieces with ropes and fittings, was 145 ft (44.19 m) long.

There are many apparent similarities between Egyptian maritime achievement and that of the northern world. The boat drawings in the deserts resemble some of those found in Scandinavia and Brittany. The river transport of the stone obelisks is paralleled by the voyage of the Stonehenge bluestones, and the boat burials in Egyptian tombs are somewhat similar to the Saxon and Viking ship-graves. But neither oars, sails, steering oars, quarter rudders or hogging trusses appear in the Scandinavian rock carvings, so there is no reason on present evidence to consider these similarities as more than vague resemblances in techniques used by peoples widely separated in space, time and cultural development. The bluestone catamarans were not poor men's copies of Egyptian barges but some inkling of the highly developed southern naval architecture may have drifted along the routes of migration and trade.

The brilliant civilisation of Crete lasted from about 3000 BC until Knossos was destroyed around 1550 BC. Because it was unfortified it has been suggested that a Cretan navy made land defences un-necessary, but it is unlikely that any government of the time could have maintained a large enough standing fleet or that small galleys with lookouts only a few feet above the sea could have guaranteed security.

Drawings and models of Cretan boats or ships which have come down to us show vessels with a sort of 'beaver tail' at one end and a high vertical post at the other. Nobody knows which was the bow, but some boats have a fish weather vane on top of the post with the tail pointing into the boat. This suggests that the upright was the stem post and the 'tail' a steering oar. Since it is unlikely that a genuine navy existed in ancient Crete there is little possibility of the tail being a ram. Similar ships (without tails) are depicted on 3rd millennium artifacts from the islands between Greece and Turkey.

R W Hutchinson in *Prehistoric Crete* notes that there does not seem to have been any word in the ancient Greek language for a paddle so the invention of the oar seems to have been very early in the Mediterranean. The crew, who number up to thirty in contemporary illustrations, seem to be rowing in the Cretan vessels which also carried a sail.

When the Neolithic peoples made their way along the northern shore of the Mediterranean around 3000 BC, there were little more than farmer/fisher communities in Greece and the Aegean. Yet around 3400 BC Egypt had changed from an advanced Neolithic peasant culture to a dynastic state with a civil service capable of organisation on a great scale. Shipping was confined to Asia Minor, the Levant, Egypt and Crete. But there were plank-built ships sufficiently close to the eastern end of the route to suggest that sheep and grain were carried to the west in small planked craft.

Only that part of the northern Mediterranean from Crete to the Asiatic shore had achieved any great level of civilisation by 1000 BC and this was on a very small scale. Troy, probably besieged about 1240–1230 BC, was about 200 yards across. Helen's face hardly needed to launch a hundred ships let alone a thousand, to carry the Greeks to the little city near the entrance to the Dardanelles.

Colonisation of the western Mediterranean began about 1000 BC when Phoenician traders began to sail westwards along the north African shore. Ezekiel says that their hulls were made of cypress from Mount Herman, masts from cedar of Lebanon, oars from oak of Bashan, and the sails from Egyptian cotton.

Carthage was traditionally founded by the Phoenicians in 814 BC though archaeologists have found nothing there dating before 750 BC. By this time they had also settled in Sicily and Sardinia. Greek traders were at Cumae in the Bay of Naples in 750 BC and had tapped one of the early sources of copper. There were other Greek 'colonies' in southern Italy; Syracuse in eastern Sicily was founded in 733 BC, Massilia (Marseilles) was established before 600 BC, and from there the Greeks sailed on to the Spanish coast where they built Mainake, a small trading post near modern Malaga.

Although Neolithic peoples from the east had settled in the Iberian peninsula before 4000 BC, it was not until the Greeks and Carthaginians reached the western Mediterranean that trade developed on a scale that could directly affect northern Europe. The Carthaginians established trading posts or watering points about every 50 miles (a day's sail) along the North African coast. Around 500 BC they occupied Gades (Cadiz) and superseded a local people who had traded to the north for centuries from Tartessus. Ancient writings suggest the Phoenicians traded here in 1100 BC. The newcomers sought tin, gold and silver.

The first meeting of Mediterranean and northern shipping must have taken place in the Cadiz region, not later than 500 BC and perhaps a few centuries earlier when an occasional Phoenician ship had called. The Mediterranean ships already carried properly rigged square sails, and in a few generations the art of sailing must have passed around the Iberian peninsula to where the Pyrenees meet the Atlantic and on northwards to where the Garonne reaches the sea.

By now the metalworkers from the Levant had tapped all the local sources of metal—Sinai, Cyprus, Etruria and Spain—and wealth and population were growing. Carthage ruled 500,000 people living in 40,000 square miles of Africa, and Athens governed a territory the size of Hampshire, in England or Long Island, in the USA with a population of 400,000 living in an area of about 3000 square miles. Some Greek and Carthaginian colonies in the central Mediterranean contained 10,000 people. Rome was still insignificant, but on the shores of Asia Minor there were millions of people of far older civilisations who traded east as well as west.

The sophisticated governments of the eastern Mediterranean built specialised warships. Egypt, Persia, Assyria, Carthage, Athens, Sparta and Rome all had large galley fleets.

Freight can be carried in galleys, but there is little room for bulk cargoes like grain, oil and wine. Even a small galley carried thirty oarsmen who had to be fed and paid, or shackled and guarded. The cargo got wet from water breaking in through the oar ports and the sanitary problems from large numbers of men immobilised for long periods were acute. Galleys were long and narrow and liable to work and leak. They had to be dried out and scrubbed off or they became too heavy to row.

So we are not surprised to find a picture of a small sailing ship on an Etruscan vase of 500 BC. Until recently we could not judge her size nor make any worthwhile attempt to draw her lines, but in 1967 the wreck of an ancient Greek ship was found in 16 fathoms off the harbour of Kyrenia in Cyprus. In 1968–9 divers excavated the mound of silt that covered her and found that most of the port side and all the cargo still remained. The stem and stern, decking and hatches had all disappeared. Robin Piercy, who is directing the reconstruction in Kyrenia Castle, showed the author all that has been recovered, enabling him to make the drawings and calculations in Fig. 7.

The basis of the reconstruction is the almost intact curved keel and the section drawn in great detail by the excavation's modelmaker from the planks, frames, keel, keelson etc. The position of this section was based on Mr Piercy's estimate of the mast position and the hull lines followed naturally using the drawing on the Etruscan vase as a guide. The result is not unlike a modern full-

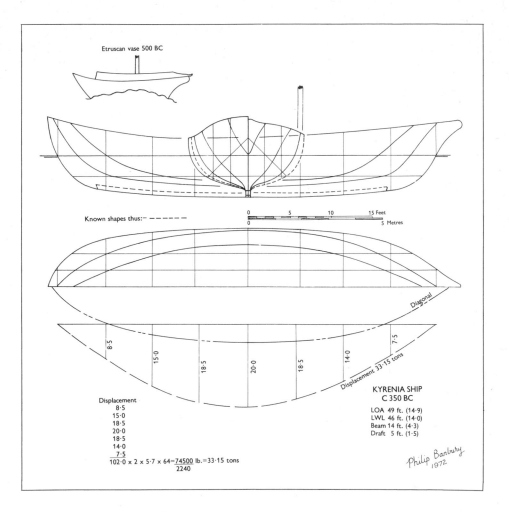

Etruscan vase 500 BC

Known shapes thus:— — — — — —

0   5   10   15 Feet
0   5 Metres

Diagonal

8·5

15·0

18·5

20·0

18·5

14·0

7·5

Displacement 33·15 tons

KYRENIA SHIP
C 350 BC

Displacement
8·5
15·0
18·5
20·0
18·5
14·0
7·5

LOA 49 ft. (14·9)
LWL 46 ft. (14·0)
Beam 14 ft. (4·3)
Draft 5 ft. (1·5)

$\overline{102·0 \times 2 \times 5·7 \times 64 = \underline{74500}}$ lb.=33·15 tons
2240

Philip Banbury
1972

7 Kyrenia merchant ship ca 300 BC (author's reconstruction)

bodied yacht. Today's vessel would be fuller aft and finer forward, but all known ancient ships were symmetrical. A modern yacht would be lower at the stern, but ancient ships sailed mainly with the wind abaft the beam and this sort of sheer and the full bow may have suited them better. When Saint Paul's ship was gale-driven towards the shore 'they cast four anchors out of the stern and wished for day'.

The cargo of the Kyrenia ship was 400 amphorae each weighing about 70 lbs (32 kg) full, and 29 millstones; 9000 raisins were also recovered. She had apparently come from the Aegean via Rhodes. The weight of the ship unladen was calculated at 33,650 lbs (15,264 kg), and the cargo weighed 39,600 lbs (17,962 kg), a total displacement of 73,250 lbs (33,226 kg). She was completely sheathed in lead, a cheap by-product of the silver mines. The sheathing weighed 6000 lbs (2722 kg) and with the 11,600 lbs (5262 kg) weight of the millstones stowed over the keelson, is the only ballast included in the calculations. She floated deep, and perhaps on the fatal day around 325 BC she was running before a rising gale and shipping water over the bow, filling as it penetrated the hatch covers. They lowered the sail to slow her up—too late.

The planks were fastened edge to edge with tenons and fastened to the heavy frames by bronze nails nearly a foot long, driven through wood pegs and turned over on the inner face of the frames. The nail points were then turned over again and hammered into the wood. This became Roman practice and we shall find it again in the London ships. The draw tongue joints lead back to the early Egyptian ships. How the Kyrenia ship was steered is not yet known, nor how she was rigged. Four cups, plates and oil bottles were found in her and this was presumably the number of the crew, who would only have been able to row her very slowly in a dead calm. She has been dated by C_{14} to about 300 BC and shows us what a Greek merchant ship was like a few hundred years after Greek merchants had begun to trade into the western Mediterranean.

We now have the reports of Mediterranean explorers sailing the outer seas. The most important were the Carthaginians Hanno and Himilco, possibly brothers from one of the leading families. Hanno made a voyage of trade or colonisation to the Atlantic coast of North Africa and what is said to be the Greek version of his report has survived. According to this he sailed with sixty 50-oared ships carrying 30,000 men and women; a certain exaggeration in view of the total population of Carthage.

The Elder Pliny criticised the report severely, for if it is true at all it appears to have been written not to reveal Hanno's discovery but to mislead rivals. It is now thought that while the voyage did take place it can no longer be maintained that he circumnavigated Africa or got close to the Cape of Good Hope. Himilco, on what seems to have been the northern part of the same project, sailed round Spain to Brittany.

There is no archaeological evidence that the Phoenicians or Carthaginians ever came to Britain but there is little doubt that Himilco made the voyage, probably on behalf of his government, in the 5th century BC. If he also used galleys, they may have been the first ships to demonstrate the superiority of oars over paddles in northern waters. For a voyage such as this the galley was ideal; able to keep out of trouble in uncharted waters and with a large crew for protection unless she was rowed by slaves.

We can follow Himilco in imagination from Gades (Cadiz), a great natural harbour commanding the exit from the Mediterranean and where the Carthaginians minted coin from local silver. His galleys (Plate 13) would have reached the sheltered roadstead of Huelva after the normal daylight voyage of 50 miles. The second day would have taken them to the sheltered lagoons at Faro where the hills a few miles inland rise up to 1000 ft. The third night would have been spent on whichever side of Cape St Vincent gave a lee; the fourth night 40 miles north, the fifth in the great haven of Setubal and the sixth in the roadstead of the Tagus. If they had had bad weather the voyage might have taken three weeks (Map 6).

Four more days would have taken Himilco's fleet to Oporto past magnificent harbours every 50 miles where he could have anchored each night. From Oporto to Finisterre the river mouths and creeks are only about 10 miles apart and from Finisterre to the inlet where Corunna now stands is another 50 miles. So far the voyage would have taken 13 days if they had little rest and time ashore, good weather and provisions for the asking.

The times suggested are an absolute minimum, for conditions off the west coast of Spain and Portugal present special problems. In addition to a $\frac{1}{2}$ knot south-going main current, the prevailing wind —the Nortada—blows from the north and causes a further 2 knot south-going surface current. The Vikings cruised successfully along this coast using a single square sail rigged in much the same way as the one on the Phoenician or Carthaginian galley shown in Plate 13. But suggestions of a busy trade route between Spain and Britain in early times may not always have taken local conditions into account.

The northern coast of Spain, cliffbound and backed by mountains as far east as the Pyrenees, would have been passed in six more days. Then the ships would have turned north for two days or so, past the great salt etangs along the sandy shore to the Gironde estuary. This part of the voyage was far from easy for a pioneering captain. The normal current, an eddy from the Gulf Stream, flows southward and westward but strong winds far out create a counter-current which flows at up to 5 knots along the coast where Spain and France meet. A heavy swell develops which breaks dangerously near sunken rocks even in deep water and pounds heavily on the bars which lie across the entrances to many of the harbours. Tides are small. The coast from here to Brittany has already been described in chapter 3.

The total voyage from Gades could have been done in 24 days, but would have been more likely to take two months. A trader

WAR GALLEY of VIIth CENTURY B.C.

אניה קרב מן המאה ה-7 לפני הספירה

FIGHTING SHIP BUILT BY PHOENICIAN SHIPWRIGHTS

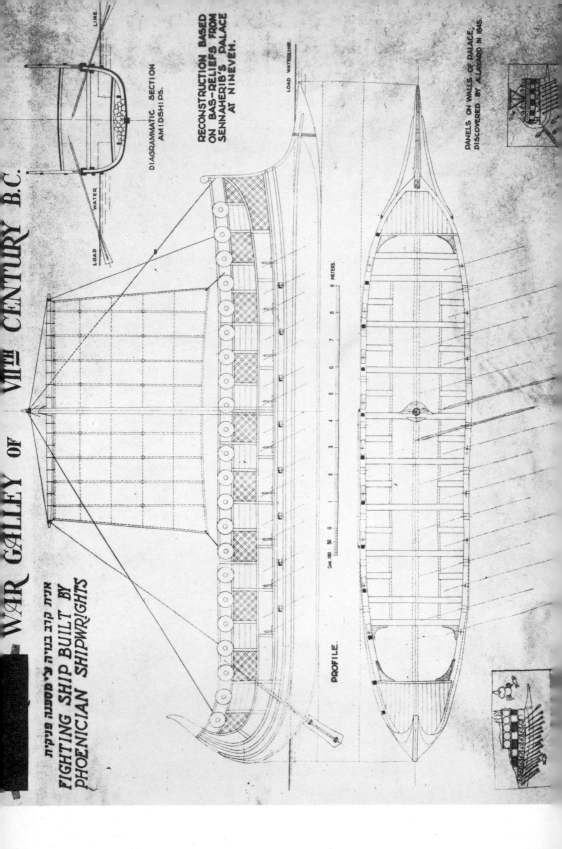

RECONSTRUCTION BASED ON BAS-RELIEFS FROM SENNAHERIB'S PALACE AT NINEVEH.

DIAGRAMMATIC. SECTION AMIDSHIPS.

LOAD LINE.

WATER

LOAD WATERLINE.

PROFILE.

Cms. 100 50 0

0 1 2 3 4 5 6 7 8 9 METERS.

PANELS ON WALLS OF PALACE, DISCOVERED BY A. LAYARD IN 1845.

might have made only one round voyage a summer and laid up his ship all through the winter.

Avienus, a Roman writer using sources from the 5th century BC or before, wrote of trade between Tartessus and Brittany, but in spite of this and the confident statements of modern writers it is unlikely that there was any very serious trade between Britain or Brittany and southern Spain before 500 BC and not much for centuries after. Britain and Spain produced tin, copper, lead, gold and silver and the Carthaginians had found all they wanted in Spain. Brittany also produced tin. If the Mediterranean world got objects or materials from Britain or Brittany, it is more likely that they travelled across Europe via the Garonne.

At every one of those two dozen or so anchorages used by Himilco, the local sailors would have seen ships under sail and oar, whether the 50 short oars of a galley or the four or six long sweeps of a sailing ship. We may take it as a certainty that both oar and sail came into use in northern Europe between 500 and 400 BC unless they were already there.

Himilco claimed that his ships were stopped by calms, mists, shallows and sea monsters. Perhaps he was just trying to frighten off rival explorers. But he had reached the entrance to the English Channel, a region of vicious tides with an enormous rise and fall. He may have run his ships aground several times and made no progress against ever-changing contrary streams he could not understand. The Mediterranean was full of fine seamen, but the slight tides there are often obscured by other changes in the water level and currents, and even the scientifically minded Greeks did not recognise them.

We meet the 'sluggish sea' again. Pytheas, a Greek from Massilia (Marseilles), made an extensive voyage of discovery between 310 and 304 BC. He is vouched for by several well-known contemporaries, and was an astronomer and a geographer who measured and recorded the length of daylight at the places he visited and the latitude of the place from which he started. He slipped past the Carthaginians and sailed the Atlantic coast of Europe as far as the Shetlands (where the longest day is 19 hours). Here he heard of a land six days' sail to the north where the sea was sluggish and congealed. Other writers say this was Thule, where there was perpetual night or day and plenty of bees and honey. It could have been Iceland or north Norway, but perhaps because of colder weather there are now no bees near either place.

The voyage is recorded by Strabo and again much of it is plausible. Pytheas is said to have seen tin in Cornwall cast into knucklebone shapes for export, and later on he is supposed to have reached

13 Reconstruction of Phoenician or Carthaginian galley such as Himilco may have sailed to Brittany, 7th century BC. Based on bas-reliefs from Senna-cherib's palace at Nineveh. (Crown copyright Science Museum, London)

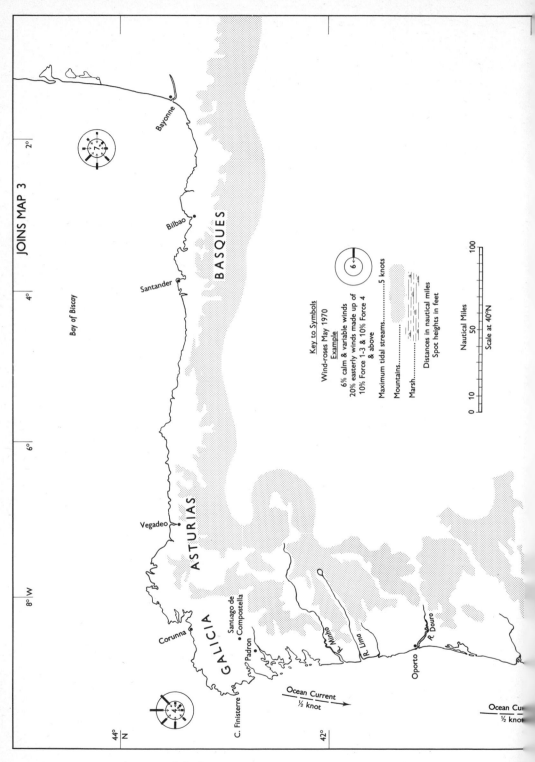

2°

4°

6°

8° W

Bay of Biscay

Bayonne

Bilbao

Santander

BASQUES

Vegadeo

ASTURIAS

Corunna

GALICIA

Santiago de
Compostella

Padron

C. Finisterre

Minho

R. Lima

Oporto

R. Douro

Key to Symbols

Wind-roses May 1970
Example
6% calm & variable winds
20% easterly winds made up of
10% Force 1-3 & 10% Force 4
& above

Maximum tidal streams............5 knots

Mountains..............

Marsh..............

Distances in nautical miles
Spot heights in feet

Nautical Miles

0   10   50   100

Scale at 40°N

44°
N

42°

Ocean Current
½ knot

Ocean Cur
½ kno

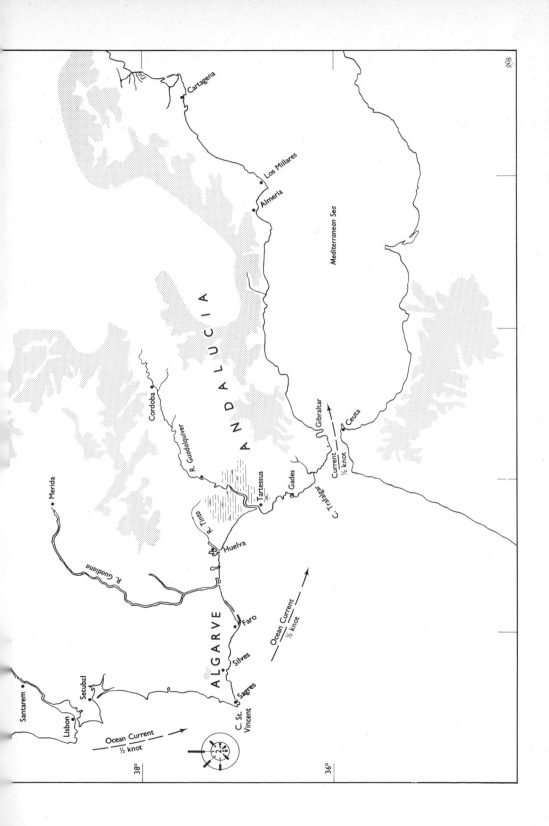

Denmark and Frisia where he saw tall blond men dressed in skins and discovered the source of amber. Nansen compared the 'sluggish sea' to the sludge formed in the Arctic when drift ice is ground to pulp by waves. Tacitus in his *Agricola* describes how the Roman fleet found the sea near Orkney 'sluggish and heavy to the oar'. In all three of these voyages the poor progress could have been due to tides, the exhaustion of cold and frightened sailors too far from home, or to incipient scurvy which disappeared after a few days in harbour and a change of food.

We are left with the probability that Iceland was visited very early indeed, perhaps even in the Bronze Age. Visited by someone who came back alive and passed on the information to the Shetlanders who told Pytheas. Geographical information was not very freely given in ancient times, and we wonder whether they told him because they thought the place was useless or just to get rid of him. Or did they have kinsmen there and asked Pytheas to deliver supplies?

Whatever happened, there is no doubt that from the 5th century BC onwards the northern seas were alive from Gibraltar to the Northern Isles and Ireland to the Baltic, and that the long slim canoe was giving way to the round-bodied sailing ship. There were professional sailors on the northern seas carrying as supercargo merchants from the southern seas, and from the mingling of the two wealth was born.

10 Julius Caesar and the Channel Shore

*One must first become an oarsman
before handling the rudder*

L CORNELIUS SULLA

Julius Caesar first saw the cliffs of Dover in 55 BC. He had been in Cadiz in 68 BC and Portugal in 61 BC; in 56 BC he had defeated the maritime tribes of western Gaul and subdued those of the northern coast. He had been captured by pirates when he was 28 and had later sailed against them. He had studied astronomy and seen many of the great ports of the known world. He was soon to rule the greatest naval power of the time, with hundreds of galleys and thousands of merchant ships at his command. When he wrote about the sea and ships it was as a logistics expert who had commanded great enterprises by land and sea, and as one of the greatest travellers of his time.

The naval organisation in the Mediterranean between 500 BC and the year when the Roman legions first crossed to Britain is impressive even to us. It is often said that the Romans disliked the sea and did not understand it. The majority of Romans like the majority of present-day Britons were probably neutral, but the Roman fleets were handled by expert professionals who had defeated all the other powers in the central sea. A few examples show the level of maritime technique that the Romans brought to the north when Caesar conquered Gaul.

Galleys with three banks of oars were introduced into the Athenian fleet soon after 550 BC. They were about 115 ft (35 m) long overall and 100 ft (30 m) on the waterline. The beam of the hulls was 12 ft (3.7 m) and the width over the outriggers, which increased the leverage of the oars, was 16 ft (4.9 m). The draft was 4 ft (1.2 m) and the displacement about 80 tons. There were 85 oars on each side, 170 in all. The cruising horsepower was about 51 and the maximum 72, power/weight ratios of 0.64 and 0.90 h.p. per ton giving speeds of 7 knots for long periods and around 9 knots for the dash into battle. These speeds are probably more accurate than those given by Thucydides, who gives 168 miles in 24 hours, and Xenophon, who gives much more.

The information we have about Roman galleys consists largely

of distorted representations in carved stone and imprecise statements by historians. There were no Fred T Janes in the classical
world. Fig. 10 is based on the dimensions of the Athenian ship-
houses and is correct for a *Greek* trireme within narrow limits:
Roman triremes were similar. The swivel catapults shown are
guesses based on firm literary evidence. They were undoubtedly
carried on *some Roman* ships in the Channel and the North Sea,
but how many, how large and how they were disposed is not known.
Roman field artillery fired iron darts of about 2 lbs weight; accurate
range was approximately 200 yards but the rate of fire was slow.
Much larger Roman warships existed, but they were not used in the
north as far as we know.

How the oarsmen were arranged is only important to the specialist. The author's suggestion in Fig. 10 is only one of many possible
solutions. How many students of the steam warship can remember
whether the *Warrior* had siamese engines, horizontal return piston
or double trunk engines? The important thing is the horsepower.

Galley machinery needed fuel and suffered from fatigue like any
other machinery, but it had other defects as well. We tend to
think of poor whip-driven wretches captured in battle or taken from
jails, always ready to turn on their captors. Roman oarsmen did not
necessarily conform to this pattern. Ancient economy depended
on slaves, mostly ignorant but some highly educated and trusted.
Most were born to it, married slaves, and had slave children. They
were not shackled and moved free. The men who rowed the Roman
galleys were presumably slaves; whether they were shackled to
the oar or just kept there by savage discipline like the men of the
Royal Navy in the 18th century (who were almost slaves) is not
certain. The oarsmen of the Rhine flotilla in AD 70 were apparently
recruited like the army auxiliaries.

The chief problem was excrement and disease. If 170 men were
locked to their oars for 24 hours, the state of their ship hardly bears
thinking about. Other ships always tried to pass to windward of
galleys. Even allowing for much lower standards of hygiene than
our own, one essential dockyard job must have been cleaning out
the ships. The oarsmen must have lived ashore and only gone on
board when the ship was ready to sail. And in the Roman and similar
navies it would have been necessary continually to check the men
for contagious disease or whole crews could be quickly lost. Above
all a trireme crew had to be fit and trained; it was not a job for
amateurs: their energy output was enormous and they had to be
sufficiently if not daintily fed.

The ships were delicate and had to be kept ashore under cover
for most of their lives to prevent water soakage. Ship sheds were

built in continuous colonades over gently sloping slips at the water's edge. Surviving naval lists show that Athens had 372 ship sheds, mostly double, backed by walled and guarded dockyards which strangers entered on pain of death. There were 220 ship sheds at Carthage with store sheds over them, which stretched round the harbour for a mile or more. The Romans had ship-sheds at Vitruvium.

In the first war between Carthage and Rome (265–242 BC) it was Rome that won the sea battles between fleets sometimes totalling nearly 500 ships. Most were quinqueremes carrying up to 300 rowers and 120 soldiers. Most of the battles were fought close to land and many of the defeated ships were driven ashore. This was seafaring on a much higher technological level than that of northern Europe, but voyaging was still along the coast where possible. In AD 253 a Roman fleet attempted to sail direct from Panormus on the western tip of Sicily to Rome, about 250 miles, and was caught by a gale which sank 150 ships. A passage of over two and a half days was beyond the range of their weather forecasting, and warships were not yet seaworthy enough to ride out bad weather.

In the second Carthaginian War (219–202 BC) the Carthaginians never attempted to command the sea, and Hannibal marched his troops from Spain to Italy where he fought for 13 years. The Romans, with remarkable naval sense, built 200 ships at the outset and maintained them throughout the struggle, but they could not stop troopships and supplies reaching Hannibal. No doubt the Roman captains tried hard enough, but their warships were too unseaworthy and uncomfortable to stay at sea for more than a few days. And what the Roman navy could not do then even the sailing navy of Britain could not do until nearly twenty centuries later.

The second Carthaginian War ended about 100 years before Julius Caesar was born, and during that period Rome had absorbed the art and learning of all the ancient civilizations of the eastern Mediterranean. Yet when Caesar saw the ships of the Veneti prepared for battle off the southern coast of Brittany he was deeply impressed. This is what he wrote:

> On learning of his arrival…the Veneti and other tribes… began to make ready for war…They knew that the roads were intersected by tidal inlets and that sailing would be difficult for us on account of our ignorance of the waterways and the scarcity of harbours…they had a strong fleet, while we had no ships available…and sailing in a wide ocean was…very different…from sailing in a land-locked sea. They fortified their strongholds and assembled as many ships as possible on the coast of Venetia

[southwest Brittany]. They secured the alliance of various tribes in the neighbourhood and of the Morini [near Calais] and the Menapii [near Rotterdam] and summoned reinforcements from Britain.

Caesar was faced with a very large operation: the whole passage reveals the coming and going of ships along 150 miles of European coastline, and back and forth to Britain with envoys and troops. His headquarters were at Angers. The sea battle was probably in Quiberon Bay.

The young Decimus Brutus was placed in command of the fleet, including the Gallic ships that Caesar had ordered the Pictones, Santoni and other tribes to provide. Brutus's orders were to sail as soon as possible for Venetia. Caesar himself marched there with the land forces.

The Pictones and the Santoni were from the coast of southwest Gaul which the Romans had occupied a few years before.

The Gauls' own ships were built and rigged in a different manner from ours. They were made with flatter bottoms to help them ride shallow water caused by shoals and ebb tides. Exceptionally high bows and sterns fitted them for use in heavy seas and violent gales, and the hulls were made entirely of oak to enable them to withstand shocks and rough usage. The cross timbers...a foot wide, were fastened with iron bolts as thick as a man's thumb. The anchors were secured by iron chains...They used sails made of raw hides or thin leather, either because they had no flax...or because they thought that ordinary sails would not stand the violent storms...The only advantage our ships possessed was that they were faster and could be propelled by oars...We could not injure them by ramming because they were so solidly built, and their height made it difficult to reach them with missiles or board them with grappling irons...They could bring to in shallow water with greater safety and when left aground by the tide had nothing to fear from reefs and pointed rocks...to our ships all these risks were formidable.

Caesar may have been exaggerating. He had run into more trouble than he anticipated and was excusing himself by this story of ships of nightmare strength and size. It is difficult to believe that the Veneti ships were so high that their crews could not be reached by sling-stones, arrows or javelins, or that the Romans could not grapple and board them quickly. And very few ships can sit on a rock with impunity.

'Caesar decided that he must wait for his fleet to be brought up' suggests that a few unsuccessful attacks had already been made against superior numbers. 'Directly it hove in sight some two hundred and twenty enemy ships sailed out of harbour and took up stations facing it.' This is a very specific figure: can we really accept this account of such a host of ships, shallow bodied and therefore poor sailers (though adequate for trade), assembling and manoeuvring like a crack legion on the parade ground?

Neither Brutus nor [the captains of his ships] could decide what to do…when they tried erecting turrets they found they were still overtopped by the…lofty sterns and were too low to make their missiles carry properly…One device proved very useful, pointed hooks fixed into the ends of long poles…With these the halyards were grasped and pulled taut and then snapped by rowing hard away. This…brought the yards down and since the Gallic ships depended wholly on sails they were at once immobilised.

We are tempted to say that we do not believe a word of it, but most ancient history has a substratum of truth.

When the yards of an enemy ship were torn down, two or three of ours would get alongside and soldiers would board it. When the natives saw what was happening, and after the loss of several ships could still find no answer to these tactics, they tried to escape by flight. They had already put their ships before the wind when such a dead calm fell they could not stir…It enabled us to complete the victory by pursuing [sic] and capturing the vessels one after another.

What really happened? Fig. 8 attempts to show the probable appearance and size of the opposing vessels. The Veneti ships cannot have been much more than 50 ft long by 15 ft beam (15 m by 4.6 m). The Mediterranean sailing ship described in the last chapter was about this size, displacing 30 tons laden to 5 ft (1.5 m) draft with 2 ft (0.6 m) of freeboard. The large Viking knarr at Roskilde in Denmark is about the same size, displacing 20–25 tons.

The Veneti anchor in the Dorchester Museum weighs about 190 lbs (86 kg) and, if it held as well as a modern 'fisherman' type, would have suited a 50 ft (15 m) ship. It was probably much less efficient but, as ancient vessels carried at least twice as many anchors as we do, it may well have belonged to a 50-footer. By the laws of chance it was probably a conventional size, though of course it may have been larger or smaller than usual. The ship was

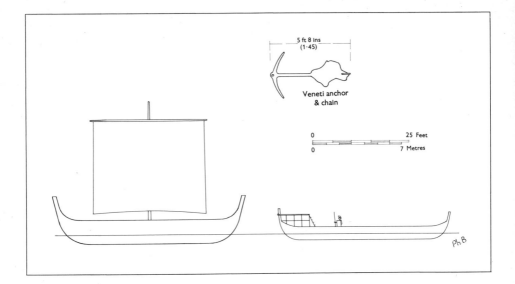

5 ft 8 ins
(1·45)

Veneti anchor
& chain

0   25 Feet

0   7 Metres

Ph B

moored to it by an iron chain, confirming this detail of Caesar's story.

8 Probable sizes of Veneti ship and Roman galley 56 BC

During the battle the Veneti ships were probably sailing light with about 5 ft (1.5 m) freeboard and their crews were crouching down out of sight. The Romans were standing in open boats and their heads may not quite have reached the enemy gunwales. The Veneti bows may have overtopped the Roman helmets by 6 ft (1.8 m). Bearing down in close formation, 220 ships would have looked terrifying to men waiting in low rowing craft, and the high bows would have sheltered the Veneti crews from the Roman missiles. Caesar's account becomes plausible when we remember that he was not there himself and had to rely on the accounts of badly shaken officers.

It is fairly certain that the Celtic peoples of Gaul used long, low rowing craft for piracy, intertribal warfare and trade in confined waters. These must have been the type of vessel that the Romans had built by the Pictones and the Santoni: far too small to carry any elaborate boarding towers and not fitted with rams. If the Romans had been using their standard Mediterranean galleys displacing 80 tons and fitted with bronze-shod underwater rams, they would have smashed anything.

At the end of the battle the Veneti ships turned away downwind. Until then they must have had the wind on the beam. When the wind dropped they did not attempt to row out of danger so they must have carried few oars—as Caesar says. Whether the sails were really leather—he does not seem to have been sure what leather—or were heavily tanned flax is a moot point, and he may have been mistaken. The size of the nails he quotes is quite possible, spikes of this size were used in the construction of the Veneti forts and in the Kyrenia ship and the Blackfriars ship, both of about the same size. The Veneti ships must have been carvel built, for if they had been clinker built he would almost certainly have said so.

That they had only one mast and sail does not make them primitive. All northern ships were rigged this way until the 13th century, when a second mast was added not for efficiency but because ships had got too big for one. More masts and sails, other things being equal, can produce less efficiency not more.

Roman punishment for rebellion was savage and there is considerable evidence that those Veneti chiefs who would not submit voyaged to southwest Britain, where they persuaded the inhabitants to increase the defences of their hill forts. Fighting men from the Channel shore of Gaul also crossed to Britain. Perhaps there were only a few hundred altogether who turned up unheralded, like the French fishing boats which crossed to Britain in 1940. They might well have raided Gaul from their new base if Caesar had not invaded Britain.

On 26 August 55 BC he sailed to Britain from the country of the Morini near Boulogne. 'He had ordered ships to assemble there from all the neighbouring districts as well as the fleet which had been built for the Veneti campaign....In due course about 80 transports were obtained and assembled and also a number of warships.' The transports were to carry two legions which if they were up to establishment would have totalled 12,000 men or 150 to each transport, a figure confirmed by Caesar in a later passage.

The transports were presumably native vessels like the ships of the Veneti. To have set up full Roman dockyard and design facilities for all the ships would have taken too long and it was already late in the summer. But Caesar does specify some warships which were quite unfamiliar to the Britons and scared them 'by the strange shape, the motion of the oars and the unfamiliar machines' (catapults). Since some Britons had seen the warships used against the Veneti it is possible that a few new warships were built under the supervision of Roman naval shipwrights for the invasion.

If the 150 soldiers per ship had been packed very tight they might have been squeezed into vessels about 70 ft by 25 ft (21 m by 8 m). The baggage was left behind so the legions must have sailed with only arms, armour and iron rations. There were also 18 transports for the cavalry.

Caesar questioned merchants about the southeast coast of

Britain and sent a warship on a four-day reconnaissance. Did Captain Volusenus stay over the horizon by day and row in to test the landing beaches by night? We only know that he was 'a suitable man for the job'.

The eighty infantry transports sailed at midnight. Caesar was in the leading ship, which closed the English coast at 9 o'clock the following morning somewhere east of Dover where high cliffs rise up from a narrow beach. Here he anchored and waited for the others. At 3 o'clock in the afternoon the whole fleet sailed east about 7 miles on a favourable wind and tide and the transports were run aground near Deal on an open beach, Mediterranean fashion, but risky even there. They touched bottom far enough offshore to frighten the soldiers, probably seasick and terrified at the thought of jumping fully armoured into four or five feet of water.

There are other horrors in modern warfare, but to wade slowly ashore towards a ferocious enemy screaming for blood at the water's edge must have been an equal terror. Caesar ordered his warships to beach on the enemy's flank and fire their ballistae into the defenders; they may have been standard Roman war galleys with swivel catapults in their bows. Discipline took command again and the standard bearer of the 10th Legion leaped into the water with the soldiers surging after him.

The eighteen cavalry transports had been slow in loading and missed the midnight tide. We can imagine the scene, with the frightened horses screaming and shying in the dim light. In the cavalry transports of the 18th century the horses had separate stalls, but Caesar's horses were probably packed close to hold one another up, perhaps with each rider at his horse's head to calm it; a terrifying prospect to a non-horseman. On the basis of the words on the French railway wagons of World War I, *Hommes quarante, chevaux huit,* ships of the size illustrated would have carried 20 horses.

The ships did not sail until four days later and, although the wind was light when they weighed anchor, it blew up when they were in sight of the main fleet and drove them away westward until they anchored to ride out the storm. But they shipped too much water, and as darkness fell they stood out from the coast and returned to Gaul.

It was full moon and Caesar admits that the Romans did not yet understand the tides. The high water and strong winds caught the infantry transports moored offshore, driving them together and carrying away their anchors and cables. But the soldiers worked manfully and made all but twelve ships seaworthy again with 'timber and bronze' from the wrecks or fetched from Gaul. The

Romans were dogged by bad weather and, although they beat off all attacks and penetrated inland, their situation was precarious. Caesar arranged a truce and took the fleet back to Gaul a few days before the autumnal equinox (23rd September).

At the real invasion in 54 BC, Caesar tells of the transport of five legions, 30,000 men at full strength and 2000 horses. There were 800 ships including 28 warships and he mentions artillery and ships' boats. The number of ships seems too great; on the previous basis we would expect about 400. The transports were built to Caesar's own specification, confirming that those used the year before were ordinary Gallic merchant ships. The new ships had lower sides so that the soldiers could row, and row they did when the wind failed (Fig. 9). But it is unlikely that Caesar interfered with the construction, which would have meant retraining the local shipwrights in the very short time available. Some of the ships were privately built, presumably for Roman officers or officials.

We accept the building of these enormous fleets too lightly. The ships were built all over northern Gaul; sixty were built on the Marne 80 miles from the sea and sailed or towed down to the Seine and out to the coast to sail up to Boulogne. The vessels were caught by storms and never got there. The Meldi who built them were presumably barge builders.

This time Caesar hoped to cross early in the sailing season. But he was delayed several weeks by a northwest wind, which shows what poor windward sailers his ships were. He finally set sail on 20 July with a light southwesterly, which fell away at midnight and left him drifting in the strong tides of the Dover Strait. Is it coincidence that all four of the great cross-Channel invasions mentioned in these pages sailed at night?

This time Caesar disembarked his troops between Sandwich and Deal unopposed, and struck inland immediately with his main force, leaving his ships anchored off on a sandy bottom. A day or two later he was 12 miles from the sea when despatch riders brought news of a gale and ships driven ashore or foul of one another, with immense damage and loss of gear; forty were total wrecks.

One is tempted to say that he deserved it for making the same mistake twice, but this is too easy. He wanted to catch the enemy off balance and he had done so. It must have been a sudden gale quite beyond his ability to predict. Some writers have suggested that the story was a fake to cover up a military reverse, but there were too many men involved to have kept up the deception.

He tackled the situation like Brunel. He had plenty of men and skilled artisans in the army and he had all those 800 ships drawn

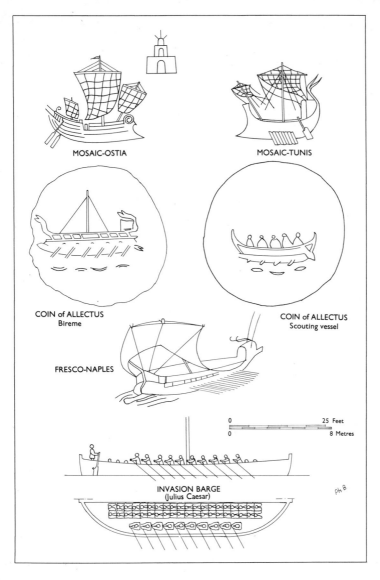

MOSAIC-OSTIA

MOSAIC-TUNIS

COIN of ALLECTUS
Bireme

COIN of ALLECTUS
Scouting vessel

FRESCO-NAPLES

0   25 Feet
0   8 Metres

INVASION BARGE
(Julius Caesar)

9 Roman ships

high up the beach and surrounded by a defensive wall. If they lay in trots of four there would have been 200 rows of them and the whole fortified area would have covered 50 acres. And we can be sure that the ships were drawn up in rigid formation with the lanes between them running at right angles like every Roman camp or city; 6000 men had been guarding the ships from the moment of landing.

After a summer's successful campaigning Caesar withdrew.

None of the replacement ships he had sent for had succeeded in crossing, though not a single laden troopship was lost in either campaign. As he had hostages and a large number of prisoners to bring back and some of the transports had been wrecked on the beaches, the ships were even more tightly packed than before. Once again it was near the equinox and once again he set sail at dusk, landing safely as the day broke.

Roman Sea Power in the North

Keep the Seas we must, live if we can

POMPEY

East of the Rhine were the ever-increasing Germans; first the Batavi, then the Frisii as far as the Ems and the Chauci from there to the Elbe: peoples to be known later as Frisians, Saxons and Jutes. Caesar crossed the Rhine in 55 and 53 BC, and Drusus made the Roman presence felt as far as the Elbe in 12 BC. He created the Rhine flotilla and had a canal dug between the Waal and the Ijssel so that his ships could sail inland all the way from the Rhine's mouth to the northern entrance of the Zuider Zee. In AD 5 Tiberias sent a fleet to reconnoitre the coasts of Germany and Denmark as far as the entrance to the Baltic. But in AD 16 the tribes were still restive and the Roman general Germanicus 'saw that …their forests and swamps favoured [the enemy]…long baggage trains were vulnerable to surprise. The sea provided a better route… easily controlled and inaccessible to German intelligence…cavalry could be taken upriver from the coast and landed in mid-Germany.'

So wrote Tacitus in the perfect appraisal of an amphibious operation. Germanicus lost no time: 1000 ships were built, 'some short and broad—with little prow and stern—to stand up to rough seas. Some flat bottomed for beaching. Others had rudders fore and aft so that they could move either way and land on either side of the river. Many had decks for catapults and could carry horses and supplies. All the ships could be sailed or rowed.' They assembled at an island in the Rhine delta and rowed west along the Drusiana canal to the river Ijssel and on to the Zuider Zee. There was nothing to fear from the Batavi, who provided the Romans with assault swimmers. From the Zuider Zee the ships sailed through waters so perfectly described in *The Riddle of the Sands* and landed their troops far up amid the tidal marshes of the river Ems.

After victory in Germany, near-disaster came on the way home when the ships met a southerly gale and a hailstorm. They were scattered among the islands and shoals and, when tide and wind ran together, their anchors dragged and the ships began to fill. Horses and baggage were jettisoned and ships were sunk and wrecked. Germanicus himself was driven ashore between the Ems and Elbe and almost lost his nerve. But the damage was not so bad as it seemed. Ships that had lost their oars were towed or sailed back under jury rig. The islands were searched for shipwrecked soldiers, who were ransomed when necessary. They brought back stories of monsters.

Early Roman naval operations depended on good weather. The ships were not seaworthy by our standards having neither continuous decks nor efficient pumps. They also suffered from low freeboard, oar ports that let in the sea, and the windage of the artillery on deck. Some were carrying horses and the soldiers got in the way of the crews. It is about 130 miles on the open sea from the Elbe to the Zuider Zee and they would hardly have dared to sail at night along the treacherous north German coast. The voyage would have taken at least three days including a day to get out of the Elbe. Force 6–7 winds and short steep seas breaking on the reefs and in the shallows would have been enough to play havoc with the ships. However, the Normandy landings nearly 2000 years later ran into serious difficulties despite all the scientific weather and sea state forecasts provided by the Allied staffs, and we have no right to criticise the Roman planning or seamanship.

The number of Roman troops involved is not recorded, but over 60,000 were engaged soon after the disaster among the islands. The expedition may well have carried 50,000 men and the minimum number of ships would have been 500. Allowing for horse transports, fodder, artillery and small craft, a total of 1000 vessels of all sorts and sizes is quite possible.

The Rhine frontier having been secured, all was clear for the Imperial occupation of Britain in AD 43, and much had happened since the reconnaissance of 54 BC. Julius Caesar could find out very little about Britain before landing there, but Claudius had reliable information about conditions from normal commercial contact as far north as the Humber. Trade with Gaul had vastly increased and the aristocrats of the Iceni of Norfolk, the Catuvellauni of Essex and the Thames valley, the Cantii of Kent, the Regnenses of Sussex, and the Belgae of Wessex imported silverware and pottery, wood and bronze furniture, glass, jewellery and wine. Strabo says they paid with 'corn, cattle, gold, silver and iron, hides, slaves and hunting dogs'—enough bulk cargo to maintain a flow of sizeable ships to and from Southampton Water, the havens of Sussex and Kent, the Thames and Essex creeks, the rivers of Norfolk and Suffolk, the Wash and the Humber. The coins of the Catuvellauni, minted at their capital and port of Colchester, bore an ear of wheat. Those of the Regnenses carried a vine leaf. Many British nobles crossed to

Gaul and back—some to obtain the support of Rome or the benefits of her culture, malcontents to seek Roman aid. They wore rich dress and fine jewellery and travelled with baggage and attendants on voyages of up to a week. They must have demanded some sort of private accommodation and paid well for it. But there were no passenger ships and they would have had to put up with the stink of slaves, hides or cattle from the open holds.

The main Roman fleet was based at Boulogne and it was probably from there that the squadron sailed to the Baltic in AD 5. There were other fleets based on the Garonne and the Somme, and river flotillas on the Rhine, Seine and Danube. Wherever ships could best guard the Imperial frontiers, the Romans used them.

Preparations to invade Britain in AD 40 came to nothing. British craft, probably small galleys or curraghs, then raided the coast of Gaul and Roman preparations started in earnest. The II, IX, XIV and XX Legions from as far away as Hungary assembled at Boulogne with a great force of auxiliaries, 50,000 men in all. The thought of leaving the girls and comforts of the eastern frontier for indefinite service in the northern mists drove the troops to mutiny, and news of this put the Britons off their guard.

Once again the coast of Europe echoed to the clunk of adzes and the thud of caulking hammers from the Seine to the Rhine, a din that was to occur again and again down the centuries. There was an even greater tonnage of shipping than in 54 BC for the legions sailed with full equipment, transport, artillery, engineers, and maintenance and medical personnel. Great quantities of stores, administrative staff and civilians followed in the wake of the invasion fleet.

Claudius crossed a few weeks later with part of the Praetorian Guard, advisors, servants, slaves and elephants for his triumph. (The form and scantlings of an elephant carrier were known to Mediterranean naval architects.) The main fleet, in three divisions, followed Caesar's example and crossed at night, to Richborough in Kent and probably to Dover and Lympne as well. A small force may have gone to Chichester harbour to support the pro-Roman king of the Regnenses. Work started immediately to turn Richborough into the fortified supply base that was to link Britain with Gaul for 400 years. Part of its great walls still stand.

The fleet played little part in the campaign, which ended in the capture of Colchester. The only point of maritime interest is that the Romans crossed the Thames via a bridge; probably constructed of boats built by their engineers or left unguarded by the retreating Britons, as there is no evidence of large fixed native bridges of this date in Britain. Some of the fleet supported Vespasian's drive to the

West Country, and Roman ships used Fishbourne at the head of Chichester harbour very early indeed. Poised at Chichester, Vespasian must have thought long and hard about the first 40 miles of his march. Cousins of the Veneti, the Britons were daring sailors with great fleets in the Hampshire harbours. There were deep creeks all along Vespasian's route up which they could row while protected by marsh and hidden by sedge. They could attack under cover of mist or dark and be away on the tide faster than the Romans could march. Until the Isle of Wight was occupied the Britons could come and go with little hindrance and the Roman supply ships would have to sail in hostile waters.

Vespasian knew he must first take the Isle of Wight. Unfortunately we do not know the details of the operation, but he had about 10,000 men and could scarcely have spared more than a quarter of these. Perhaps two or three thousand men were rowed down Chichester harbour in twenty or thirty ships and across to Bembridge haven which then penetrated right in to Brading, forming a secure base at the eastern end of the Wight. Whatever the exact route, the Romans fought the islanders to a complete surrender and no doubt captured or destroyed every British ship or boat they saw.

Further north the Menai Strait was crossed in specially built landing craft in AD 59, and the Romans pushed on to Holyhead. They never occupied the Isle of Man, and although Agricola in AD 78–84 planned to invade Ireland, the scheme came to nought. But he sent ships up both coasts of Scotland, and the fleet that explored the Western Isles carried the geographer Demetrius of Tarsus. Agricola's son-in-law Tacitus wrote, 'Fearing a general rising…he used his fleet to reconnoitre the harbours. It was first employed by Agricola to increase his striking power…and made an excellent impression. The war was pushed forward simultaneously by land and sea, and infantry, cavalry and marines… would mess and make merry together…The Britons, as was learned from prisoners, were dismayed by the appearance of the fleet now that the secret places of their sea were opened up.'

He tells of a German cohort which mutinied and captured three small warships. Then they 'sailed round North Britain', were reduced to canibalism, wrecked, taken for pirates and 'cut off' by the Suebi (North Germans) and the Frisians. Some were sold as slaves and finally reached the Rhine. What tremendous story is hidden behind those few titbits of fact?

There were 600 men in a cohort, but perhaps this one was under strength when it mutinied and killed its officers. There were perhaps 400 desperate men left whose only hope was to escape by sea beyond the reach of punishment by crucifixion or some such awful penalty. Each of those 'small warships' had therefore to carry 130 mutineers as well as any necessary crews. They can hardly have been smaller than a bireme with 100 oars or as large as a trireme with 170. Certainly the so-called Pictish style scouting ships of 20 oars could not possibly have accommodated the soldiers however tightly packed. Never was discipline, leadership and obedience needed so much as in an overcrowded galley in enemy waters, and all these were lacking. Those unfortunate Germans could only sail on to progressive dissolution and disaster.

While Britain was being conquered there was serious trouble on the Rhine. In AD 69 a Batavian noble named Civilis raised a rebellion of the Germans between the Rhine estuary and Cologne. He sent to Britain for help while the Cannenefates and the Frisii carried out seaborne raids on the coasts of Roman Gaul; 24 ships of the Rhine flotilla were captured by their Batavian rowers and delivered into Civilis's hands. There is no suggestion that this was a major Roman disaster, so the Rhine flotilla must have had a lot of ships.

The Roman commander Hordeonius Flaccus travelled down the Rhine with another squadron, an 'elderly invalid marshalling his men from the pillows of a sickroom' (it sounds more like a comfortable cabin). Everything went wrong. A large corn ship was captured by the Germans near Cologne, a legion deserted, and Flaccus was murdered. The garrison at Cologne was forced to allow free crossing of the Rhine and free trade along it. Petilius Cerialis took command of the Roman troops, and the VI and I Legions were brought from Spain and the XIV from Britain. It landed safely but its transports were destroyed in the North Sea by the Cannenefates.

The Germans were routed in AD 70, but Civilis escaped and there was further trouble. Cerialis was nearly taken when his flagship and many other vessels of the Rhine flotilla were captured. He only escaped (it was said) because he was ashore with a German woman called Claudius Sacrata. Her name like that of Civilis shows how deep Roman influence was beyond the Rhine. Civilis then collected all his biremes, single banked vessels, and liburnians carrying 30 to 40 men each. Where the ships had no sails they were improvised for them. These Germans at least knew all about sails. The Roman fleet was smaller but their ships were larger—triremes probably; their oarsmen and helmsmen were better. The 'battle' took place in the estuary of the Maas and Waal; the Romans rowed north with the current while the Germans sailed south, and the fleets passed with neither side making much effort to engage. The heart had been knocked out of the Germans and the Romans were content to let them go.

In Britain, Hadrian's Wall from Tyne to Solway, with signal stations and probably a fleet base on the Cumberland coast, was completed by AD 128 to keep out the hordes of Picts, who could draw allies from Ulster via the short sea crossings to Galloway and the Mull of Kintyre. The Picts and the Irish were the principal enemies during the Roman occupation and they joined with the untamed tribes of Wales in surprise attacks. A naval base with a fortified beaching point like those on the Rhine and Danube was later built at Caer Gybi, Holyhead; there were other bases at Cardiff and Lancaster and probably one at Brough on the Humber. It was against the Picts, not the Saxons, that the signal stations were built on the Yorkshire coast in the second half of the 4th century. In the 1st century AD there were coastal signal stations at Old Burroughs and Martinhoe, high up under Exmoor on the north Devon coast. These seem to have been to watch for seaborne reinforcement from South Wales to the Britons of Devon and Cornwall. They were presumably abandoned when the fleet bases on the South Wales coast came into operation. The Antonine Wall from the Forth to the Clyde was built in AD 142, and there were almost certainly fleet bases on both estuaries.

Around AD 195 there began a series of invasions and counter-invasions on a scale that the history books treat too lightly, scarcely pausing to consider the shipping involved. Albinus, the governor of Britain, decided to try for the purple while Emperor Septimus Severus was campaigning in the East, and he crossed the Channel with the VI and XX Legions—possibly the whole garrison. What transports he used to carry this force of at least 10,000 men we do not know. Nor do we know what the Classis Britannica was doing while it happened: probably nothing, while its commander waited to see which emperor to obey. In the first act of the drama at least 100 troopships crossed to Gaul, and a fleet of powerful warships waited in the wings at Boulogne or St Valery or both. Albinus marched to defeat at Lyon in AD 197, and the Picts swarmed over the Wall and ravaged as far south as York. Severus sent a new governor to Britain in AD 197, and the much-travelled VI Victrix and XX Valeria Victrix went back with him, no doubt with new officers. Once again 10,000 men crossed the narrow seas and this time the watching warships knew who was master.

The new governor could barely hold the North, however, and in AD 208 Septimus himself crossed with very considerable re-inforcements to conquer all Scotland. The depot at South Shields was stocked with enough corn to feed 40,000 men for three months, and from there it was shipped to Cramond on the Firth of Forth. Detachments of the Rhine and Danube flotillas were transferred to

Scotland. It is unlikely that any of the Danube guardships were brought to the Scottish border, so their crews must have travelled overland to the Rhine flotilla.

The crews of the Roman navy had lower status than the legions and we can picture the Danube sailors on the march, officers with provincial accents and men rolling along out of step. Local craft, new-built or requisitioned, must have been waiting for them when they reached the Tyne. The Classis Britannica stayed in the Channel and this time the commander would have had simple orders: 'Guard the Straits or else...'.

From Cramond supplies were shipped to Carpow, a new legionary fortress on the south bank of the Tay. Here the army, probably about 10,000 men including cavalry, artillery and sappers, prepared to advance into unknown country. The Tay was crossed by a bridge of boats half a mile long, a structure which would have needed over a hundred pontoons, each anchored upstream and down; a nice mass-production problem for both the boatbuilders and the anchor makers, shaping and assembling hundreds of wood stocks and flukes and weighting them with lead. Over the bridge went the wagonloads of materials for the staging posts at Inchtuthil, Cleaven Dyke and Kirkbuddo.* The army thrust north amid the heather and rocky outcrops to make its final rendezvous with the fleet at Raedykes, the furthest north the Roman storeships ever went in an army support role. Pictish resistance was broken and the frontier made secure for several generations.

The Saxons began to make trouble in the 3rd century and a Roman officer called the Count of the Saxon Shore was appointed to defend those parts of Britain and Gaul subject to Saxon raids. Nine Saxon Shore fortresses were built in Britain and a somewhat similar defensive line in Gaul. Each of the 'British' forts stood at the water's edge in a strategically placed harbour or creek; a combined castle, storehouse and fleet base to deny the haven to Saxon settlers or pirates. With the exception of Portchester at the head of Portsmouth harbour these forts are high and dry today. The other eight are Brancaster on the Wash, Burgh and Bradwell on the Suffolk and Essex coasts; Reculver, Richborough, Dover and Lympne in Kent and Pevensey in Sussex. There are impressive remains of all except Dover, the foundations of which have recently been uncovered. A fort about 2 acres square was built in the early 2nd century for the Classis Britannica whose tiles were found on the site. A much larger and more modern Saxon Shore fort was built ca 275 lying over the top of one corner of the older work and

* The forts north of the Tay had been built by Agricola and later abandoned.

enclosing the site of modern Market Square. Sand dunes covered the area after the Romans went.

The Roman fort at Carisbrooke on the Isle of Wight, while inland and not designated a Saxon Shore fort, must have formed part of the sea defences of this gateway of Britain which has been ringed by forts of every type and period since.

The Saxons eventually settled 10 miles south of Boulogne and at the mouth of the Loire, but it seems unlikely that the Roman forts west of the Seine were built primarily to stop them (Maps 2 and 3). There was an enormous length of coastline to guard and the forts could only have been intended to cover selected areas: they may tell us a lot about contemporary shipping when we know more facts. There were twelve forts on the Gallic coast and one on the north coast of Spain.

Boulogne was the base of the Channel fleet and Rouen the headquarters of the Seine flotilla. They must have had dockyards and there must have been another for the Somme squadron though no fort is linked with it. Caen is inland and may have been a distribution or collecting centre for cargoes through any of the little harbours of that Normandy shore. Coutances, Avranches and St Servan, only 20 miles apart, suggest an important centre of trade, or a constant threat connected perhaps with the Channel Islands and western Britain. From St Servan to Brest is 120 miles as the galley rows. Carhaix looks like a headquarters for the whole Breton peninsula, Vannes covers Quiberon Bay, scene of the earlier sea battle with the Veneti, and Nantes is on one of the great trade routes. (Avranches, Carhaix and Brest are close to important Veneti hill forts.) Blaye guards the shortest route to the Mediterranean and must have been the base of the Garonne flotilla.

It is probable there were galley squadrons at Coutances, Avranches, St Servan, Brest, Vannes and Nantes. A galley cruised at about 5 knots and the 'machinery' had to sleep: to send a squadron from Blaye to deal with a raid near Vannes would have taken a week. And on this coast of difficult tides local knowledge was essential. Again, there must have been slipping and repair facilities. The whole organisation, while probably designed to deter raids from across the sea, may have spent most of its time searching out pirates and smugglers among the multitude of havens on this long and difficult coast.

Although we think of the people around the coasts of Britain as living in terror during those centuries, the majority probably never saw a Saxon raid, though alarms and rumours were rife during the summer months.

Carausius, a Roman officer of Flemish origin, became Count of the Saxon Shore in AD 284, and some historians believe that he strengthened the British coastal defences before declaring himself Emperor of Britain and part of Gaul in AD 286. The Imperial Roman fleet sent against him met with disaster which it blamed on bad weather, but it may have been defeated in the Channel by the Classis Britannica under the control of Carausius and Britain for a short while was part of a breakaway northern empire. Carausius was murdered in AD 293 by his finance officer Allectus who, to judge from the warships portrayed on his coins, was another believer in naval power (Fig. 9). But perhaps his ships were not so good as his coins, for Roman fleets under Constantius sailing from Rouen and Boulogne to the Hampshire coast brought Imperial rule back to Britain in AD 296. This is almost all we know, and it is difficult for us to realise now that hundreds of ships and thousands of men were involved in a twelve-year series of naval campaigns.

After the great British attack of AD 367, when Picts, Irish and possibly even Saxons combined against the Romans, Count Theodosius sent a fleet to Orkney to show the power of Rome in the Northern Isles. If there really were Saxons in the alliance of 367, then even at this date their ships were sailing at least as far as Northumberland in considerable numbers. And the triumphant riposte of Theodosius means that the Romans still had a large fleet available.

Why go so far north to punish a confederation whose focus was in south Scotland? Is it possible that sea raiders from Jutland were coming north-about and that Scapa Flow was already the crossroads of the northern seas? There is no other evidence that Saxons or Angles came this way, but there seems no other reason for this sudden Roman counter-thrust. Whatever the reason, Scapa Bay heard the sound of Roman trumpets and saw the discipline of Rome. But we can feel the uneasiness of the Roman navigators as they watched the ebb surging at 6 knots in the Sound of Hoxa, thankful that their galleys could slip out at slack water whatever the wind direction. Lupicianus, their commander, must have been glad when the operation was over.

Daring though it was, it was little more than an empty gesture. The Romans were six days' sail from their nearest base and by way of the Western Isles the voyage would have taken eight; in either case they would have been at the mercy of the weather in uncharted and hostile seas. Just over thirty years later the Romans were gone from Britain altogether.

The Classis Britannica had squadrons of triremes, each about 115 ft (35 m) long with 170 oars and a bronze-sheathed ram.

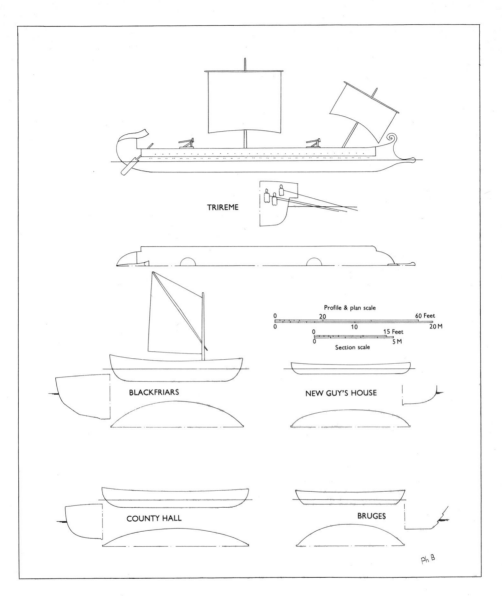

TRIREME

Profile & plan scale

BLACKFRIARS

NEW GUY'S HOUSE

COUNTY HALL

BRUGES

Ph B

10 Roman ships

Displacement was about 80 tons (Fig. 10). Caesar's experience against the Veneti in 56 BC had shown that quite small merchant ships could be a serious threat to light single banked galleys. Merchant ships had increased in size since the days of the Veneti and, crammed with men in temporary 'castles' fore and aft like medieval cogs, might have been too powerful for anything less than a trireme to tackle. When Caligula planned a fake triumph in Rome he ordered some of the Channel fleet triremes to be transported back overland. Since he had a passion for doing the impossible, they must have been the biggest ships available. According to Suetonius he had ships of ten banks built for his own use in the Mediterranean. The triremes of the Channel fleet may well have mounted swivelling ballistae like those in the forts on the Saxon Shore. The story of the mutinous cohort suggests that there were biremes of about 100 oars operating in Scottish waters. A cornelian intaglio that fell out of a ring near the Saxon Shore fort at Caister shows a galley with ram and two banks of oars. Martin Henig has

14 *Caister Intaglio*
(Norwich Museum)

suggested that the 'oars' may be only a wave pattern, but the true wave formation would be vee shapes running aft from the bow and not forward. He suggests that the ring might have belonged to an officer of the Classis Britannica and says that the workmanship is probably British (Plate 14).

The coins of Allectus (Fig. 9) show galleys with ram, parados and the arched shelter for the captain or helmsman peculiar to Mediterranean galleys down the ages. (On Roman galleys this was apparently covered with leather and shows the desire of the designers to keep top weight to a minimum.) Only seven oars are shown but the shape of the coin cramped the artist's style and there were probably at least 20 in a ship of this sort, or 50 if it was double banked as this one appears to be.

Vegetius in *De Re Militari*, written about AD 390, mentions liburnians. Originally this term meant a small galley, usually a bireme, used by the Liburnians. Later it became a loose name for a small warship, and some are said to have been built on the Rhine for Constantius's attack on Allectus. The river flotillas may have consisted of such ships. Galleys were rigged either with two masts as in Plate 14, in which case the larger one was sent below when the ship went into action (Fig. 9), or with one mast amidships as on the coins of Allectus.

Vegetius also mentions scouting vessels in ambiguous terms usually translated as Pictish or painted boats but sometimes as pitched. Painted is more likely since the Picts were the 'painted people' and the boats are later described as painted blue, with blue sails and blue-clad oarsmen. The best camouflage against lookouts at sea level is white, but the Roman scouting vessels may have been painted to hide them from men watching from the cliff tops. Vegetius says they had about 20 oarsmen, in which case they must have been single banked with 10 oars a side. The Vikings used warships of just this size on lakes and rivers because they were manageable on portages from one stretch of water to another.

One of Allectus's coins shows a boat with a lively sheer and very different from the traditional galley, which may represent one of the 'Pictish' ships. If the scratch on the waterline is only meant to be the bow wave, she is like a small version of the Nydam ship of the same date which pulled 14 oars a side. Whether Allectus's scouting ships would have been clinker or carvel construction we cannot say, but they would not have been curraghs, for the Romans were shipbuilders in wood who only used skin boats in exceptional circumstances.

A name often used by ancient historians was *lusoria* which usually meant a small warship like those used in the river flotillas: some boats on the Allectus coins might be lusoria. During a winter campaign on the Meuse ships of this sort were rowed up and down all night, breaking the ice to cut off the enemy's retreat.

At least 500 warships must have guarded the northern frontiers of the Roman Empire. Compared to modern ships they were very slow and often delayed by wind and tide. They were so delicate that a high proportion of them must always have been undergoing repair. The alerting system had a very short range, and therefore squadrons and individual guardships must have been closely spaced around the coasts and along the rivers.

The Rhine, Meuse, Somme, Seine and Garonne flotillas may have numbered 250 ships and the full strength of the Classis Britannica could easily have been 100 triremes. In addition there were the squadrons in the Bristol Channel, the Irish Sea, Morecambe Bay, Solway Firth and the Firths of Forth, Clyde and Tay. There must have been yet more ships stationed round the coasts of Spain.

Roman sea power depended on the legions and flotillas being able to hold the Rhine frontier. Boulogne was only a hundred miles to the west, and once the Germans closed in behind, communication with Britain broke down. The Roman withdrawal took at least twenty years. Bitterne (Southampton) replaced the fort at Porchester after AD 369 and Southampton seems to have been occupied at least until 428. Roman ships sailed from there to the Somme and then to the Seine as the German peoples moved west.

Many of the warships in Britain were probably abandoned or passed over to the Britons, and operated by them wherever the elaborate organisation necessary was maintained. In remoter regions the delicate biremes and triremes probably rotted in the mud or sank at their moorings. On the Continent the Garonne flotilla was taken over by the Visigoths. The Seine and Rhine flotillas may have passed into German hands and as they no longer served any strategic purpose were left to rot.

In considering the limitations of Roman sea power we must forget what Nelson would have done. The Royal Navy of the Napoleonic Wars mustered over 400 ships able to stay at sea in all weathers. The country was immensely wealthy for that day and could afford to maintain such an enormous fleet against the constant threat of total defeat. Ships' lookouts swayed over 100 ft above the sea and in clear weather kept continuous watch over a radius of 20 miles; signal flags fluttering from topgallant yardarms relayed messages from ship to hull-down ship until they reached the flagship.

The Roman scouting ships could neither see nor signal to anything like the same degree, but the system of galleys, shore signal stations, and troops ready to march along good roads to the point of attack was probably the best that could be done in the 3rd and 4th centuries AD. The Romans were professionals with four centuries' experience of watch and ward off the coasts of Europe.

12 Roman Britain— Shipbuilding and Trade

Roof and floor tiles, like those used on land, are found on all large Mediterranean wrecks, also…lead piping for pumps or plumbing

HONOR FROST
Under the Mediterranean

No ancient warship has yet been found.* They spent a lot of time in harbour where conditions were not suitable for preserving the hulls. When they sank in deep water and became buried in sand there are no tell-tale amphorae to mark the spot. But we know from other sources that the design of Roman warships was standardised and whole fleets were built very quickly, 100 ships in 60 days, 220 ships in 90 days, and so on.

Some were built in naval dockyards by skilled slave labour under the direction of naval shipwrights, but when great numbers of ships were required in a hurry other naval shipwrights must have moved into private yards taking with them the standard galley moulds. And when the Romans set up naval bases at Boulogne and Dover, on the Gironde or in the Bristol Channel, at Holyhead or on the Clyde, their shipwrights must have come north with the moulds in their baggage. Alternatively they may have been able to construct a mould by some rule-of-thumb geometrical method such as naval shipwrights used in the 17th century AD.

There is no positive evidence that moulds were used in ancient shipbuilding or that complete frames were set up to provide the correct hull shape round which to bend the planks. All the merchant hulls examined indicate that separate side frames were inserted as the planking proceeded, these frames being neither connected to the floors nor continuous across the keelson. In most cases they stop short several feet from it. The Kyrenia ship is an example of this practice which may also be seen today in native shipyards in Southeast Asia and elsewhere.

Such simple methods produce useful merchant ships without the use of moulds but the vessels are peculiar to the builder and even then probably vary so that some sail better than others. It is inconceivable that scores of identical warships could have been built at different shipyards by this means. Weight, hull shape and

---

* Honor Frost is now excavating off western Sicily what may be the first ancient warship to be found. It appears to bear the marks of prefabrication.

strength were all critical and stability could be marginal in the best of galleys. In addition the hulls had to be carefully strengthened forward to withstand the shock of ramming. The rather untrustworthy evidence of a ship-shaped lamp from 4th century BC Greece suggests that some galleys had hollow waterlines forward which could only have been formed by building on moulds.

There are several accounts of Roman fleets being built to the design of captured Carthaginian vessels. This could only have been accomplished with moulds of some sort, though they may have been little more than bent rods held against the new ship at intervals during the building. The Romans should not be criticised for copying: the British Admiralty did it all through the 19th century. And just as the Romans were not too proud to borrow from the Carthaginians, so in Scotland they may have taken off the lines of a fast Pictish rowing ship, perhaps substituting Mediterranean style 'peg and nail' fastenings for whatever simple lashings or spikes the natives used.

It seems safe to assume that after a period of improvisation with native craft Roman naval overseers were sent for and worked in commandeered shipyards, specially built dockyards, or selected private yards, setting up their moulds and checking that the new galleys conformed to them. Fifty identical thoroughbred warships could only have been built by high class builders under supervision.

These Roman shipwrights, who may have been highly skilled slaves, brought with them the Mediterranean method of fastening planks together and to floors and frames. Without ancient warship remains to guide us we have to assume that they were built in the same way as Greek and Roman merchant ships, of which some have been excavated. Six of these—Kyrenia, Congloué, Titan, Nemi, Chrétienne A, Antikythera and others— all had a projecting keel, however rudimentary, and their planks were joined edge to edge by closely spaced tenons set in mortices in the mating faces and dowelled in position. The planks were fastened to the floors and ribs by long bronze nails usually driven through wood treenails and in most cases turned over on the inside of the floor or rib. We should expect to find evidence of these practices in ships built in those parts of northern Europe where the Roman fleets operated.

From the age-old shipbuilding centre around the Tagus there is no evidence at all about any of the vessels built there. Neither have we any knowledge of the ships built between the Gironde and Brittany other than Caesar's description of the Veneti ships, and he gives the impression that in 56 BC they were purely Gallic.

Nor is there any evidence of how ships were built between Brittany and the Rhine save one fragment, but we know that transports were built by almost all the boat-using peoples in the area for Caesar's invasions. No doubt they also provided transports for Claudius and Severus and Constantius in later centuries.

The Thames at London has yielded remains of three Roman or Romano-British merchant ships. The best preserved was excavated in 1962 by the old entrance to the Fleet River between Blackfriars Bridge and the nearby railway bridge, just over half a mile above where London Bridge spanned the river in Roman times. She was 50–55 ft long by 22 ft beam (15–17 m by 6.7 m) and a fragment of knee-shaped timber suggests that she was decked at least from stem to mast. A step in one of the floor timbers positions the mast at about 17 ft (5.2 m) from the bow. A bronze coin of AD 88 or 89 was found in the step. It was usual to put one under a mast when it was first stepped and this one had been in circulation for some time.

Unlike any of the Mediterranean style merchant ships quoted there is no keel or keelson but a backbone of two very heavy planks edge to edge (Fig. 10). Fundamentally she was a round bilged ship though there is a slight chine making an angle of about 160° in way of the mast. Because the frame here is curved the plank seam at this point does not touch the timber. The bottom planking was up to 3 in. (8 cm) thick and the floor timbers 12 in. by 8 in. wide (30 cm by 20 cm). The ceiling (lining) was only 1 in. (2.5 cm) thick, as in the Kyrenia ship.

She was built of oak and the strakes were attached to the floor and frame timbers by iron nails up to 2 ft (0.6 m) long, driven through wooden treenails as in the Mediterranean ships but with a strange difference—the treenail penetrates the frame or floor only and the nail was apparently driven blind through the plank to pick up the peg. The shipbuilder probably had some simple method of location long since forgotten. Each nail was a blacksmith's masterpiece, with a coned head and round shank except for a short square section near the end which was turned over on the inside of the timber and then turned again and driven into the wood. Modern boatbuilders when clench-fastening planks drill small for square-section copper nails to prevent them bending when being driven. Modern iron nails are driven direct and Saxon and Viking boatbuilders did the same. There seems no reason to drive an iron nail through a peg unless the iron was very soft or the builder was copying a process he did not understand. The planks were not held together by tenons like those in the Mediterranean ships but lay edge to edge as in modern carvel practice. The seams were often considerably open and caulked with hazel twigs.

The heavy plank backbone of the ship calls to mind the Ferriby boats built on the Humber ca 1000 BC (Fig. 6) and the Saxon Nydam ship (Plate 19). The Ferriby boats, which were of sewn chine construction, were built over 1000 years before and 200 miles distant from the Blackfriars ship: it is hardly wise to draw any conclusions. The Nydam ship, although quite different apart from the wide, thick, flat plank that took the place of a keel, was built only about 200 years later and such ships might have rowed to Britain even in the time of the Blackfriars ship.

15 Model showing construction of the Blackfriars ship, 2nd century AD. (Crown copyright Science Museum, London)

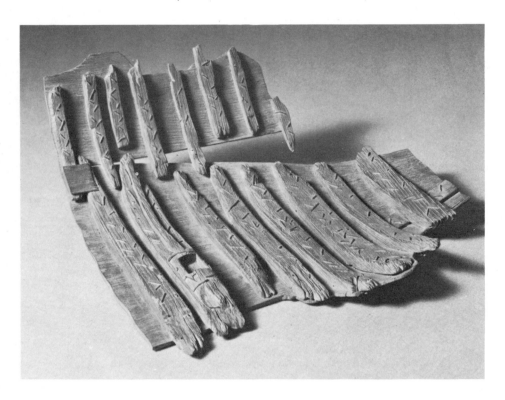

The Blackfriars ship displaced about 70 tons and because of her small size and simple rig she has been called a river barge. The position of the mast a third of the length from the bow instead of near amidships suggests a fore-and-aft sail and the same difficulty arises with the Kyrenia ship. Douglas Phillips-Birt in *Fore and Aft Sailing Craft* produces conclusive evidence for both lateen and spritsails in the Mediterranean in the 2nd century AD. The Blackfriars mast does not seem to have been arranged for lowering and presumably would have had to be unstepped for passing under London Bridge.

River barges or not, ships of this size and shape were used for transport round the coasts of Europe right up to the end of the 19th century and this one had brought a cargo of Kentish ragstone from somewhere near Maidstone when she sank at Blackfriars. There is no reason why she could not have gone across or down the Channel. Modern Thames barges have carried a similar cargo on

16 Nail from Black-friars ship, $\frac{1}{2}$ full size.

the same route one week, taken a cargo of grain to Holland the next, and loaded with cement for Hull the week after. A Thames barge, in spite of her name, was a seagoing ship.

The second London ship, the County Hall ship, was found there in 1910 and is dated by coins and pottery to the late 3rd century AD. She is estimated to have been 60 to 70 ft long (18.3–21.3 m) and 15 or 16 ft beam (4.6–4.9 m). There was a centre keel $8\frac{1}{2}$ in. wide and

$6\frac{1}{2}$ in. thick (21 by 16 cm) and probably two heavy stringers two or three feet (0.6–0.9) out from the keel though only one remained. This had mortices for stanchions every three feet and there are remains of deck beams, suggesting that she was fully decked. There is no evidence of a mast, though the centre 40 ft section (12.2 m) of the ship was recovered. However the remains are too small to be conclusive and both the deck and the way the planks are joined

to each other by mortice and tenon joints like the Kyrenia ship suggest very strongly that the County Hall ship was far more than a lighter. The planks were fastened to the timbers by treenails alone.

The remains of the New Guys House boat, found at Bermondsey, London in 1958 consisted of 22 ft (6.7 m) of one end of a round-bilge vessel about 50 ft (15 m) long, 14 ft (4.3 m) beam and 3 to 4 ft deep (0.9–1.2 m). The planking was about 1 in. (2.5 cm) thick and the timbers were 3 in. by $4\frac{1}{2}$ in. (8 cm by 11 cm) spaced at about 24 in. (0.6 m) centres. Like all the London ships she was built of oak. There may have been a slight external keel and the planks were

17 Model of a Roman merchant ship ca AD 200. (Crown Copyright Science Museum, London)

fastened to the ribs by long iron nails turned over on the inside and then turned again and hammered into the timber. This time there were no treenails (pegs) and the nails, square section with round heads, were hammered direct through the plank and frame. The ceiling planks were only $\frac{3}{4}$ in. (2 cm) thick. The ship was abandoned about AD 200 (Fig. 10).

The three vessels were almost certainly built by British shipwrights using a mixture of native and Mediterranean techniques. Although they were carvel built, moulds were not used and the frames were added after the bottom planks were in position and during the planking up. Only the Blackfriars ship provides real evidence of her shape, which was probably like the beamy canoe-sterned fishing boats of Scotland and Scandinavia. Nearly all ancient merchant ships were like this and the other two probably looked much the same. They were different ships for different purposes, from different builders. By this time Mediterranean methods must have been well known in the north, at least near the harbours used by the Romans, and how much was adopted would have depended on the shipwright and his clients.

There may have been a few much larger ships on the main crossings between Britain and Gaul (Plate 17). There were certainly some very large contemporary merchantmen in the Mediterranean and the cargoes of some of them have been recovered. But their hulls were destroyed in the process and the early excavation records were poor, making it difficult to reconstruct the ships.

Three thousand amphorae were recovered from the Congloué wreck off Marseilles, and Cousteau estimated that the total must have been 10,000. Strabo mentions ships carrying 10,000 but contemporary laws normally limited the number to 3000. An amphora full of liquid weighed between 70 and 110 lbs (32–50 kg) giving a cargo weight of 94–148 tons for a 3000-amphora ship and 310–490 tons for one carrying 10,000. In the 400-amphora Kyrenia ship the weight of the hull etc about equalled the cargo weight, so the full load displacement of a 3000-amphora ship was between 200 and 300 tons and of a larger ship 600 to 1000 tons. Since there is a considerable possibility that there were two ships close together at Congloué it is safer to assume a total displacement of 300–500 tons for each ship of which 80–120 tons was actual wine.

Plate 17 shows a London Science Museum model of a ship of about this size. Figure 9(A), a sketch of a mosaic from Ostia, shows a three-masted ship which may have been larger still and Fig. 9(B) indicates that triangular raffee topsails could be set on all masts. Thus a three-masted ship could have carried a very large spread of canvas split into areas small enough for her crew to handle. Why this ship, which is apparently a merchant vessel, should have had such an aggressive-looking ram is a mystery.

A Roman grain ship described by Lucian seems to have been nearly 200 ft by 50 ft (61 m by 15 m) and there are wrecks of Roman ships loaded with tiles, an enormously dense and heavy cargo. Some had private cabins in the stern, with tiled and mosaic floors.

However, Rouen, Lyon, Boulogne, Strasbourg, London and York were only small provincial cities by the standards of Rome and Alexandria and would not have required wine, grain or building materials in anything like the quantities needed in the south. If the population of Britain was one million and one in every hundred persons was a wine drinker consuming a gallon a week, then two ships of 200 tons displacement would have been sailing every week in the summer season between southwest Gaul and Britain.* We might also safely postulate a few ships over 100 ft (30.5 m) long with well appointed cabins for senior administrators and their staffs, sailing between Gaul and Britain, and chapter 11 shows that troop transports of considerable size were necessary.

Britain was only Ultima Thule, a frontier province or buffer state, held with minimum force and minimum drain on the Imperial treasure. Normal trade would have been carried on by local ships and crews. Military transports would probably have been laid up in quiet times and fitted out in a fury of improvisation when the Irish sailed up the Bristol Channel or the Picts rowed down the Yorkshire coast in strength.

The deep query remains: why did this excellent shipbuilding technique vanish so utterly when the Romans went that planks were not joined edge to edge in Britain for a thousand years and draw-tongued joints were never seen again? It can only be that the less sophisticated people beyond the Rhine with the simplicity of genius found a better way. By laying each plank along the face and not the edge of the previous one they had a mould to determine the shape of the hull. The overlap provided an ampler mating surface which remained watertight after shrinkage, and to fasten the joint by riveting was ten times simpler than the exquisite marine joinery of mortice and tenon. The Saxons were already using clinker planking in the 3rd century; is it possible that the Romans found the Picts doing it too?

There is something more, something intangible. For all their sophistication the Romans never seem to have achieved in their ships that symphony of increasing curves that makes a sailor catch his breath. Compared to a big Roman merchant ship the Roskilde

---

* Production of wine in Britain may have reduced the amount imported.

knarr was just a small open boat, but her shape was as a sonnet to an inventory.

But we must be so very careful. Almost all traditional ships and boats had this magic quality. Perhaps the Romans had it too but it is lost to us because almost the only representations we have of their ships were carved in stone or set in mosaic by men who could not feel the sea.

Note: Since this chapter was written, a very large Roman ship has been uncovered at Zwammerdam in Holland. Full details are not yet available, but she seems to be a merchant ship and is massively built with a flat bottom and lowering mast. I am indebted to Mrs Valerie Fenwick, MA, of the National Maritime Museum, for this information.

13   Franks, Frisians and Saxons

When Caesar's sun fell out of the sky
And who so hearkened right
Could only hear the plunging
Of the nations in the night

G K CHESTERTON

In the final years of the 4th century Rome must still have seemed immensely strong. A dozen legions stood along the Rhine and warships rowed between them and the barbarians of central Europe. At Boulogne galleys of the Channel fleet stood ready to close the seas around the northern flank. Flotillas lay in the Somme, the Seine and the Gironde. There were fortified harbours all along the northern shores of Gaul and round the southeastern coasts of Britain. Yet more squadrons searched the seas off Scotland and patrolled the Irish Sea and the Bristol Channel.

But by AD 400 the pent-up German peoples had spilled over; the Rhine flotilla had disappeared and the Channel fleet had retired to the Somme: after AD 450 it is not mentioned at all. By AD 407 or a few years later, the legions had left Britain and any remaining naval forces had passed into British control.

The Franks attacked Roman Gaul from across the middle Rhine and their King Childeric was buried in 482 with a mass of jewellery similar in style and pattern to the Sutton Hoo ship treasure. By 550 a Christian Frankish kingdom stretched from the Danube to Spain, and from the Channel to the Alps and the Mediterranean, controlling the great trade routes along the Rhine, Meuse, Seine, Rhone, Garonne and Loire. It may have taken over the Garonne flotilla from the Visigoths, who had taken it over from the Romans—a fleet last recorded in AD 475. Three great centres of shipbuilding were in Frankish hands: the coast of Gaul from Brittany to Spain, the Mediterranean coast from Marseilles to Narbonne, and the deltas of the Rhine and Meuse. The origin of French excellence in naval architecture may be in the interaction of these three traditions.

Nobody knows the precise difference between the Saxons, Angles and Jutes. The Saxon homeland was probably to the south of Denmark, but in the early centuries AD they seem to have expanded west along the waterlogged coast of northern Germany where people lived on 'terpen' built up above the surrounding marsh.

The Angles, according to Alfred the Great quoting a merchant named Wulfstan, came from Denmark, the home of the best organised of the Vikings in later centuries. A land with a long ship history and the country of the Als boat, the Nydam ship and those from Roskilde Fjord. A land with its own Bronze Age ship pictures, separated at Elsinore by only three miles of sea from Swedish Bohuslan which is also covered with rock carvings of ships. Bohuslan was often under Danish rule and was the home of Beowulf.

The Venerable Bede wrote that the Jutes came from Jutland as their name suggests, but they are now thought to have come from near the Rhine. Those who settled in Kent had a higher culture than the other Saxon peoples, and there were links between them and the Rhinelanders who lived on the fringe of the Roman rule and had absorbed some of the Roman achievement.

The Frisians were neither settlers nor warriors, but traders. They were the most westerly of the German maritime peoples and traded all along the northern coasts from Dorestad near Utrecht. When the Vikings burned it in 836, Dorestad covered 30 acres spread out for half a mile along the banks of the Rhine.

It is sometimes said that the Saxons, Angles and Jutes were poor seamen and provincial boatbuilders who never used the sail. But the Angles enjoyed the same stimuli as the Vikings and were heirs to the same tradition stretching back into the 2nd millennium BC. The Saxons stood across the age-old trade route to the Baltic now marked approximately by the line of the Kiel Canal, and the Jutes lived cheek-by-jowl with the greatest merchant sailors of the day. If environment and technological tradition mean anything the Jutes, Angles and Saxons were in the forefront and not the background of the seafaring of the age.

The Saxons were raiding both sides of the Channel and up the east coast of England from the beginning of the 3rd century AD. The forts and fleet of the Saxon Shore were organised against them and Carausius, Count of the Saxon Shore, was alleged to have turned a blind eye in return for a share of the spoils. It is now suggested that these defences were more concerned with an intra-Roman power struggle and it is difficult to see the need for these great fortresses with their swivelling catapults when even in the 5th century, according to the *Anglo Saxon Chronicle*, there were never more than five Saxon ships together. Whatever their exact purpose, the Roman defences were able to stop the Saxons settling but unable to stop occasional raids by pirates who could sneak in, burn and pillage before the defenders mustered by sea and land.

Once the Roman rule began to crumble Gaul proved an easier settling ground than Britain and, while the Franks flooded into Gaul by the inland routes, the Saxons moved along the coast and settled in Flanders just before 400. Was the Roman Rhine flotilla withdrawn or did it go down fighting in one more naval action lost to history? Whatever happened, the Saxons settled as far west as the Loire until the Franks seized the whole coastline of Gaul and made their sea frontier secure.

The Saxons who then turned their attention to Britain were pirates, mercenaries and aggressive immigrants, and according to the *Chronicle* the two former acted as scouts for the latter. The ship type commonly associated with them is the big rowing ship like the Nydam ship found in a peat bog in Holstein in 1863. She is 73.8 ft (22.84 m) long overall and 59 ft (17.98 m) on the waterline; beam is 10.7 ft (3.26 m), depth amidships 3.3 ft (1.02 m) and draft 1.64 ft (0.50 m). Empty weight was computed by the Schleswig Holsteinisches Landesmuseum as 3.2 tons, ballast 1.0 ton, and total load 4.4 tons, giving a full load displacement of 8.6 tons. There were 30 oarsmen, one to each oar, who with the helmsman would

18 Replica of the Nydam ship. (Schleswig-Holstein Museum)

have weighed about 2.8 tons. The remaining 1.6 tons of load could have been made up of another 18 fighting men or 25 women and children. Plate 18 shows that they would have been as tightly packed as survivors in a ship's lifeboat.

The Nydam ship was clinker built, planked with only 11 strakes altogether, and with no external keel, deadwood or keelson. Instead there was a broad thick plank lying flat to which the raking stem and sternposts were scarphed. Each plank ran in one piece from bow to stern and heavy frames every 3.5 ft (1.07 m) held the planking to shape. Nothing was sawn. Enormous tree trunks were split into rough planks 50 to 80 ft (15 to 24 m) long, 15 in. (38 cm) wide and 4 in. (10 cm) thick; the keel plank was 18 in. (46 cm) wide and 6 in. (15 cm) thick. The outer faces of the planks were then dubbed smooth with adzes and the inner faces dubbed down to leave two lugs about 6 in. (15 cm) long standing 3 in. (8 cm) proud at each rib position. Nineteen frames, V-shaped at the ends of the hull and part circular amidships, were made of thick grown oak crooks finished by adze. Up to three futtocks (shorter sections) were scarphed together to form one frame. The stem and sternpost were adzed out of curved oak branches.

The planks were joined to the frames by lashings through the lugs, and fastened to each other by iron clench nails through the overlap in the strakes, riveted over roves in the modern manner. The plank ends were fastened into the rabbets at stem and sternpost by rivets. The oar crotches were claw-shaped grown oak crooks spiked to the gunwale strakes. There was no inwale or rubbing strake. A deep paddle-shaped rudder hung over the starboard quarter, supported in leather loops and turned by a short tiller projecting inboard (Plate 19).

The modern method of constructing a clinker-built boat is to join the keel, keelson, deadwood, stem and sternpost together to form the backbone and then set up two or three moulds (temporary ribs or frames) on it, round which the planks are bent and fastened to each other and the stem and sternpost. Very light ribs are then bent into place and the moulds removed. It is tempting to think that the Saxons and Vikings set up their heavy frames first as in modern carvel practice, faired them with long battens and then planked up. But this does not agree with the methods of simpler boatbuilders, and Basil Greenhill shows in *Boats of Pakistan* that clinker boats are still built there, planking first in spite of the difficulty of shaping the grown frames later to fit the curves of the skin. The shipwrights use no drawings, no moulds, no lofting and proceed entirely by eye. No doubt no two boats are ever quite the same.

Such practice gives little chance for innovation, and boats so built must follow a traditional pattern so that the builder can carry the shapes and dimensions of the parts in his memory. The Saxon hull would not have been a precision job and the method of fastening the frames to the planking would have allowed a good deal of latitude in fit. The Saxon emigrant ships were almost certainly built 'on the beach' like so many of our own 19th century inshore boats, as described by R C Leslie in his *Waterbiography*. The work would have been done by the emigrant crew under the direction of an itinerant shipwright.

But we cannot be sure that the Nydam ship was the only type of vessel used. Only two Saxon ships have been found complete, the Nydam ship of AD 300 and the Sutton Hoo ship of AD 650. The first belongs to the period *before* large scale migration began and

19 Nydam ship AD 400. (Schleswig-Holstein Museum)

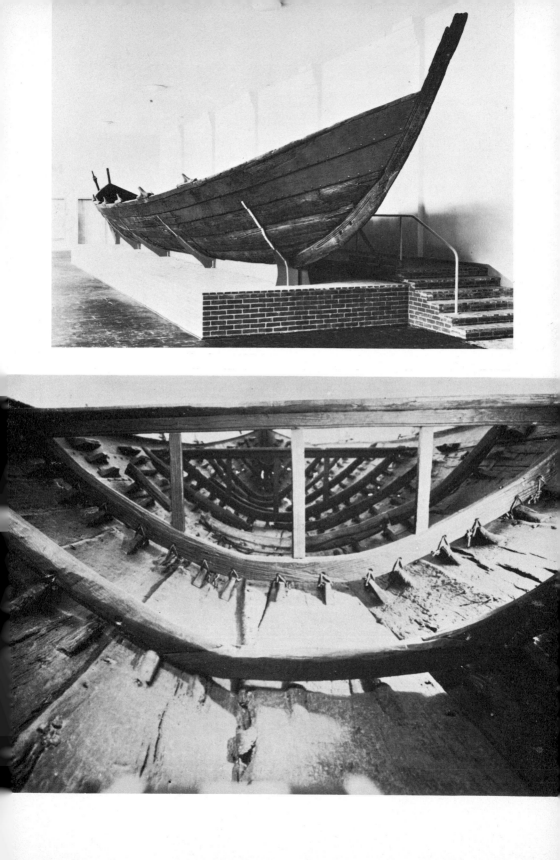

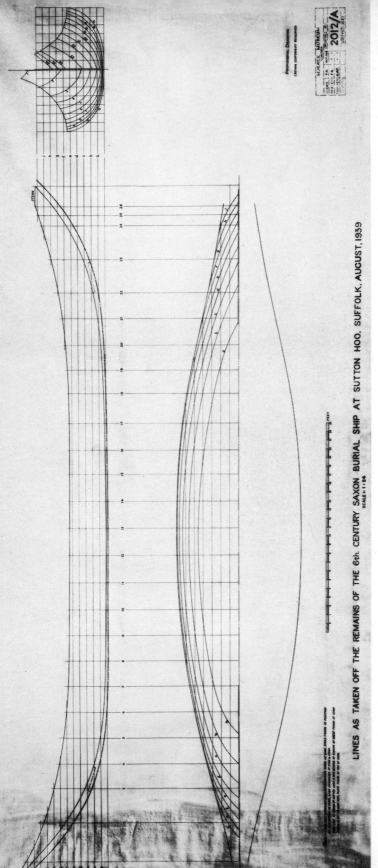

LINES AS TAKEN OFF THE REMAINS OF THE 6th. CENTURY SAXON BURIAL SHIP AT SUTTON HOO, SUFFOLK, AUGUST, 1939

SCALE ⊢1:24

*20 Lines as taken
off the remains of
the Sutton Hoo
Saxon burial ship,
AD 600. (Crown
copyright Science
Museum, London)*

was found on the *Baltic* shore of the Danish mainland just north of Flensburg. It contained a number of fine swords and a few pieces of rich jewellery. The Sutton Hoo ship was built *after* the principal migrations and was found in Suffolk, England. It was not an immigrant ship, but the property of a rich and well established prince or king. It was used finally (like the Nydam ship) for a ship burial and contained the richest collection of Anglo Saxon jewellery ever found.

Like the later Oseberg ship it may have been a state barge, though since all the wood was totally decayed we cannot say if she was carved in the same rich manner. Neither the Nydam nor the Sutton Hoo ships had any mast fittings though sails had been used in north Europe since at least 100 BC and the Saxons were certainly using them by this time. A Roman fleet had reached the entrance to the Baltic in AD 5 and its ships would certainly have carried sails, if only the small square sail the Roman galleys carried for cruising. It is just possible that the mast step of the Sutton Hoo ship, like the thwarts, had been removed to make room for the burial treasure.

Saxon raiders and mercenaries such as Hengist must have used sails. Suppose that they had raided a Roman villa near Poole Harbour. After rowing all day they had rowed into the lagoon with muffled oars at night and walked several miles inland, only to find the inhabitants awake. They then lost several men and had to carry their wounded back to the ship. By now the countryside was raised against them and they would have had to row back up-Channel, tired and shorthanded, struggling over each foul tide while the watchers on the cliff tops scanned the sea and lit beacons to warn the galleys to make all speed to the Straits to cut them off. How much easier and safer to have sailed back at 5 knots with a southwesterly force 5 on the starboard quarter. They would have been almost home before the first galley reached the rendezvous. If the wind had gone east the raiders could have turned south and been lost in the empty sea in two hours.

Everyone else used sails, and it is inconceivable that the Saxon sailors and raiders would have courted suicide by sticking to oars alone. Migrating farmers from inland (although they could never have been far from the sea) might have come to Britain in simple rowing craft like the Nydam ship. The use of sails on long narrow boats requires experience, and landsmen who only intended to make one voyage may not have troubled to obtain it.

Between 460 and 530 the Saxons spread over most of south-eastern Britain and began to settle north of the Humber around the beginning of the 6th century. The number of Saxons may have been about half a million at the end of the migration era. Allowing for those born here perhaps 250,000 landed in 100 years; about fifty shiploads a year during the summer months, scarcely more than two ships a week on average. During the first half of the 6th century it seems that southern England could take no more people and there is evidence of Saxons actually sailing back to Germany.

That is the picture of Saxon seafaring pieced together from archaeological evidence and the obscure statements of a few British and Roman writers. Although for the first 100 years they came as raiders and mercenaries, they did not come in fleets nor, judging from Plates 18 and 19, did they carry shields along the gunwales (if they had they could not have used the oars). Later they came as a steady procession of individual ships or small groups, crossing by the short routes to England, though they may have avoided the Dover Strait as being too easily guarded and rowed across from the mouth of the Rhine to Essex and up the coast. There are no records of fighting on the beaches or large armies landed.

They probably walked inland keeping away from settlements in the sparsely inhabited countryside and settled on land the inhabitants were too lazy or inexpert to farm. As the Saxon numbers built up they would have wanted more land and tried to take it; then King Arthur, or whatever British chief his legend stands for, would have been summoned with his companions to drive them back.

The main settlement routes seem to have been up the Thames valley almost to Oxford, down the Fenland rivers from the Wash, and into the Humber Estuary, down the Trent and up the Yorkshire rivers. For many of them the voyage was far from ended when the coast of Britain was sighted; they would have faced a further 100 miles of coasting followed by 50 miles of river rowing.

Without sails it would have been a one-way traffic, for the big rowing ships could not have been taken back by skeleton crews. Most of them must have been abandoned when the crews moved inland, or passed on to others whose ships were damaged or overcrowded and who were going further.

The ships were a triumph of ingenious construction with simple tools, but in spite of the incredibly long life of the Nydam ship the average useful life of Saxon ships must have been short. They would have worked in a seaway even if the lashings were taken up as the material stretched. All the other fastenings were of untreated iron, and rust and the working of the parts must have produced chronic nail-sickness quite soon. The great planks must have split frequently. The construction of the Sutton Hoo ship proves this. Each strake was now made up of four or five lengths scarphed together. There were 19 narrower strakes instead of 11 wide ones, which again allowed a more careful selection of timber and produced a smoother curve to the mid-section. She was 89 ft (27.13 m) long, 14 ft (4.27 m) beam and 4 ft 6 in. (1.37 m) deep amidships (Plate 20). There were 40 oarsmen. As in the Nydam ship the oars were 10 to 12 ft long (3–3.7 m).

How fast could the Nydam ship be rowed? Thirty men over a long period develop about 10 h.p., nearly 1.2 h.p. per ton displacement. This is better than the power/weight ratio of the liners mentioned in chapter 5 which had cruising speeds of $0.8\sqrt{\text{waterline length (ft)}}$. The same formula applied to the 59 ft Nydam ship gives about 6 knots which seems reasonable for a ship with a block coefficient of only 0.29.

She could only have reached that speed in a smooth sea with neutral wind and tide. Maximum speed over the ground with a favourable wind might have reached 8 knots. With 50 adults aboard a 30-oar ship, 20 of the crew would always have been resting and each oarsman would always have been at full efficiency. No doubt the women took turns with the men. In clear weather they might have rowed on through the night and covered 70 miles on two tides. Even if they were not a trained crew when the voyage began they would soon have become one. And they belonged to an age when common people accepted backbreaking work throughout the daylight hours as normal. Their chief need was for concealment, and they must have spent a lot of time rowing just out of sight from shore, over the horizon, perhaps another reason why they did not set sails. As a measure of what can be done by oars alone we have records of prodigous rowing by 'modern' longshoremen. In 1804 a crew of Gravesend watermen rowed from Gravesend to the Nore Light and back—67 miles—in 8 hours 17 minutes.

But however they came to England there is little doubt that the Saxons everywhere soon used sailing ships for trading. Although overseas trade declined in the chaos that followed the Roman collapse it did not cease, and soon began to mount again; and while there were fewer merchant ships than at the height of the Pax Romana there were hundreds of round-bodied single masted sailing ships carrying cargo and passengers for Britons, Saxons, Frisians and Franks.

In the late 6th century Pope Gregory found English boy slaves in Rome, and Bede thought they would find a ready sale in Roman markets though some Saxon kings forbad it. In 8th century England there were already elaborate trade regulations and tolls; and

Athelstan (924–939) forbad the export of horses. The fact that horses had been carried tells us something of the sort of ships used. In the 11th century a lady was accused of shipping girls to Denmark. Two 8th century Northumbrian churchmen made many journeys to Italy and brought back furniture, vestments, pictures and books.

Offa of Mercia, which maintained trade with the continent via the Humber, made a treaty with Charlemagne and others for the protection of traders and the freedom of trade. Edgar, first king of all England, regulated the entry of ships into his ports by fines of £2 per crewman. In the 8th century an English merchant named Botta was living in Marseilles and Englishmen were trading in the Baltic. Wulfstan, an English trader, described a voyage to the Frisches Haff to King Alfred, and Ethelred's treaty with the Danes further shows that English ships sailed in northern waters. There was a Frisian community in York, which could then be reached directly by ship. Before the 10th century London and York were great ports; documents mention cargoes of fish, timber, wine, wool, cloth, garments, building stone, jewellery, slaves and horses. Whaling products like blubber and fat are also mentioned.

Nearly all the later Anglo Saxon kings maintained fleets and could levy large numbers of warships in time of need; but the maintenance of a standing fleet large enough to intercept and destroy any Viking fleet was beyond their means. 'Search and destroy' was a very difficult naval doctrine in Anglo Saxon times and we read in the *Anglo-Saxon Chronicle* 'King Edward had forty small boats…at Sandwich [to] keep watch for Earl Godwine who was in Bruges that winter. But…he got into the country without them knowing…'

In the early 7th century Edwin, overlord of Saxon Britain, captured the Isles of Man and Anglesey, and in 684 Ecgfrith, King of Northumbria sent a fleet to Ireland to teach Irish raiders to stay away from Britain. Alfred the Great made little use of ships in the main struggle with the Danes because he had few secure bases to work from. 'He went out to sea and fought against seven ships in 875', and his ships were in action again in 882 and 885 with varying success. In 896 he built the fleet that earned him the title of 'father of the British Navy'. The *Chronicle* says, 'Then King Alfred had long-ships built to oppose the Danish warships. They were almost twice as long…Some had sixty oars, some more. They were…swifter and steadier and…higher than the others. They were built neither on the Frisian nor the Danish pattern, but as it seemed to him himself that they could be most useful.'

Most of the figures quoted in the *Chronicle* ring true, and no doubt the ships were much larger than the *general run* of 9th century Viking ships which probably pulled 30–40 oars. Alfred's ships were therefore probably about 100 ft (30 m) long.

Viking warships were slender; Frisian ships were full-bodied traders. Alfred's ships were perhaps between the two and possibly inferior to either. The Bayeux Tapestry, embroidered 200 years later, shows English ships with one bank of oars before the mast and another bank abaft, with 20 ft (6 m) or so of blank hull between. The Norman ships have a continuous row of ports. This may be just to distinguish one ship from another, but it would have been so much easier to have done it by ensigns or figureheads, that it may represent a real difference. Frisian merchant ships, although they had sails, may have had a fair number of oar ports fore and aft of the cargo space for working them up the narrow waters that led to Dorestad. If the English ships were big and beamy they would have been heavy to row, so the oar ports may have been in pairs close together and with every second oar a long one rowed by a man well inboard and slightly astern of his fellows, a layout that has recently been successfully tried in a converted naval cutter. Double banking like this would have made up for the loss of oar space amidships.

Nine of these new ships blockaded six Danish ships which had been plundering between Devon and the Isle of Wight; some say they were caught in Brading Haven at the east end of the Wight. Three of the Danes tried to slip past but only one succeeded, and there were only five men left alive in her when she made the open sea. The tide was on the ebb and the nine English ships ran aground 'very awkwardly', three on one side and six on the other. The crews of the three Danish ships on the mud further in came and fought the three English crews on their side while the others looked on helplessly: 62 English and Frisians and 120 Danes died.

When the tide turned it floated the smaller Danish vessels first although they were further up the estuary, and they rowed out past the stranded English ships. But the Danes were so weary and so few 'they could not get past Sussex, and the sea cast two of them on the land and the men were brought to Winchester to the King and he ordered them to be hanged'. So ended the fight in that estuary of bloody and muddy misfortune. Alfred's ships were perhaps too large for the shallow harbours of the time.

Later kings proclaimed full ship levies, one ship for every 310 hides of land, at a standard price of 8 marks a rowlock. Sometimes 100 ships were built, and the ship tax came to over half as much as the army tax. In Edward the Confessor's time the nails for the King's ships were forged at Gloucester, perhaps a hint of an 'establishment'. In 936 Louis d'Outremer crossed to Boulogne with an English naval escort, to receive the crown of France, and in 939 Athelstan sent another English fleet across the Channel to his aid, the first time an English fleet went to the help of a Continental ally.

Meanwhile, on the Continent a new naval threat had appeared. By 711 the Arabs had conquered all North Africa and most of Spain in the name of Allah and his prophet; in 720 they crossed the Pyrenees and took Narbonne on the Mediterranean end of one of the greatest of the north–south trade routes. As Gibbon said, 'the Arabian fleet might have sailed...into the mouth of the Thames'.

The Mohammedan armies were stopped at Poitiers by Charles Martel, but henceforth the Frankish empire needed one fleet in the Mediterranean and another based on the Garonne or the Loire and a third in the Rhine–Cap Gris Nez area. To the student of shipping the Arab explosion means that yet another foreign influence was introduced into the Iberian peninsula, and the slave trade was given a boost and an even more heartless twist with the demand for eunuchs for the Arab harems.

In AD 800 Charlemagne began to build a complete land and sea defence system from Frisia to Spain. The eastern fleet, partly built at Ghent in 811, was stationed at Boulogne to guard the narrows; harbour defences denied the use of the Rhine and Meuse to enemy fleets. Charlemagne's son, Louis the Pious, built a navy on the Loire and Garonne to protect the western shores of the new Roman empire in 810. Carolingian fleets also operated in the Mediterranean.

The warships of Charlemagne and Louis may therefore have been influenced by three or four streams of naval architecture. Charlemagne, crowned Emperor by the Pope in Rome in AD 771, was deeply influenced by Roman tradition and may have brought Mediterranean galley forms to the northern shores. But Frisian ships were clinker built as is shown by coins. The merchant ships of the west coast of France, on the slender combined evidence of Julius Caesar, Gregory of Tours and Strabo, seem to have been carvel. Tempting as it is to build up a picture of Charlemagne's fleet from these scraps we cannot allow ourselves to do so.

One thing is certain: the fleets of Charlemagne and Louis held the northern frontiers of the Empire firm and the Vikings were badly beaten in western France in 799 and 820. Not until Louis died in AD 820 were the coasts of France open to the men from the northeast who were to settle, intermarry and reappear as the Normans, one of the most dynamic peoples in the making of Christian Europe.

The serfs and peasantry of Saxon England and Carolingian France may have lived their lives within a few miles of where they were born but the nobility were great travellers. Kings and queens often went to Rome; Alfred went twice, once with his father, the king. Bishops and archbishops went to Rome to have audience of the Pope and others were appointed in Rome and journeyed to Britain, Ireland and Scotland. A frequent sentence in the *Chronicle* is 'Archbishop...received the pallium [the stole of office] from Rome', or 'King...sent to Rome for the pallium'. One meticulous Pope even wrote to say the pallium was on its way. Missionaries crossed and recrossed the seas and masons journeyed from Gaul to build stone churches in England. The most precious relics—a portion of the true cross, a fragment of the crown of thorns, and of the lance that pierced the side of Christ—were sent across the seas at the height of the Viking period.

Some of the Frisian vessels had cabins and, when King Harald of Denmark found himself sailing in company with a Frisian ship, he went aboard and finished the voyage in the comfort of not one cabin but two. The term 'cog' was used for a merchant ship in the 9th century and we shall probably be not far wrong if we imagine such a ship with cabins as being like a smaller version of her namesake of the 13th century, clinker built with a length/beam ratio of three or four to one and a single mast and square sail amidships.

Perhaps this is the proper note on which to end the chapter: fighting always steals the pages of history but law and faith and honourable trade are the basis of human existence.

14 Celtic Shipping in the West and North

Migration, piracy and amazing grace

To talk of the Celtic fringe of Britain in the 1st millennium AD is a misleading simplification. The people who lived in Scotland, western Britain and Ireland were not all Celts; and it was more than a fringe, it was over half the total area. The Celts had once covered most of Europe from the Rhine to the Pyrenees with their heroic, barbaric, tribal culture. But Julius Caesar's defeat of the Veneti fleet was the end of Celtic domination in France, and by AD 80 most of Britain south of the Forth–Clyde line was Romanised too; the Celts were still there, but the old tribal system was gone.

But there remained a Celtic world where Celtic kings, warriors and bards still ruled the remains of earlier peoples; a world of many lands divided by sea and deeply penetrated by river and sea-loch. It included Cornwall, Wales, part of the Lancashire coast, the Isle of Man, nearly all Scotland, the Northern and Western Isles, and all Ireland. Some of these people later settled in the Faroes, Iceland, possibly Greenland, and the remote islands off the coasts of Britain including probably St Kilda. The whole network of principalities and settlements has been called a thalassocracy, from the Greek *thallos* meaning sea. It was neither an empire nor a federation but a network of Celtic lands linked by sea. The Celts were among the greatest sailors of the north but their ships are a mystery, known only from legend and the chance remarks of historians who were writing about other things.

Many of the Veneti defeated by Caesar in 56 BC fled to Devon and Cornwall in the heavy full-bodied ships he described; and Celtic Cornwall, whatever craft it had before, now had vessels like small medieval cogs together with expert shipbuilders and sailors. These must have traded westwards, around Lands End and across to Wales. Many of the Celtic chiefs in Gaul and Britain who would not bow to Roman or Saxon rule fled west to plan revenge or live as pirates.

Wales was raided by the Irish before the Romans left Britain, and Niall of the Nine Hostages, king of the northern half of Ireland

AD 379–405, was the son of a British princess carried off by his father. Niall almost certainly raided the Isle of Wight and probably the Continent using curraghs. There is no doubt that the skin-covered wicker framed boat was extensively used by the Irish, and there is evidence of wooden galleys and sailing ships as well.

The *Lives* of Saint Brendan agree that a 6th century curragh like his could carry 20 to 30 men, so that ten or twenty boats could have carried enough men for a hit and run raid. But Niall's fleet may have numbered many more for he was High King of Ulster and would only have engaged in great enterprises. He may have taken Veneti-type sailing ships as well to carry stores and perhaps tow the curraghs used in the actual raids.

Niall's father must have seen and avoided the Roman galleys and scouting craft that operated from their naval base near Cardiff, and like other Irishmen would have dodged or fought Roman warships from the bases at Holyhead and Lancaster built to counter Irish raids across Morecambe Bay. They could have copied these ships even if they only made inferior copies.

There is a description of Saint Brendan's curragh in the *Navigatio Sancti Brendani*, probably written in the 9th century. He was born about 484 'in the marshy region of Munster' where there were perhaps few trees but plenty of osiers. He made his boat in the Dingle Peninsula, still famous for its curraghs. 'Brendan and his companions made a coracle using iron tools. The ribs and frame were wood as is the custom in these parts, and the covering was tanned ox hide stretched over oak bark. They greased all the seams on the outer surface of the skin with fat and stored away spare skins inside the coracle, together with fat for waterproofing the skins, tools and utensils. A mast and sail and various pieces of equipment for steering were fitted into the vessel.' There were eighteen monks on this voyage and they sailed when the wind was fair and 'rowed and rowed until their strength failed' when it was not. This describes a boat able to carry 18 men and considerable stores, about $2\frac{1}{2}$ tons in all, with a useful sail and a proper rudder.

In the London Science Museum there is a model of a boat seen and drawn accurately by a Captain Phillips in Ireland in 1685 (Plate 6). This is a true wicker sailing boat 34 ft (10.36 m) long by 7.5 ft (2.29 m) beam. The mast is rigged with shrouds and forestay and the hull is heavily reinforced with a timber stem, keel and dead-wood. There are hoops aft for a canvas or hide tilt. The bow carries a bull's head figurehead and a small cross stands up from the port quarter. She appears to have been covered with fourteen hides or parts of hides. This was without doubt a descendant of the Irish wicker boats of early Christian times and was obviously seaworthy enough to make long voyages in rough weather. The earlier boats' maximum size could only be determined by practical experiment but it must have been at least 40 ft (12 m). Some Eskimo umiaks are said to have reached 60 ft (18 m) but umiaks have built-up frames of heavy timber.

A carving on an early Christian stone near Bantry is remarkably like the Phillips boat even to the little cross on the gunwale aft (Fig. 11). There is also a model of an Irish boat made of beaten gold about 200 BC (Plate 21). This has eight oars, thole rings, and a steering oar with tiller socket. There is a feeble mast and yard. This may well represent a skin-covered wicker boat of similar shape. Both show that the steering oar was on the port side.

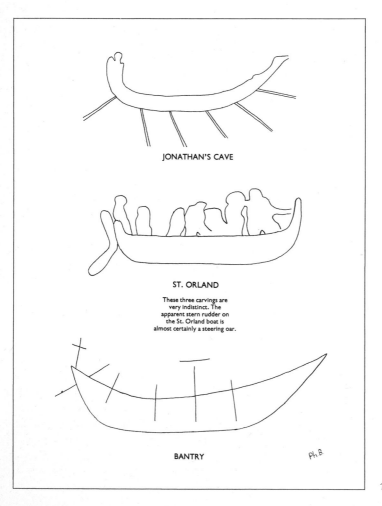

JONATHAN'S CAVE

ST. ORLAND

These three carvings are
very indistinct. The
apparent stern rudder on
the St. Orland boat is
almost certainly a steering oar.

BANTRY   Ph.B

11 Celtic boats

There are plenty of contemporary accounts of curraghs used for trade and war. Niall's grandson, Breccan, had fifty curraghs trading between Ireland and Scotland, and as mentioned above, on one terrible day the whole fleet floundered in the Corrie-vrekan whirlpool on its way to Scotland. When Lughaid MacCon fled to the Scottish court the chronicler says a great host of ships, barks and galleys was assembled and 'betwixt Ireland and Scotland was a continuous bridge of curraghs'.

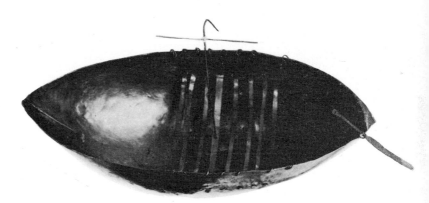

21 Broughter boat model ca 200 BC. (Crown copyright Science Museum, London)

Ireland for all its artistic achievement and religious fervour in the centuries between Roman and Viking was a pastoral country without towns or native seaports. But trade, though small, was continuous. There have been finds of eastern Mediterranean amphorae near Waterford as well as in Cornwall, Devon and south Wales. Ships may have brought eucharistic wine or holy oil direct by sea from the monasteries of the Middle East. If the rich sipped wine at the altar they doubtless drank plenty of it at home, and fine red table ware was also found on the same sites. Wine was probably shipped in barrels from southwest France. Horse racing was an Irish sport even in those early centuries and the nobility were already judges of horseflesh: good bloodstock must have travelled across the Irish Sea.

Wine, horses, cattle, hides and pottery, with perhaps grain for flour or whiskey, needed larger vessels than curraghs and the Veneti type of sailing ship is the most likely answer. Something of much the same shape as the fishing boats that work among the islands of Scotland today but probably a little smaller.

The ancient Irish laws, drawn up by professional jurists, refer to longships, baircs and curraghs and these were no doubt precise terms, unlike the ship terms used carelessly or ignorantly by monastic scribes or general historians. The longship must have been a wooden galley, and a bairc, barca or bark a beamy sailing ship.

There were plenty of passengers. Young Irishmen went to Continental seminaries, often to the Mediterranean shore. Palladius, the first bishop, was sent to Ireland in 431 according to Pope Celestine's secretary, so missionaries must have gone to Ireland well before his time. Patrick arrived as bishop in 432. He had been plucked from north Wales or the Lancashire coast by Irish raiders and taken to Ulster whence he escaped to southern Ireland and shipped with a cargo of hunting dogs bound for the Loire. Ordained possibly at Lerins off the Marseilles coast, he returned to Ireland to urge episcopal rule on the native Irish Christianity which centred round the monasteries. Soon a stream of Irish monks and missionaries crossed to Britain and on to Europe. There were also mercenaries and emigrants from Ireland, and sometimes soldiers of fortune and people hard-pressed by Angles and Saxons went the other way. And there were always slaves.

In the 5th and 6th centuries AD great numbers of Celtic Britons from Cornwall led by men of royal stock from South Wales resettled peacefully in Brittany and they must have made the crossing in Veneti-type ships. They seem to have gone because of Saxon pressure, and Gildas says they went singing sad songs 'beneath the swelling sail'. Jordanes wrote in AD 551 that about AD 470 12,000 British were invited over to fight the Visigoths and settled along the Loire.

The journeys of Saint Sampson of Dol are an astonishing tale of land and sea travel in 6th century Europe, a century in the middle of what is called the Dark Ages. In Dublin he planned a trip to Paris with such a load of books and holy vessels that he took a two-horse trap or gig with him in the ship. Surviving vehicles suggest wheels 3 ft in diameter and a track of 4 ft. He sailed direct from Howth to Caldy Island in southwest Wales (150 miles) and thence to Padstow on the north Cornish coast (70 miles). Here he harnessed horses and drove across to Fowey. From here he sailed to Dol near St Malo (160 miles); thence he drove to Paris.

The whole account suggests merchant shipping on regular routes accepting bulky and awkward loads as a matter of course; and travel by good roads with livery stables at convenient intervals. Notice how in the Bristol Channel Lundy Island lay as a refuge on the route, and how the Channel Isles served the same purpose between Cornwall and Brittany.

Sampson's cart, Patrick's ship carrying a pack of hounds, cargoes of wine, and passengers of the rank of bishop all point to full-bodied wooden sailing ships of at least 20 or 30 tons in the Irish Sea.

Voyages of 160 miles might easily have lasted three days on the open sea where reasonable beam and freeboard and shelter below would have been essential.

The shortest passage between Ireland and Scotland is from Antrim to the Mull of Kintyre, a mere 12 miles, and a vanguard of 150 Irishmen from the little kingdom of Dalriada in Antrim crossed it in the 5th century, squeezed out by the Ui Neills who now ruled nearly all Ulster. Dalriada was reborn in southwest Scotland and gradually extended to embrace many of the Pictish peoples.

An allied tribe, the Dalfiatach, made the 30 mile crossing from Belfast Lough to the Isle of Man about the same time. In the 6th century AD the two peoples sailed their fleets between Ulster, Kintyre and Man fighting both in Belfast Lough and Man. However small and remote these little empires seem now they involved prodigious seafaring.

Tradition states that Columba consecrated Aidan King of Dalriada at Dunadd near Crinan in 574. It may have been at Iona but Dunadd is much more probable. If you stand by the Crinan Canal about three miles from its western end and look north you see the flood plain of the little river Add stretch out before you. On the river bank about two miles away, on the northern side of the marshy fields, stands Dunadd, Aidan's capital and now a mound about 200 yards in diameter standing 176 feet above sea level—Troy was no larger. There are other duns nearby and the standing stones and burial cairns of older peoples.

On that coronation day in 574 the hill must have been a close-packed jumble of huts surrounding the king's house, all huddled within a defensive wall. But the normal population of a few hundred had been swelled in the weeks before the ceremony by visitors arriving by ship and boat. The saint himself may have come 50 miles from Iona in a curragh, passing close to the whirlpool between Jura and Scarba. He could have sailed or rowed right up the river to the landing stage at Dunadd.

It was the first Christian coronation in Dark Age Britain and petty chiefs must have come great distances, including kinsmen from Antrim, whence had come at some time the coronation stone itself (the stone at Westminster is probably a copy). Again we have to rely on strong tradition, but there is nothing improbable in the men of Irish Dalriada bringing their sacred stone with them, even though it weighed half a ton.

Delegations from the Clyde and the Ayrshire coast would have slipped through the Kyles of Bute and up Loch Fyne to Loch Gilp. In the 6th century it was not much more than three miles from Dunadd and the actual portage less than two. But it is not very likely that they would have dragged their ships over on a state visit. Nor is it likely that traders did so, for trade would have been vested in the hands of the tribes on each side of the isthmus and the cargoes transhipped. Ship portage was probably restricted to raiders or to foreign merchants in barbaric countries, like the Vikings in Russia.* The visitors, like the Wise Men of the Gospels, would have brought presents—jewellery, dogs, slaves, wine, or a good bull boar or stallion to sire Aidan's livestock. Hostages may have been sent by submissive tribes and spies by rivals. There would have been wooden ships as well as curraghs and by this date some of the curragh owners may have landed at a hidden bay nearby and walked to Dunadd claiming they came in a fine plank-built ship. It was a simple world and as we imagine the visitors departing we think of King Harold in the Bayeux Tapestry, barefooted and holding up his tunic as he wades out to his ship at Bosham. Some of Aidan's guests no doubt departed in pomp sitting under canopies and when they were round the corner stripped off their shirts to take over the stroke oar.

The ancient kings of Scotland were buried at Iona and this gives us another picture of early Celtic shipping; funeral processions making the long voyage among the islands with the king's coffined body amidships in the curragh or galley.

It is natural that in an aristocratic warrior society there were also saints, leaders of equal stature but opposite psychology. Saint Columba of the blood royal of the Ui Neills crossed from Ireland in 563 via the Mull of Kintyre. He and his little band crossed in one curragh. The story says he buried it in the sand so that it would not remind him of Ireland where he had clashed with his superiors and lost. Or was he afraid it would reveal his presence, or the greased hides be eaten by rats? His 'footprints' in Carskey Bay point away from Ireland. He did, however, return to Ireland several times. Columba was no hermit monk but one who crowned the King of Dalriada and made Iona famous throughout the Christian world. We can imagine the lading of that curragh—a portable altar, rich vestments, church plate, gospel books and communion wine, perhaps from the eastern Mediterranean, in carefully stowed amphorae. The Book of Kells was being written in the Iona scriptorium at the time of the first Viking raids and was secretly shipped to Ireland for completion.

Columba was only one of many Irish saints including Saint Moluoc who founded a monastery in Scotland in 562 and Saint Maelrubha who settled at Applecross on the mainland opposite

* P A Macnab in *The Isle of Mull* states that skiffs were portaged by the Crinan route in the 17th and 18th centuries, before the canal was built.

Skye in the following century. Saint Cormac sailed from Ireland to the Orkneys around 570. Luckily Columba was visiting Brude, the Irish king of the Picts, at the time and begged safe conduct for Cormac. Brude's dominion over the Northern Isles was real enough for Columba met a vassal king of Orkney at Brude's court at Caithness. It is unlikely that Columba defeated a monster in Loch Ness, but the story (which is pre-10th century) and the terrain suggest that he made the journey to Caithness by boat along the route of the Caledonian Canal. There must have been much sailing across the Pentland Firth, including an expedition sent by Brude in 580 or 581.

Adamnan, the ninth abbot of Iona and the biographer of Columba and Cormac, was no stranger to the western seas. He tells of another voyage when Cormac ran for fourteen days before a southerly wind. Whether he reached Shetland, the Faroes or Iceland is not known but his crew were attacked by clouds of stinging creatures. These Irish saints made voyages of enormous distance and duration and Adamnan says the monks of Iona used wooden boats as well as curraghs.

They were the finest sailors who ever stepped into a boat. Like the Biblical prophets they wanted to spend forty days in the wilderness and they were proud to suffer for Christ. Short rations enabled them to mortify the flesh. And how could the saints be frightened when God was so near? Sometimes the crews were terrified by wind and sea and then, according to the stories, their leader called upon the waves to be still and they subsided. There is nothing unlikely here except the time factor; he remained calm and confident in the turmoil and kept them bailing or rowing until the storm blew itself out—six hours later perhaps—but they were too busy to notice the time.

They saw great visions and we cannot say they lied. After days at sea, hungry and exhausted but firm in simple faith, how can we know what they saw or thought they saw?

There has been much speculation as to where Saint Brendan went and one writer has sought to prove that he went to the Hebrides, St Kilda, the Canaries, the Bahamas, the Caribbean, the Faroes, Iceland, Jan Mayen Island and Greenland. All we know is that the Irish 'illuminati' lived on the Orkneys, Hebrides and Faroes, Iceland and probably Greenland.

We can guess a little at these voyages by applying practical boatmanship. It is stated that the hides had to be greased every three days to keep them watertight. It is just possible that this could have been done at sea by careful boat trimming. The Faroes to Iceland is 300 miles and they might have done it on one greasing, perhaps bailing steadily towards the end of the voyage. Saint Brendan in the 'Book of Lismore' is said to have taken forty days from Ireland to Iceland, but this is probably a poetic use of the traditional forty days in the wilderness.

The nearest point to Norway is Shetland, the route of the 'Shetland Bus'*, and they must have made the 190 mile voyage for Irish monks are known to have reached Norway. Iceland to Greenland was within their range. But we can rule out the Bahamas even though men have rowed and drifted across the full width of the Atlantic in recent years. Neither the monks' provisions nor their curraghs would have lasted out the voyage.

Curraghs are usually described as light buoyant boats, but these would have been very heavy at the start of their voyages. And as stated before, if the crews were seeking some lonely spiritual refuge they would have carried books, sacred vessels and perhaps the croziers by which their sites have been identified in Iceland and probably Greenland. Apart from such small finds, the names of Papa Westray in Orkney and Vestmannaeyjar (Island of the West Men) in Iceland provide proof of the outward urge of the Irish 'papae' or priests. Saint Brendan returned to Ireland after five years, and later his foster mother advised the use of a wooden boat for his next voyage from 525–527 AD. This may reflect and date a change from wicker to wood in Irish boatbuilding.

The Picts, the inhabitants of Scotland before the Angles moved into the Lowlands and the Irish crossed into Kintyre, have their own place in history as shipbuilders and sailors. The name is more convenient than exact and is used here for the peoples who built the broch forts, and those who fought the Romans and finally came under the sway of the 'Scots' who crossed from Ireland to found the kingdom of Dalriada. There is no good evidence for Pictish ships but their design may be inferred from what we know of the northern peoples in the later centuries of the Roman occupation. On more than one occasion the Picts with Irish help swarmed down over northern and central Britain and the building of the Roman signal stations on the Yorkshire coast shows that some of them moved by sea.

Although contemporary writers describe armies of 30,000 these are greatly exaggerated. Modern scholars believe that even the great Gothic invasions of Europe only numbered 8000 warriors. The Pictish invasions of Britain can only have numbered a few thousands, and the ship-borne wing that crept down the east coast probably no more than a few hundreds. There is only one probable

---

* The route taken by Norwegian patriots in the Second World War.

picture of a Pictish ship, an engraving on stone in Jonathan's Cave, East Wemyss, Fife in the heart of the Pict country (Fig. 11). This shows what is possibly an eight-oared craft with a steering oar and high bow and stern. It may of course have been rowed by only four men each pulling two oars. There are prehistoric pictures in the same cave but the oars shown on this particular one suggest that it is Pictish.

The proto-Pictish peoples had been subjected to considerable influence from the world of wooden shipbuilding. Refugees from Roman conquests in Gaul and southern Britain seem to have come by sea and landed on the banks of the Tweed, the Forth and the Tay. An incised sandstone disc from Jarlshof in Shetland, ca 3rd century AD, shows very crudely what appears to be the high-peaked bow of a clinker-built ship with a single square sail. Ships portrayed on Celtic crosses in Ireland also include what seem to be clinker-built vessels with a high stem and sternpost and a central mast. Sometimes a single bank of oars is shown.

It will be remembered that the Romans employed Pictish types of scouting vessels, probably camouflage painted with their crews dressed in blue. These were obviously not the big Roman naval galleys, and Vegetius says they had about 20 oars. The Pictish ships were no doubt similar, and we know that the Irish used sails extensively. We can infer that the Irish-Pictish longships had at least 20 oars and a steering oar, a high bow and stern, and possibly carried a total crew of 30. The Roman signal stations therefore were looking out for fleets of about a dozen vessels. From the heart of Pictland to the Wash is about 150 miles and they would have had to row about 50 miles a day and keep over the horizon to maintain any element of surprise. A Pictish raid must have been sudden and sharp, before the local defences could muster. Some cattle would have been butchered for provisions, valuables and a few women taken, the village burned. Then they would have been away. There was not enough room aboard for much booty, but it is almost certain that the treasure buried at Taprain Law in Scotland was captured in a pirate raid on the coast of Gaul.

As early as 1000 BC there was an important centre of wooden shipbuilding in the Humber area of England and finds of very large dugout canoes with sternboards, and probably washstrakes, have been made in the Midlands and the north of England. There are also dim records of such dugouts and possibly a plank boat of the Ferriby type discovered in the foundations of Glasgow in the 19th century. The tradition of wood shipbuilding in Scotland may be very old.

Northern Scotland is famous for its brochs; drystone forts about 30 ft in diameter and 60 ft high with stairways in the walls and no openings at all except a low doorway. They look like modern cooling towers and were probably built in the 1st century AD. Like the later Irish round towers they were passive defences too strong to be stormed without heavy casualties, and in which the local inhabitants could take refuge. Brochs cluster thick round the coasts of northeast Scotland, are found in fair numbers around Skye, and less frequently on Lewis and the Orkneys and Shetlands. They suggest that even then there were a lot of small galleys cruising around looking for provisions, slaves or easy plunder but whose crews were not intent on long sieges; galleys with only 20 or 30 men aboard who could not afford many casualties because they had to row away afterwards. If the local people and their cattle could take shelter in time they were safe.

As the Irish from Dalriada spread their rule over the Picts of northern Scotland the scale of their operations increased. In 578–582 Aidan waged naval warfare in the sound of Jura and in 590 he led an expedition to the Orkneys. Galley warfare in the Western Isles became a tradition, and the seal of Islay of AD 1156 shows the ship of Somerled, a Celt from Argyle whose fleet of 58 galleys defeated the Vikings under Godred on the night of 6th January, 1156, in Loch Gruinart, Isle of Islay—probably the only ancient sea battle fought in winter at night! The seal shows a ship with a single square sail amidships and very high stem and stern post. A ratline ladder enabled the crew to reach a fighting top at the masthead. There appears to be a central rudder, which is unknown for this date from other sources. No oars are shown but she is almost certain to have been a galley. She has the earliest known central rudder.

Ships like this were called 'nyvaig' or 'little ship' in Gaelic, which suggests that there were 'big' ships (probably sailing merchant ships), and a nyvaig-big ship battle would have been like the Veneti-Roman battle suggested in Fig. 8. Somerled took the romantic title of Lord of the Isles and as late as 1545 Black Donald of the Isles raised 180 galleys to fight against the Scottish Crown. But all Pictish seafaring was not piracy or war, and in 729 according to the Annals of Tigernach, 150 Pictish merchant ships were wrecked, possibly in the course of trading with Norway.

As the Irish infiltrated from the west, the Saxons moved up into southern Scotland and considerable numbers of Britons, i.e. the original Celtic inhabitants, seem to have gone to North Wales. The Lancashire coast with its deep sea inlets was not an easy land route and there was considerable sea traffic across Morecambe Bay between Wales and the Scottish lowlands. North Wales was presently ruled by King Merfyn who was probably descended from one of these north Britons, and his capital became a staging post for Irishmen on the way to the court of Charles the Bold at Liége. From Wales they journeyed overland, perhaps to the Humber and on from there. Merfyn's son Rhodri became famous by slaying the Danish Viking Horm off the coast of Anglesey, presumably in a sea battle, but in 876 he was defeated by the Vikings in Anglesey and fled to Ireland. He must have returned for he and his son were killed by the Saxons in 877.

Many Irish settled in south Wales and a tribe called the Deisi migrated en masse to Pembroke in the 4th century, led by a king called Eochaid Over-sea. Other Irishmen went to Cornwall, west Devon and the Scillies where there have been pottery finds similar to those in Ulster. And there is considerable evidence of an Irish colony in Spain which in 572 had a bishop with the Celtic name of Mailoc. Chapter 13 describes how the Saxon King Edwin captured the Isle of Man in the early 7th century and how Ecgfrith sent an expedition to Ireland in 684. The Isle of Man was obviously of great strategic importance and was colonised from Ireland and Wales at an early date. The movement of Celtic shipping back and forth across the seas from Biscay to the Shetlands was enormous. Breton ships, Roman ships, Irish ships, Pictish and Saxon ships mingled and good points in the design of each must have been copied by the others.

The coming of the Vikings belongs to a later chapter. Ireland suffered more than any other country except England, but the Norwegians and Danes did not have it all their own way and after the middle of the 9th century they met with fierce resistance though there is little evidence of sea battles.

Except for Wales, which was subdued by the genius of Alfred, the Celtic fringe of Europe maintained its integrity, and this strange pastoral world with its heroes and saints, its artists and poets, made a very real contribution to western civilisation. As sea explorers the Irish monks excelled the Vikings. Wherever the Northmen went in the Atlantic, apart from Vinland, they found the papae were there before them. The Norse were not racialists and many of them were Christians: some think that their sagas owe much to Celtic poets. Niall's Saga bears a Celtic name and in the Vinland Saga we read of an Irish Christian in a Viking crew. The boats of the wandering saints were small and frail, and to have ventured so far shows outstanding seamanship. The men who sailed them eschewed all comfort, and all women save one—she whom later romantics were to call 'Our Lady Star of the Sea'.

15 Fishing Boats, Ferries and Barges

*The general characteristic of long-line fishing is
that it consists of a long-line with shorter lines...
attached at intervals, the whole affair being sunk or
moored by stones or anchors*

PETER F ANSON

The northern seas are much richer in plankton than the waters of the Mediterranean and the consequences of this may have provided added stimulus for boatbuilding from the earliest time. But although the pattern of biomass suggests interesting possibilities it does not supply a conclusive reason why boatbuilding techniques seem to have developed more in some areas than others.

There are three areas of exceptional plankton concentration. The first is a narrow belt along the coast of Norway from Bergen to the North Cape. The early boat petrographs come from the centre of the coast (Fig. 1, Nos. 1–5). The second area runs from Sierra Leone to south Portugal where there are some remarkable fortified settlements of the 3rd millennium BC and trading stations were founded by Phoenician and Carthaginian merchants who traded fish as well as tin and silver into the central Mediterranean. The third area includes the English Channel and the North Sea to beyond the Arctic Circle. A westward arm encloses Iceland, creeps up the western coast of Greenland and down across the Newfoundland Banks continuing south along the New England coast beyond the farthest limits reached by the Vikings. There are two other extensions of this great belt of fish food: one stretches down the west coast of Scotland and includes the northern coast of Ulster and the whole of Morecambe Bay. The other, even richer, penetrates the Kattegat and Skaggerak as far south as Copenhagen.

The bulk of the Bronze Age ship pictures are on the Norwegian and Swedish side of these straits, though there are others in northern Sweden and Karelia. Norwegian Vikings settled on the Orkneys, Shetlands, Faroes, Hebrides, Iceland and the *west* coast of Greenland. The Irish Sea, the other waters round the Atlantic coasts of Europe and the Baltic are adequately supplied with plankton but of nothing like the same richness. The waters off the east coast of Greenland are barren and the Mediterranean is generally a poor fishing area. But the Sea of Azov and the Caspian

Sea are the richest of all and were an important factor in the early Greek settlement of the shores of Scythia.

This of course is an oversimplification of the complex inter-play of marine biology and human endeavour, and considerable fishing took place in poor areas as well as rich. Meat was rarely available to the mass of the population until quite recent times and dried or salted fish was an important article of diet for many thousands of years. Some sea fish were caught in Palaeolithic times and by the close of the Ice Age there were many coastal communities living mainly on fish from Brittany to the Baltic in one of the plankton-rich areas. There were other fishing communities by the sea between Scotland and Ireland. In historic times the city of Rome provided a huge market and the wealthy could afford fresh fish, which was brought into Ostia in fishing boats with wet wells like those found during the excavations of the Claudian harbour. Similar boats may have supplied the needs of senior Roman civil servants and retired army officers in their coastal villas in Gaul and Britain.

The earliest evidence of trading in fish along the Atlantic coasts of Europe is in the 6th century AD when there were professional fishermen along English, French and Frisian shores. They worked from creeks or beaches near their homes, but in the 10th century fishermen from Normandy seem to have migrated to southern Ireland for the summer. If this is so they left an area of maximum plankton for one less well endowed. English fishermen began to go far offshore in the 11th century. By the 12th the Basques were fishing deep in the Bay of Biscay and as far afield as Norway, which suggests a boatbuilding centre of long tradition in the corner of Biscay between France and Spain. All these people fished with long-lines, but nets and traps were invented in Mesolithic times.

A W Brogger cites an amateur archaeologist, a Norwegian like himself, who compared ancient and modern fishing weights between $10\frac{1}{2}$ and 53 oz. and deduced that Neolithic peoples fished in up to 100 fathoms of water. This means that either they fished up to 10 miles out from the Norwegian coast where the bottom drops away or else crossed the deep channel and dropped their lines onto the bed of the North Sea, 50 miles out. Edgar J March records in *Inshore Craft of Great Britain* that 19th century Shetland sixerns, small open boats, went 40 miles offshore to fish with long-lines on the teeming bed of the North Sea.

In Stone Age times this sort of fishing would have been done from skin-covered boats. Plank boats had not been invented and dug-outs are heavy and unseaworthy in *small* sizes. Some of the boats in Scandinavian carvings seem to be one-man kayaks which were probably used for seal or walrus hunting—both animals appear in the carvings and there are Neolithic harpoons from Scandinavia. For line-fishing they would have needed an open boat with room for tubs to hold the lines, hooks, bait and catch, and room to move about.

One of the most delightful of the Bronze Age rock carvings, from southeast Sweden, shows what looks like a husband and wife fishing from a boat (a fishhook has been found in a woman's grave). And the vessel rides to a proper anchor, not just a stone (Fig. 12). One of the lines seems to have two hooks; other carvings show up to a dozen. Fishing in 100 fathoms would have needed many more hooks otherwise the catch would not be worth the labour of handling the lines.

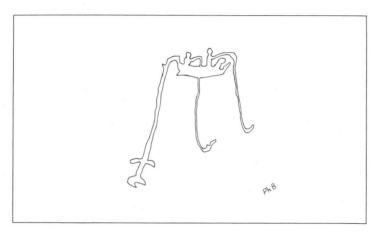

12 Prehistoric fishing scene

Fishing is notoriously hard on boats and men, who go out every day unless the weather is impossible. A skin boat is easily damaged, needs constant attention, has a short life and may be eaten by rats. Where timber was available fishermen would have changed to plank boats as soon as they knew how to build them and the skin boat would have survived only in treeless regions like western Ireland, where we find it today.

Before the overfishing of modern times and before the thud of steamer screws scared the fish away from inshore waters, the seas around northern Europe were teeming with fish. We cannot know how easy it was to catch them in prehistoric eras but we have figures from Saxon times when careful counts were made to assess the fishing revenues. Rent was usually paid in herrings—Southease, a tiny village in Sussex, paid 38,500 and Dunwich in Suffolk 60,000. At Wisbech seventeen fishermen paid a rent of 59,260 eels. There is a reference at this time to a cargo of blubber indicating whaling or sealing on a considerable scale.

Surplus fish had to be cured. In Scandinavia, winter cold will do it unaided. On the Atlantic coasts of France and Spain summer sun will evaporate sea water in shallow pans and leave pure salt behind. Britain is not so happily placed and salt often had to be produced by burning expensive fuel. 'Bay salt' was therefore imported very early into southern Britain from France and Spain and travelled in clay containers.

The coracle was widely used for river fishing in Wales, Ireland, Scotland, the Hebrides and the English counties along the Severn up to the end of the 19th century. In its original form it must date back unchanged to Neolithic and even Mesolithic or Palaeolithic times, and may have been used all over Europe. The modern coracle is an open framework of laths (or even aluminium strips) covered with canvas whereas in earlier times it was always a wicker basket covered with hide, heavier than a modern coracle but still carried by the fisherman across his shoulders. There were also two-man fishing coracles in Scotland and Wales. We read of other large coracles for ferrying. In some the passenger stood behind the seated ferryman, with his hands on his shoulders, and some carried two or three passengers who also paddled. There is an account of timber being towed downriver by coracle.

During the Irish wars of the 16th century a troop fleeing from the enemy built large ferry boats of osiers and timbers. The skins of eleven horses provided the covering of one boat which crossed the Shannon with thirty men at a time, towing the remaining horses behind it. There were ferries all over Europe which carried a heavy traffic and the profession of ferryman must have grown up in Neolithic times and been handed down from father to son. The ferry across the Humber has yielded most evidence, and what is true of the Humber would have been true, with local variations, for ferries across the Seine, Rhine, Elbe, Garonne or among the islands and bogs of Ireland and the Low Countries, or across the fjords of Scandinavia.

The Humber Estuary forms a barrier to travel which stretches inland for 30 miles from the North Sea, 7 miles wide at the mouth and 1 mile wide at the inner end where the rivers Ouse, Aire and Don join it. They rise in the Pennines so that in the days before bridges every man, beast, load and cart had to cross water to go from the Midlands to the North or vice versa. In pre-Roman times this was between the Brigantes and the Parisi to the north, and the Coritani to the south. In Saxon times it was between Northumbria and Mercia. The main routes lay across the estuary, and from the richness of the boat finds there the principal crossing place was between North and South Ferriby, about 8 miles west of Hull. The Roman road from York is aligned on the estuary about 3 miles to the west, and west again the land forms a flat flood plain for 30 miles, impassable in early times for anyone without local knowledge. To the south the Ermine Street from Lincoln and London reaches the estuary opposite Brough, once a Roman settlement called Petuaria.

This was the most important ferry in England, though whether the principal crossing was where the Roman road was divided or at Ferriby where the boats were found cannot be ascertained for certain, but there were ferries at South Ferriby and Barton (4 miles east) in Saxon times, which were valued at £3 and £4 per year in the Domesday Book. The estuary is 2 miles wide here whereas at Goole 15 miles further inland it is only 300 yards. Clearly organised crossing must have been impossible anywhere in the vast area of swamp and saltings west of Brough. Between Brough and Ferriby but close to the south shore is Reads Island, low and flat, about $1\frac{1}{2}$ by $\frac{3}{4}$ mile, which might have provided useful shelter in bad conditions of wind and tide (Map 2).

The three boats found at North Ferriby and described in chapter 7 may have been ferry boats, though if they had thwarts they could just as well have been used for coastal cruising or migration. The date was 1400–1000 BC, cattle and sheep existed in considerable numbers, and two and four wheeled carts were probably in use in Britain. The slave trade was already in being and corn, hides, pigs, geese and passengers also had to make the crossing.

The 'rafts' found at Brigg 10 miles south of Ferriby and at Yaddlethorpe must have formed the bottoms of true ferry boats able to carry any of the loads mentioned above. The Brigg 'raft' was 40 by 10 ft (12.19 by 3.05 m) wide amidships tapering somewhat at each end and almost certainly the basis of a flat-bottomed scow able to carry about 6 tons on a draft of 1 ft (0.3 m) and 10 tons at 18 in. (45 cm). She would have been very similar to the flatboats used in North America to carry 'prairie schooners' and stagecoaches across rivers too deep to ford. Some years ago there was an old pontoon at Itchenor which used to be towed across to the Isle of Wight as a cattle ferry.

In the early days of the Roman conquest a whole legion of 6000 men must have crossed the Humber, probably in boats built on the spot by its own sappers. But once garrison duty commenced the largest unit to cross was probably a cohort of 600 men using the civilian ferry. Four 40 ft (12 m) flatboats carrying 50 men each could have carried out the whole operation in three crossings, unless there were a lot of wagons, artillery, horses and camp followers when several times that number might have been needed. The double crossing would have taken about three hours allowing for loading and unloading and the set of the tide. It would have needed a day to get that cohort across in peacetime. The Pictish invasion of AD 367 was another matter; several thousand Picts, Scots and North Britons were involved, and unless their planning was extraordinarily thorough the Romans would have removed or destroyed the Humber ferries before they arrived. By all accounts their advance was devastatingly swift. Is it possible that the Pictish fleet sailed down the Yorkshire coast to rendezvous with the army in the Humber and ferry it across? Fifty ships could have moved it all in a few hours.

The Humber crossing is a study in itself. Harold's house-carles got across it in 1066 in spite of a Danish fleet. If Harold had not marched with such lightning speed that Viking fleet would have enabled Hardradi to campaign both north and south of the estuary. Whoever wanted to rule all Britain had to control the Humber crossing all the time.

Found with the Ferriby boats was a carefully made wishbone-shaped piece of timber with holes that looks like one half of a windlass (Fig. 6). The boats could not of course have been winched all the way across the estuary, and if this really was part of a wind-lass it must have been for hauling boats up onto the shore.

The great watery maze of the Humber fens stretched from York, which is only 60 ft above sea level in the north, to Lincoln, Newark, Nottingham and Doncaster in the south; 50 miles by 30. Through it ran the rivers Ouse, Wharfe, Derwent, Aire, Trent, Don, Idle and Ancholme. Until medieval times all these were natural rivers and part of Hardradi's fleet in 1066 moored at Riccall, 10 miles south of York on a tributary of the Ouse. Three years later a Danish fleet operated from a fortified base on the Island of Axholme, 10 miles up the River Trent. This gives some idea of how rivers were used in early times.

Boats like the Brigg and Yaddlethorpe 'rafts' may also have been used as barges, which we can assume with near certainty were used all over Europe. A bas-relief at Arles in southern France shows a barge containing three large tuns of wine being hauled by three men dragging ropes hitched to a samson post forward of amid-ships—the ideal place. The boat is crescent shaped and may be a bad artist's impression of a vessel like the Utrecht ship (Plate 27). The bas-relief is Roman and the vessel suggests the probable form of barges on rivers with firm banks throughout Europe. Many barges used simple sails as recently as the 19th century. Plate 22 shows a model of a 'modern' wine barge sailing on the river Douro in Portugal. She is of a very ancient design and has some things in common with the Arles bas-relief. Strabo mentions wine barges on the Douro and they may not have been much different. There was tremendous barge traffic throughout Roman Europe and nearly every large river had its corporation of 'nautae' or boatmen. The megalith builders transported great blocks of stone, the Romans transported blocks of marble all the way from Italy, and towards the end of the Saxon period when stone church building began again there are other records of stone being carried by water. So also did the Brothers of Ely Cathedral collect a great stone for St Audrey's coffin. There are even references to curraghs as

stone boats, which may mean that they were carrying blocks of stone to be made into Celtic crosses.

But probably the banks of most of the early rivers were too soft and slippery for bow-hauling. The early rivers flooded often and wound for much of their course through swampy land. For this reason contemporary barges were probably more often poled, quanted, paddled or sailed then hauled, but hauling is so much the best means of moving a heavy barge that crews must often have built up bad sections of towpath with faggots or bundles of rushes. The flash weir, a dam built round stakes that can be easily withdrawn to make a flume to float a barge down to the next level, may even have been a Stone or Bronze Age invention and it was still

22 Modern period wine barge, river Douro, Portugal. Probably of very ancient design. (Crown copyright Science Museum, London)

in use at the end of the 19th century. The earliest one now known in Europe was in operation in Holland in 1065.

The route across southern England from Christchurch to the Severn via the Hampshire and Somerset Avons has already been described. Boats and barges could penetrate to the very heart of England and Ireland and this was much the easiest way of moving heavy loads. The Domesday Survey of 1086 refers to the navigability of the River Ouse and in the Middle Ages York was classed as an 'overseas port'. Ships sailed regularly between York and London and York and the Continent.

Chapter 10 describes how sixty ships of Julius Caesar's second invasion fleet were built on the Marne and taken down to the Seine. The builders could only have been bargebuilders and their crews bargemen. Most of the Roman merchant ships excavated in the Mediterranean were carrying amphorae, empty or full, and others were carrying tiles. Pottery and earthenware is traditionally a barge cargo, for water transport provides the smooth passage which prevents breakage. Timber, stone, wine, grain, bricks and ingots are also typical barge cargoes to which we can probably add hides, vinegar and salt. Nearly all of these belong to the latter end of our period, from a few hundred years BC onward for wine, grain, salt, hides and timber; with bricks, tiles and metal in large bulk added in the Roman period.

Salt was mined at Hallstatt in Austria in the 7th century BC at least and the crude punt-like barges that transported the salt on the rivers Train and Danube until recently had probably changed little from very early times. There is a model of a 19th century Hallstatt salt barge in the London Science Museum which is 26 by 5 by 2 ft (7.9 by 1.5 by 0.6 m) with a flat bottom and vertical sides. The bow is pointed and upturned and the stern is square. Propulsion was by a pair of sweeps. Boats like this, of heavy planks simply joined into a crude trough-like shape, may have been in use on most of the great rivers of Europe before the more shapely round-bilged seagoing planked ships were developed.

Except in out-of-the-way places it is doubtful if the rivers carried any regular passenger traffic once the Roman roads had been built and as long as they were maintained. River transport on natural rivers is usually very slow. Where there are no locks there is often a strong current and much shallow water. In the dry season weirs or dams have to be built to increase the depth of water and if already there have to be broken to let the barges pass. Occasionally no doubt someone would take passage on a cargo barge on some deep fast reach of say the Danube or the Rhone and cover an exciting 50 miles in five hours. But generally if a road existed it would be quicker and surer to go that way, and there was always the possibility that on a cargo barge the passenger would find himself on the end of the towrope.

In Britain there was a network of drainage channels which served as waterways in the Cambridgeshire and Lincolnshire fens. The Fossdyke connected Lincoln with the river Trent. I R Richmond suggests that tribesmen of the Iceni were made to dig this after Boudicca's revolt in AD 61. Remains of canalside granaries are sure evidence of considerable barge traffic. The Cardyke joined the Cam to the Ouse and the Ouse to the Witham. It was 7 ft deep, 28 ft wide on the bottom and had sloping sides. There is no trace of locks on Roman canals but they were well within the capacity of Roman engineers. Honor Frost has described and drawn the remains of guillotine-type sluice gates built by the Phoenicians at Tyre several hundred years BC. The earliest known true lock in Europe is dated 1373 and was in Holland.

Nero Drusus, the creator of the Rhine flotilla, had a strategic canal dug to connect the Waal near Arnhem with the Ijssel in about 5 BC and began construction of a dam to control the Rhine. Another Roman governor planned a canal linking the Saone with the Moselle but could not get permission to build it. In AD 47 Cnaeus Corbulo was responsible for a 23 mile long canal between the Rhine and the Meuse. In Italy there seems to have been a canal tunnel. Bridgebuilding across the Euphrates was covered by fortified catamarans mounting considerable artillery and it is more than likely that similar craft were used on the Rhine and Danube.

A steering oar found at Newstead, the great legionary fortress on the Scottish border, shows that there was barge traffic on the Tweed. The length of the oar, 5 ft 5 in. (1.65 m) would have suited a barge of about 30 by 6 by 3 ft deep (9 by 2 by 1 m).

Every river and lake in Europe had boats from the earliest times for fishing, wildfowling, the carriage of goods and animals, and away from the roads or ridgeways, for people. Settlements may not always have been beside the rivers for fear of dampness, flooding and 'marsh sickness', but there would have been landing stages where the river banks were firm, and from these, animals, goods and humans would have set out through forest or swamp on voyages of tedium and toil upstream or excitement and danger downriver.

16   The Vikings—Part I

*The great prince saw ahead
the copper roofs of Byzantium*

King Harald's Saga

*King Athelstan…fought in ships and slew
a great army at Sandwich…and captured nine
ships and put others to flight*

Anglo-Saxon Chronicle AD 851

The Viking era looks so simple and is so bafflingly complex. Even Scandinavian philologists do not know what the word means, and no one is sure what made the Vikings leave home to trade and raid across the western world. It may have been overpopulation; during the migration period Norway, for example, seems to have been cultivated to the maximum possible until the great farming improvements of the 18th century, and there were no large towns to breed disease and compensate for a healthy birthrate.

Yet why did the Norwegians cease to emigrate after the 12th century? It is not even certain that any large proportion of them did go overseas for good. Their footholds in Ireland were largely trading posts and the Irish drove them out about the year 1000. The total number in the Hebrides, Orkneys, Shetlands and Faroes was only a few thousands and about 20,000 settled in Iceland in 60 years. The Norwegians who settled around Rouen do not seem to have been in any great number and their language had died out by 1025.

Vikings whether Norwegian, Danish or Swedish, were not heathen fanatics. Many became Christians in the 9th century and most seem to have been ready to be baptised, lapse and be baptised again. One man had twenty baptisms, and traders are said to have travelled 'half-baptised' so that they could be Christian or pagan according to customer. In their time they were represented as monsters. This was an exaggeration. As Salvador de Madariaga says of the Conquistadores, they were ordinary virile men in an age and place not where there was no law but where the law could not control them. This is the real meaning of the Dark Ages. There was plenty of sound local law, but all-pervading, universally enforceable law was lacking.

Their magnificent longships seem to have burst on the rest of Europe like a secret weapon. But their very excellence is evidence of long development, though we take them for granted, rarely asking how this provincial corner of Europe could suddenly spring these remarkable ships on an unsuspecting continent. The myriads of islands round the coasts of Norway, Sweden and Denmark may have favoured the oar and sail combination for many purposes, and the Sagas tell us of fiercely independent families and individuals whose customs allowed them to take the law into their own hands, to take a life for a life and a farm for a farm. The Viking longship in a smaller form may have been developed to take part in family feuds and inter-village squabbles among the islands. The key to the problem may be the islands of Oland, Gotland and Bornholm which were attacked by sea raiders time and time again in the 5th and 6th centuries AD, as evidenced by coin hoards, burned farms and fortified refuges. Gotland is especially rich in ship carvings of the 5th to 11th centuries showing both oared ships of the Nydam and Sutton Hoo types and sailing ships of the Viking period.

The Baltic was a galley sea. Although galleys died out in the rest of northern Europe in the 16th century they still went into battle in the Baltic in the 18th. And these were not obsolete leftovers in a northern backwater, but the inspired creations of the greatest naval architect of his time. Something about this island studded sea demanded the swift oar-sail combination.

Towards the end of the 8th century the Scandinavians were a people in search of change. They had exhausted life in their own lands and were ripe for new ideas, new scenes, new religion and new trade, only to be had across the sea. They took with them a folk art of high achievement. Many of the wealthy men, the leaders and the thrusters, were polygamous and the number of their sons, cast in the same mould, was high. The poorer man took only one wife, all he could afford. It was the sons of the rich, too bored and too proud to farm, who led the ships overseas. When Christianity really took hold and all men normally had only one wife and fewer aggressive sons, the situation changed. This perhaps as well as the rise of strong kingdoms in Britain and France and the levelling out of the population put an end to the Viking age.

The Swedes were the first to move. Southern Sweden is many times larger than Denmark and much more productive than Norway. It is separated from Russia by 150 miles of sea. Gotland, a third of the way across from Sweden to the old republic of Latvia, reduces the maximum sea crossing to 80 miles, and the Aland Islands further north enabled the early Swedes to cross to Finland without losing sight of land.

Across the relatively calm Baltic Sea was a vast hinterland penetrated by huge rivers, with more timber, furs and potential slaves than Sweden could possibly use or sell. This was the country of the Slavs from whose name the word 'slave' is derived. More sinister still, it is the origin of the Arabic word for a eunuch. Nine hundred miles south of the Baltic was Byzantium, the greatest market in the Christian world.

In Finland, the Swedes were called 'Ruotsi' which according to a Scandinavian expert meant 'rowers'. The Slavs turned it into 'Rus' and supplied the future name for their country. By the middle of the 8th century Swedes and Gotlanders were in Latvia in strength. By AD 839 there was an independent Swedish or Rus state on the upper Volga and from the mid-9th to the 10th century they colonised the region round Lake Ladoga and were ready to move on down the Dnieper and the Volga. About 910 they reached the Caspian and crossed it in sixteen ships. In 912 a Moslem wrote that they came again with 500 ships, captured Baku, already famous for its petroleum, and marched inland for three days. Baku is over 300 miles south of the mouth of the Volga and 500 ships is probably an exaggeration. Perhaps the author wrote from hearsay of hordes of Rus invaders. However we can speculate a little. The Swedes made their reconnaissance in sixteen ships which seems a reasonable figure. They were no doubt small ships about 40 ft (12 m) long for ease of portage and carried about twenty men each, just over 300 in all. Probably after the first raid they retired to an island in the Volga delta, fortified it after the Viking manner, and waited for reinforcements. The second raid, which was ultimately defeated, is much more likely to have consisted of fifty ships and 1000 men. But Norway and Denmark sent out fleets of several hundred large ships and Sweden with a far greater population could have sent out even greater numbers of smaller ones.

Large number of Swedes moved along the Russian rivers. In 862 they settled in Novgorod under Rurik and in 882 they made Kiev, 600 river miles further south, their capital. They had already sailed to the Black Sea and threatened Constantinople. They were not ditch-crawlers. Plate 23 shows the river Volga near Kuybyshev where for hundreds of miles the waterway is more like an attenuated lake than a river. At Kiev the Dnieper narrows to 300 yards around islands on the right bank below the old Viking trading city. There are great lakes above the city and hundreds of miles of lakes and rapids below. All the main rapids have names of Viking origin and the portages around them were made under constant threat of attack by local tribes. Another place of ambush was Khortitsa island where the river ran fast and narrow between high bluffs.

In 912 according to the *Nestorian Chronicle* Oleg, another Viking, made a treaty with Byzantium and in 941 his son Igor attacked Constantinople with 10,000 ships (sic) which were repulsed by the Byzantine navy using Greek fire (there are contemporary paintings of this being used in ship-to-ship actions). The Vikings must have had 10,000 men for the attack to have had any chance of success, and 150–200 ships would have been needed to carry them the 400 miles across the Black Sea. In 988 Vladimir, ruler of Russia from Kiev to Novgorod, became a Christian and in 1015 this prince of slave traders was proclaimed a saint.

For a while Vladimir kept the Dnieper route safe against increasing pressure, but by about 1050 the river route that had been one of the great trading arteries of the western world was abandoned. For over 200 years Swedes had sailed rivers so wide that their ships could keep out of range of the nomads with reflex bows who watched them from the banks. But as more and more mounted bowmen rode out of the eastern steppes every night stop and portage became dangerous and the risks outweighed the profits. The Volga boatmen sang as they hauled on the towropes, and this is how the Swedes would have moved their flatboats upstream where the current ran strong—and this is when they would have been open to attack.

There are accounts of the Rus using oak dugout canoes. To accommodate the volume of trade they may have been 40–50 ft long by 10 ft wide (12–15 by 3 m) made up of several trunks pegged together like the dugouts that have survived in northeast Europe. None of these, however, is known to be of Viking date. Cargoes included honey, beeswax, fine fabrics, silver, wine and fruit as well

23 River Volga—a Swedish Viking route. (APN)

as furs and slaves. And the peacock that was found in the Gokstad ship may have come up one of the great rivers, passing southbound walrus ivory on the way.

From the beginning of the 9th to the middle of the 11th century the Swedish Vikings had a surplus of slaves and furs to sell. Holy Church taught that slavery was wrong, but it had been the custom from time immemorial and the moral issue was clouded by the fact that the Slavs were heathen. The Moslem world had no scruples. We do not know how many slaves travelled the northern sea routes but they were short-lived and expendable and liable to die of disease, brutality and despair. The survival rate of those castrated for the Moslem harems was low. If there were 5000 slaves in transit a year we can translate this into 250 shiploads of twenty each.* The next few pages deal with raiding and warfare by sea and river, but all the time we must bear in mind those hundreds of shiploads of slaves and furs sent every summer across the North Sea, down the Irish Sea and the English Channel and across the Bay of Biscay, for sale in the markets of Moslem Spain; or up the great rivers of France to the slave markets of southern Europe.

Romantic historians who saw in these centuries the glorious birth of Christian Europe were apt to regard the Vikings as heathen barbarians. But there were Christian Vikings in the early 9th century, and from the year 900 Swedish Vikings were trading with Byzantium, a Christian empire and the most sophisticated state known, a state that maintained centres of learning and armies and navies with equipment and weapons superior to anything in Europe. Viking chiefs absorbed Greek Orthodox Christianity and made it the religion of medieval Russia. And Byzantine technology flowed back along the Viking trade routes to the north. Much later, the Czarist navy acknowledged the contribution of the Swedish Vikings to the early development of Russia by naming two cruisers *Rurik* and *Oleg*.

Norwegian and Danish Vikings flooded into Charlemagne's Holy Roman Empire and into England and Ireland in a continuous invasion which was the first exercise in long-range sea power. Roman sea power had been short-range. We cannot discuss the whole history of the Viking attacks on western Europe but we can follow the principal fleet movements over the first hundred years to try to discover the pattern of the Viking assault and the forces at their disposal.

* Contemporary Arab sources state that at one time in the 9th century there were 14,000 slaves in Moslem Spain alone.

The Viking longship was not really a warship but a fast troopship able not only to sail across the sea but to penetrate far inland by river. It was even possible to drag them from one river to another, one such portage being from the Don to the Volga. The big crew could row for long periods, save the tedium of tacking in light airs, and move the ship when the wind was blanketed by hills or trees. Oars were ideal for proceeding in strange waters in the dark.

In general the numbers of ships quoted in contemporary documents such as the *Anglo Saxon Chronicle* may be taken as accurate for they check roughly against known requirements. For example modern military historians estimate William the Conqueror's army at Hastings as about 8000 fighting men plus a considerable force holding the base at the coast. It was the very minimum number for the invasion of England and only succeeded by the accident of Harold's death, the lack of a successor, and the diversionary attack of Hardradi and Tostig in the north. The Romans had used 50,000 men and 500 ships.

Against great soldiers like Alfred, Athelstan, Edgar and Edmund the Danes would have needed far more men than William had, and these they brought from Denmark and reinforced and replaced. Ten thousand fighting men needed a hundred ships, probably more, and no army, Danish or any other, has ever moved without garrison and support troops. In 892 at least they brought their own horses, and even 200 horses needed between twenty and forty ships. The Vikings often invaded after sea crossings of several hundred miles, and they could not pack their men or beasts as close as Julius Caesar or Duke William. Therefore when contemporary records say that in the second campaign against Alfred the Great the Danes came with 250 ships, or that in AD 836 sixty Norwegian ships sailed up the Boyne and sixty more up the Liffey, we can take the figures at their face value.

The large crews of the longships were totally uneconomic for trading, for which the Vikings built beamy sailing ships (knarrs). These must have gone with the great invasion fleets as supply ships sailing independently to a rendezvous, and they may have carried most of the horses. While experiments have shown that horses could have been carried in the longships, they would have travelled much more safely in the deep, fuller-bodied knarrs.

The Danes had a complete and permanent military and naval organisation. In Cnut's time (he died in AD 1035) and probably earlier there were at least four fortified military camps in Denmark holding a total of 5000 men or more, enough to man a fair-sized invasion force. Trelleborg, Aggersborg, Fyrkat and Odense were laid out with the precision of Roman legionary fortresses.* At Trelleborg there were sixteen barrack blocks arranged in a pattern of four squares within a rampart 156 yds in diameter. Each building was 100 ft long, shaped like an upturned wooden boat with the bow and stern cut off and closed in. There were thirteen other barracks outside the circle. At Aggersborg there were forty-eight barrack houses each 110 ft long. The ships were obtained by levies which laid down the number of oars and the main dimensions such as the distance between the rowlocks. There was probably a payment of so much a rowlock as in Saxon England.

According to one text of the *Anglo Saxon Chronicle* the first attack on England was by three Danish ships in AD 789. Another text says invaders first came from Norway and landed at Portland. In 793 Norwegian Vikings plundered the Abbey at Lindisfarne on the Northumberland coast, but their next attack in 794 on Jarrow was a failure. They switched to the west coast, going northabout, and plundered Saint Columba's abbey at Iona and Saint Patrick's shrine on the Isle of Man. By 820 they had colonised Orkney and Shetland and around 840 they settled in the Hebrides. In 839 Norwegian Vikings raided Dublin with sixty-five ships.

It is 170 nautical miles from Norway to Shetland and the 'Shetland bus', the fishing boats that went to help Norwegian patriots between 1940 and 1943, used the same route. Bressay Sound in Shetland and Scapa Flow in Orkney are magnificent anchorages and poised in either a ship or a fleet is well placed for a voyage to England, Scotland, Ireland, Iceland or further, as the Royal Navy showed in two world wars.

We can reconstruct a longship voyage from Norway to Dublin. Victualling schedules for 18th century sailing ships were worked on a basis of 100 miles per 24 hours and there is no reason to believe the Gokstad ship could have done any better, although she could sail 11 knots for short periods under favourable conditions with the wind on the beam, and modern full-size replicas have got close to this. That 11 knots would have been speed through the water, rarely directly on course, and only possible in the right weight of wind. The *Cutty Sark*'s maximum speed was 16 knots, her average between 5 and 8; the Gokstad ship's average was probably 4–5 knots or 100–120 sea miles in 24 hours. Occasionally a Viking fleet would no doubt have sailed from Norway to Shetland in 24 hours, but generally they would have taken two days and nights. If the nights were clear and the wind constant they would have sailed on through the dark steering full and bye, more by the

* Johannes Brøndsted suggests that these Danish camps were in use from approximately 975 to 1050 AD.

afterglow of the sun and the feel of the wind than by the Pole Star, which is of small use in the long summer daylight of high latitudes.

The passage from Bressay Sound to Scapa Flow would have been made in daylight, tides permitting. They could have reached Stornoway on day three and spent the night of day four near Loch Skiport on South Uist. On the fifth night they might have lain in one of the lochs of Mull, the sixth somewhere near Islay and the seventh in Belfast Loch. On the eighth day out from Norway they could have reached Dublin. Then they would have been ready for a run ashore, and some of them would have been rough like sailors before and since.

They would not normally have sailed or rowed in waters like these after dark, though on raids they might have traded risk for surprise. They had no compasses and we can discount stories that they ever had any success with lumps of lodestone. A successful boat compass demands a much better technology than they had, and for pilotage at night the boat compass has to be supplemented with a bearing compass and fixed lights in known positions. They dared not risk sudden mist or fog or deep dark.

Just before 810 King Godfred of Denmark descended on the coast of Frisia with 200 ships. Charlemagne retaliated by building fleets and organising defences all along the coast as far as the Seine. Louis the Pious pursued his father's policy and held France and Frisia until 834 when a great Danish fleet overran the defences and sailed up the Rhine and the Lek to capture Dorestad, the greatest 'port' of northeast Europe.

When Louis died in 840 the way was open for further Danish penetration. In 845, 600 Danish ships sailed up the Elbe to burn Hamburg and another 120 made the 600 mile voyage down-Channel and up the Seine to the gates of Paris. The Vikings made great use of island bases. Walcheren was already in their hands; Jeufosse was their stronghold for attacks on Paris; and two islands now joined to the mainland kept them safe during their assault on Rouen. Another fleet sailed round Brittany and rowed 150 miles up the Loire to Tours and 100 miles up its tributary the Loir to Chartres. Its base was the island of Noirmoutier which Vikings had occupied since 843. Charles the Bald paid Danegeld and paid Vikings to fight Vikings just as early British kings had paid Saxons to fight Saxons, but he fought manfully as well and blocked the rivers, even attempting to build a bridge below Rouen.

The number of ships and their mobility was astounding. There were already 200 Danish and Norwegian ships at Jeufosse when Charles paid 5000 lbs of silver to another Viking to bring up 200 more ships to drive them out. Yet at the same time the Danes were also attacking England.

In 835 'heathen men ravaged Sheppey' according to the *Anglo-Saxon Chronicle*. Once again the Vikings had seized an island base. From then on they attacked year after year, landing at Portland, in Devon, at Southampton, in East Anglia and in Kent. In 851 they came with 350 ships, wintered on Thanet, and stormed Canterbury and London. Saxon kings of Mercia and Wessex marching fast across the country fought them wherever they landed, and Athelstan of Wessex fought them 'in ships' and beat them at Sandwich in Kent. The fury of the Northmen was no greater than the fury of the Saxons.

The full invasion began in 865 when from the shelter of Thanet, then a real island, they ravaged eastern Kent. Another great army came from Denmark with more horses and East Anglia surrendered. Year after year the penetration deepened as the Danes moved into Northumbria and Mercia. In 871 they came south into Wessex and the first Ethelred and Alfred his younger brother were defeated at Reading.

This story of land campaigns hides the logistics of the Danish invasion. The attrition in those hard-fought battles was enormous and there must have been fleet after fleet bringing replacements and a constant outflow of despatch vessels begging for more men and horses and carrying pilots to bring them to rendezvous.

King Burgred of Mercia was driven out of England and somehow in all the turmoil managed to cross the seas to Rome where he died. Part of 'the army' (the Danes) ravaged right up into the Scottish lowlands and the remainder under Guthrum turned on Alfred. The year was 875 'and that summer King Alfred went to sea with a naval force, and fought against the crews of seven ships and captured one ship and put the rest to flight'.

If Alfred had not been surrounded on three sides by armies he might have been a great naval commander. As it was he marched and countermarched while Danish reinforcements moved along the coasts. He cornered a great host at Wareham and 'they swore on the holy ring' to leave his kingdom. But part of the Viking army rode away at night to Exeter on the horses they had brought across the sea, and part tried to sail along the coast to join them but lost 120 ships in rough seas near Swanage. Perhaps they slipped out of Poole Harbour on a night tide and did not realise how rough it was outside.

In March 878 Alfred retreated into the marshes around Athelney in Somerset. Here amid 100 square miles of fenland he made his stronghold. And like Hereward at Ely he launched raids along uncharted waterways and secret paths. By May he was strong enough to leave the marshes. He routed the Danes at Edington, stood sponsor at Guthrum's baptism, and received his promise that 'the army' would leave the land. The fens of Ely and the Humber and the marshes of the river Parret have their special place in the history of amphibious warfare. Desperate men moved about them by punt and pole vault, surprised the enemy in watery ambush, and retreated again into their fastnesses.

17 The Vikings—Part II

The first payment was 10,000 pounds
Archbishop Sigeric advised that course
Anglo-Saxon Chronicle AD 991

In 878 part of the Danish army camped at Fulham, and in November 879 it sailed away to Ghent, rowing through Danish London and out under London Bridge to the sea, a great host of undecked ships in retreat in winter. Rivers were almost as important to the Vikings as the sea, and 'the army' went up the Meuse, up the Scheldt to Condé (50 miles), and up the Somme to Amiens (30 miles). There were still Vikings in East Anglia and Kent, and Alfred did not occupy London until 886. Some Danes besieged Rochester without success, and combined with others from East Anglia camped at Benfleet, then an open anchorage perhaps sheltered by sandbanks. But Alfred 'sent ships from Kent into East Anglia' which captured sixteen enemy vessels at the mouth of the Stour after a 50 mile voyage across the sands of the Thames estuary. His ships were outnumbered and defeated on the way home but the keys to victory, harbours and warships, were in Alfred's hands.

On the Continent the Vikings were also in trouble, for a 'large naval force assembled among the Old Saxons…and the Frisians' met the Danes twice and defeated them. Though we cannot yet see the whole picture clearly, the Danes and Norwegians were apparently trying to do too much with too little. They were fighting a European war with perhaps 50,000 men, 10,000 horses and 1000 ships, and after brilliant amphibious infiltration they could not hold the ground they occupied. They had no maps and no means of feeding intelligence swiftly into a central command; they had no means to plan and direct operations over such vast distances. Each thrust was an independent campaign planned by a committee dominated by a leader of outstanding personality. There were to be two more centuries of fighting, but from the early 10th century the Vikings began to be absorbed by the territory they occupied.

In 887 a Danish force went up the Seine past the bridge at Paris, thence up the Marne to Chezy, and up the Seine and the Yonne into the heart of France. The depth of the Viking raids reveals the weakness of 10th century Europe. A hundred ships stem to stern occupied 2 miles of river. Sometimes they could move between marshes on either hand, but many reaches were ideal for ambush. We do not know in what formations the ships were rowed or lay at anchor. Wooden ships burn easily and we can only assume that at night they clustered as tight as a Boer laager on the South African veldt and that the ring of sentries was large enough to keep incendiary arrows out of range. A hundred ships and 5000 men could penetrate the ill-organised countryside too fast for local resistance to concentrate against them, but Alfred, Charlemagne and others blocked the rivers by castles, chains and bridges and maintained fast-moving armies.

In AD 892, 200 or 250* ships crossed from Boulogne to Lympne and rowed 4 miles into the Weald along a river which hardly exists today. In 896 Alfred began to build ships twice as large as those of the Danes, as described in chapter 13. The descendants of Guthrum's veterans forgot their ships and managed their farms in the Danelaw, and Alfred's descendants fought on manfully against fresh invaders. 927 saw a Saxon fleet sail up to Caithness and in 937 Athelstan defeated an alliance of Vikings, Irish, Picts and northern Britons. Then there was peace by 10th century standards until Ethelred was crowned in 978.

Southampton, Thanet and Cheshire were sacked in 980 and the Normandy Vikings gave the raiders shelter until an Anglo-Norman treaty closed the ports of either country to the other's enemies. Olaf Tryggvason of Norway landed in strength at Maldon, Essex in 991 and a treaty was made regulating the treatment of merchant ships by the belligerents. These treaties dealt with problems that have bedevilled naval warfare ever since, and the second suggests that considerable seaborne trade was being carried on in spite of the raids.

In 994 Tryggvason and Swein raided with ninety-four ships. Tryggvason's *Long Serpent*, about 140 ft (43 m) long, and the first of the giant Viking ships, was built in 999 but never came to England. Too many generals have failed in our own time for us to judge Ethelred too harshly. In 1007–9 he ordered every 310 hides of land (20–40 square miles) to provide a warship of about 60 oars, but the hundred ships built were destroyed by treachery and tempest. (According to Bede the Isle of Thanet was 600 hides and Iona 5 hides.) By 1012 Danegeld had reached 48,000 pounds.

In 1013 Swein of Denmark came to England to take the crown. He sailed direct to Sandwich, thence to the Humber and up the Trent to Gainsborough in the very heart of the Danelaw. From there he marched south and took London. Ethelred took ship to Nor-

* Texts of the *Anglo-Saxon Chronicle* vary.

mandy a few months before the all-conquering Swein died and left his ships in charge of a very young and inexperienced Cnut who sailed back to Denmark when Ethelred returned. It was like a game of chess on blue water, in which the kings moved hundreds of miles and checkmated themselves by death.

Cnut was back in 1015 and Ethelred died in 1016, leaving his embattled kingdom to Edmund Ironside who carried all before him while Cnut tried desperately to take London. His fleet seized Greenwich in May and moved up to the island of Bermondsey. London Bridge blocked all further advance so Cnut's men dug a canal round the south end and rowed into the Upper Pool. The City was on the north bank. About 100 ships and 10,000 men must have taken part in Cnut's unsuccessful assault and then retreated via the canal and the Thames to East Anglia for provisions. They were back at the old stronghold at Sheppey for the next campaign, which ended when Edmund and Cnut divided England between them. Edmund died almost immediately and Cnut was left ruler of a dual monarchy separated by 400 miles of sea, no longer the nervous youngster who had retreated before Ethelred the Unready. In 1018 he led his fleet against thirty Viking ships on the prowl in English waters, levied an enormous Danegeld, and sent all but forty of his ships back to Denmark for good.

Cnut probably made a dozen round voyages of 1000 miles each between Denmark and Britain and Denmark and Norway. He too had one of the big ships and he probably sailed in her between Roskilde and London, accompanied by a staff of advisors, some well past the age when they willingly slept on a wet deck with their boat cloaks around them. The story of Cnut and the tide is interesting for its sheer improbability. Throughout the period ships were apparently run up on the beaches rather than anchored off, though Viking ships carried both anchors and longboats. The timing of the tides was of overwhelming tactical importance and we await a new C S Forester to explain how a ship was managed in a hostile tidal estuary in the 10th century. 'Go aground on the top of the tide and you'll be there for 12 hours' must have been dinned into every Viking prince as his ship first closed the English coast. Cnut's daughter is buried at Bosham, one of the places where the incident is supposed to have taken place. Think of that glorious stretch of water at high tide and the mud at low. And think of the rise and fall at Maldon, Benfleet and Sandwich. No-one was ever so stupid as to tell Cnut he could control the tide.*

* It is possible that Cnut was famous for his ability to foretell the time of high tide and in this case miscalculated (see page 244).

Norwegian Vikings made the Irish Sea their own. For almost 200 years they fought the Irish and English, the Danes and each other. The Western Isles of Scotland were settled early and remained independent of Scotland well into the Middle Ages. The Kintyre peninsula was claimed as an 'island' by King Magnus II of Norway in 1098 when he 'sailed his ship' over the mile of land connecting Tarbert harbour with West Loch Tarbert (Plate 3). In Ireland the Norwegians laid the foundations of Dublin, Waterford, Wexford and Limerick and sailed into the heart of the country up the great rivers from the west and the east coasts. The Irish Sea became part of a great slave route from the steppes of Russia to Moslem Spain.

It seems impossible that anyone would have done business with people so warlike and treacherous, but they undoubtedly did. It may be that trade was the norm and raiding the exception, and that there were more knarrs than longships. Trade and piracy do not go together for trade depends on trust even if it follows the flag. Viking raids on Spain started at the end of the 9th century and in 844 they raided Seville. The expedition which left the Loire in 859 was probably led by Norwegians from Ireland, for black slaves were recorded there soon after its return. The Vikings may have run into a Saracen fleet with Greek fire tubes, and the sixty-two Viking ships or what was left of them sailed away to North Africa and then crossed to the Camargue for the winter. After raiding up the Rhone and down the Italian coast they met another Saracen fleet in the Strait of Gibraltar and only twenty-two ships returned to the Loire in 862.

For three hundred years Danish and Norwegian Vikings sailed along the coasts and rivers of Europe. The amount of sheer hard work in rowing up a fiercely flowing river like the Rhone, or sheer discomfort in driving before a Biscay gale in an open boat, makes one wonder if it was worth it and why—certainly not just for a few sackfuls of church plate.

The Faroes, Iceland, Greenland and Vinland

The first man to settle in the Faroe Islands was Grim Kamban
Flato Book

The Faroe Islands are 160 miles northwest of the Shetlands, and although they appear on small-scale maps as mere specks they cover the same area and support a similar population. Irish hermits had already settled there around AD 700. Like southern and western Iceland and the coast of Norway, they lie in the path of the Gulf

Stream. Temperatures therefore are far above those of Labrador, which lies in the same latitudes on the other side of the Atlantic and which because it is swept by a Polar current is bleak and inhospitable.

The northern and eastern coasts of Iceland and the eastern coast of Greenland are cooled by currents from the Arctic. In winter the ice pack is bounded by a line stretching roughly from Cape Farewell on the southern tip of Greenland to a few miles north of Iceland and from there to Jan Mayen Island which lies between the warm and cold currents. Occasionally the ice comes much lower now, but in Viking times the seas were slightly warmer. Western Greenland, although within 600 miles of Labrador, is swept by a warm undercurrent and was a desirable country, at least for men as tough as the Norwegians, until the drop in temperature which set in in the 14th century.

The mingling of the warm offshore Gulf Stream and the cold inshore Labrador Current off Newfoundland produces the fogs over the Grand Banks. But away from the fogs the Atlantic atmosphere is often exceptionally clear and the highest mountain in the Faroes is nearly 3000 ft. Tricks of the light—mirages—push the horizon back in high latitudes, and the mariner might have glimpsed the loom of the Faroes at 100 miles, and he might not have lost the Shetlands or Scotland until he was 50 miles out. The intervening 50 miles or so, ten or fifteen hours at sea, must have been a considerable strain for emigrants who had never seen a map nor been deep-sea before.

The *Flato Book* says 'In those days many people left the country because of the king's lust for power. Many of these settled in the Faroe Islands and made homesteads there'. This was in the last third of the 9th century and many hundred families made the voyage with their cattle, sheep, horses and ploughs—fifty shiploads perhaps. Norwegian settlers had already driven out the Irish monks by 825. Here we see the Vikings in a new role: their weapons were stowed, the ships were all knarrs, and the scene would have been one of single-masted trading ships proceeding on their lawful occasions.

Iceland is 240 miles from the Faroes and the landfall is a great snow-capped tableland, the Vatnajokull, 7000 ft high and 40 miles long. Under exceptional conditions such a high plateau might have been seen from well over 100 miles out, when the sailor would barely have lost sight of the 3000 ft peak in the north Faroes.

Irish monks, who had possibly sailed direct from Ireland or via Scotland, were already there. Dicuil, an Irish cleric who had himself probably been to the Faroes, states this in *De Mensura Orbis*

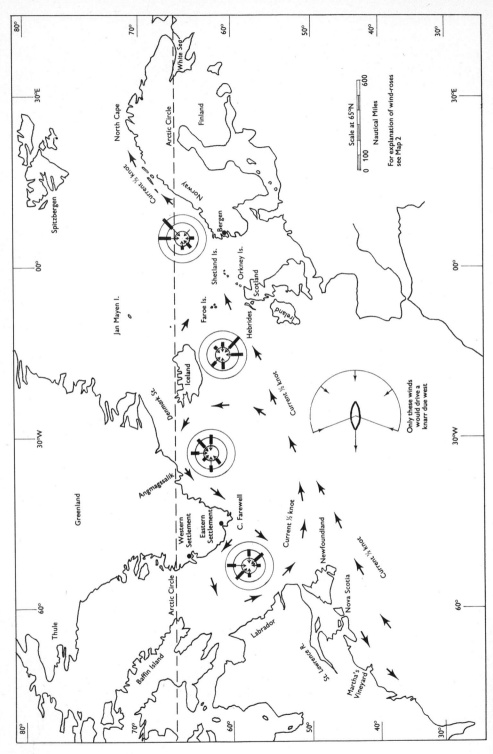

7 North Atlantic: prevailing currents and winds

Terrae, which he wrote in France in AD 825. He had probably fled to Charlemagne's court after the sack of Iona in AD 806. He claimed first-hand information from monks who had come back from the north, and gives a convincing description of the midnight sun. The monks said that Iceland was much warmer than when the first people went there: there was an improvement in climate in the 7th and 8th centuries and it is possible that the first Irish went there in the 6th century. The Vestmannaeyjar, the 'Island of the Westmen', stands out on modern maps to proclaim the Irish settlement, and names beginning with 'Pap' as in Orkney record the presence of the priests. Whether the Norwegians knew of the Irish discovery or not, Norse records suggest that Iceland was also discovered by accident by ships blown off course from both Scotland and Norway.

The first Norwegian settlers arrived in Iceland in 870 and within sixty years over 20,000 people followed, so that in 930 at the end of the settlement period the population was round 30,000. Of the several thousand Norse families who sailed to Iceland, most came from Norway but some from Ireland. With them went Celts, who may have influenced the Sagas. On average about six shiploads a year between May and September; in the peak years perhaps thirty ships went. The first settler, Ingolf Arnarson, had killed a man in Norway. Eirik the Red and his father left Norway for the same reason, and Eirik later left Iceland after another killing. This seems to have been the natural turbulence of the people of the time, and Saxons and Celts were probably the same. The fittest had survived, and the fittest were the roughest, the hardiest and the strongest willed.

The first care of the families who sailed from Iceland would have been for the animals on which their livelihood depended. Although a knarr was much deeper than a longship it was still only an open boat, and the direct distance from Norway or Ireland is nearly 600 miles, one to two weeks' sailing time. We know that the first direct crossing was made by accident, and later it was sometimes done intentionally with passengers and cargo: the *Landnamabok* gives seven days' sail from Stad in Norway to Horn in Iceland. But it would have been neither practical nor prudent to make a long crossing with cattle as their legs break easily and they eat an enormous amount of fodder which would have got sodden with salt spray even if no solid water had come on board. Undoubtedly they were carried from island to island and put ashore at each landfall to recover. The ship would leave again only when there was a good prospect of a calm sea and a fair wind lasting for several days. If they were very lucky the settlers would have put their cattle ashore in Iceland two or three days out from the Faroes. If they were unlucky it would have taken a week, and if very unlucky the humans would have landed safely after a week's voyage, cold, wet and exhausted, and the livestock would have died of pneumonia.

The Norse settlements were mainly around the west coast of the island, and to reach them from the landfall off Vatnajokull meant a voyage further than any yet made, involving tacking to windward in a square-rigged ship and coasting along a lee shore. If they had known what they were up against many might never have attempted the voyage.

The Iceland settlement soon developed into a republic which became Christian by popular vote in 1000 AD. A little later the Alting made a treaty with Norway to exempt explorers blown to the Norwegian coast from the normal landing tax, an example of how governments were beginning to control the movement of ships by the early 11th century. The end of the raiding era was in sight. The families who went to Iceland did not cut themselves off from the southern land and a small but steady trade developed—wool, cheese, whale oil, blubber, walrus hides and tusks, and sulphur being exchanged in Norway or Britain for timber, tar, food, drink, linen and metals.

Jan Mayen Island, 400 miles north of the normal direct route from Iceland to Norway, was discovered by an Icelander blown off course in 1194. Spitzbergen, 600 miles inside the Arctic Circle and 500 miles from the North Cape, was discovered around 1150. This must have been the greatest Viking voyage of all.

A few years before 900 Alfred the Great talked with a wealthy Norwegian trader called Ohthere or Ottar and wrote down the information he obtained. Ohthere lived far enough north to keep reindeer herds and took tribute of walrus teeth, bearskins and feathers from the Finns. Walrus skin, he said, was made into the best ships' ropes. From his home in Helgeland he sailed coastwise round the North Cape to the White Sea and southwards to Oslo fjord and Hedeby, the old Baltic port at the base of the Jutland peninsula. The southbound voyage took a month with favourable winds and the total distance sailed was over 2000 miles each way.

The *Landnamabok* says that Greenland was first sighted by Gunnbjorn Ulfsson, blown to the west from Iceland about the year 900. He glimpsed skerries around Angmagssalik before the wind changed and carried him back. We never know the details behind these bald statements, but we can imagine him running before the storm under a bare pole and glimpsing that awful coast through the murk, and then as disaster seemed certain the wind changed as has happened to yachtsmen in our own time. He must have been driven over 300 miles for three, four or five anxious days in a half-decked ship that required frequent bailing and exposed the crew to cold and wet, with little sleep and no hot food—all the things the modern yachtsman tries to avoid.

No-one tried to settle in Greenland until 978 when one shipload landed somewhere near Ulfsson's sighting, barely survived a disastrous winter among the snows, and went home again. In 981 or 982 Eirik the Red, having quarrelled with his neighbours in Iceland, set out on a three-year voyage of exploration to Greenland. He had left Norway with his father twenty years earlier for the same reason and now he was on the move again. They were not pirates and the people they had killed were their own. They were probably typical of the leaders of the early ventures in colonisation: tough, arrogant, short-tempered and ruthless. Early societies did not lock up their lawbreakers—they killed them or moved them on.

Eirik, an outlaw again, sailed west along latitude 65° N (the Arctic Circle is $66\frac{1}{2}°$ N) until he sighted Greenland and then south 300 miles to round Cape Farewell and find more friendly land on the west coast. In 1931 Gino Watkins and two companions made the same journey. Here is the coast in August and September as they saw it. The writer is Augustine Courtauld.

> When I first heard of this I thought it sounded mad. That an open whaleboat should traverse...the worst part of the Greenland coast...seemed the height of suicidal folly. When Gino asked me which journey I would like to go on I said any but that one... In the first ten days...we were able to make our way slowly down the coast threading...between the islands and the still icebergs... It was sunny and warm...On the ninth day we were held up by fog and thick ice. Two days later we came across the Eskimos [and] towed about thirty in their skin boats to our camp. That night the gale came down on us from the icecap, blowing foam off the fjord and smashing the ice together.
>
> After a week the pack-ice proved just loose enough to drive the boats through...Now, however, we came to the end of [it], finding nothing but large icebergs and brash ice broken from the glaciers...an impassable barrier for small boats for many days at a time.

The weather may have been a few degrees warmer in Eirik's day and he would have kept further offshore. But he would have had to put in to shore at intervals, and while his knarr may have looked more impressive than the whaleboats of Watkins, Courtauld and Lemon, she was after all only a 50 ft (15 m) open boat.

After three years exploring the west coast Eirik persuaded several hundred Icelanders to settle with him in the country to which he gave the inviting name of Greenland. They sailed in 985 or 986 in twenty-five ships. Only fourteen of them reached Greenland; some were lost in bad weather and some returned to Iceland. Perhaps this was the pattern of the Scandinavian emigrations. A violent man quarrels with his neighbours, others take sides with him. In the end they are forced to go, and out of a widely scattered community of several thousands five hundred or so leave for the new land, with a failure rate of 45 per cent of ships lost and faint hearts returning.

Eirik's farm at Brattahlid in the Eastern Settlement was surrounded by 190 other farms. The Western Settlement was 250 miles further up the west coast of Greenland and there were another ninety farms there among the deep fjords of the Godthaab area. The total population reached about 3000 and this Christian democratic state eventually became part of the archdiocese of Hamburg. The remains of the tiny wooden church built by Eirik's wife are still visible.

From the Western Settlement lying under its 6000 ft high glaciers it is 360 miles along the 64th parallel to Baffin Island. The first recorded sighting of America took place in 986, when Bjarni Herjolfson left Iceland in his own knarr to follow his father to Greenland. He was in such a hurry he did not even unload the cargo he had brought from Norway. After three 'days' (the word could mean 12 hours or 24 hours) with a fair wind they saw Iceland's peaks sink below the sea. There was fog and a northerly wind for many days and they drove before it not knowing where they were. Then the sun returned and next day they sighted a land of low tree-covered hills. Bjarni did not think it was Greenland because there were no glaciers and he turned out to sea again, running before a southwest wind for three days before sighting an island with glacier-topped mountains. Again they did not land but sailed on before a fair wind which blew up into a gale and forced them to shorten sail. Four days later they reached Bjarni's father's farm in Greenland.

Bjarni did not know where he had been, and we cannot be sure either, but it seems that he was blown over 1200 miles from Iceland to an island off North America, a voyage that must have taken at least twelve days. Possibly he had sighted Newfoundland, 700 miles or about seven days' sail from Greenland. When Bjarni told his tale in Norway there was much talk about the new land beyond Greenland though he was thought to have been a bit chicken-hearted for not landing.

Leif Eiriksson bought Bjarni's ship and persuaded thirty-five men to sail with him back along Bjarni's homeward course. They found the island of glaciers and called it Helluland, probably Baffin Island at about 64° N latitude. Putting to sea again they can only have sailed south for they came to a pleasant wooded country with sandy beaches, which they called Markland or Forest-land and was probably Labrador. They launched a boat and went ashore but soon put to sea again before a northeast wind, probably reaching fast to the southwest, until they came to a land of rich pastures and lakes teeming with salmon. On the shortest day of the year there the sun rose at about 9 am and set at 3 p.m., so we know that they were between 40° and 50° N. Leif and his crew built stone houses and sailed back to Greenland in the spring. They called the country Vinland after the wild grapes which today are found as far as 41° N (Martha's Vineyard on Cape Cod) but may have grown still further north in Viking times. Salmon are not now found south of the Hudson River.

Everyone talked of Vinland in the maritime north and soon Thorfinn Karlsefni found sixty men and five women to settle there with him. They carried 'livestock of all kinds' including cows and a bull, and made an easy passage to find Leif's houses till standing.

But the colony in Vinland was little more than an adventure which served no real purpose and it perished very soon, mainly from attacks by Eskimos or American Indians. Its history was remarkably like that of the early Elizabethan settlement in Virginia. The Greenland settlements fared well enough until trade with Iceland declined and they struggled on through centuries of worsening weather until the early years of the 15th century. Iceland remained down the centuries as a living monument to Viking seamanship: the dead monuments to their further enterprise, the remains of farms scattered all over the Greenland settlements have only been discovered in the last few decades.

18　Ships of the Viking Period

There are nine and sixty ways of constructing tribal lays,
And-every-single-one-of-them-is-right

RUDYARD KIPLING

We talk of not seeing the wood for the trees. In the study of ancient ships it is often a case of not seeing the ships for the fastenings or the lashings, of losing the displacement among the details.

Table 1 contains details of ships from the 9th to 11th century; Fig. 13 shows the size, shape and displacement of typical ships, all drawn to the same scale. Four of these are Viking ships, but the warships of Alfred's navy, the transports of William the Conqueror, and the trading cogs of Frisia all probably followed one or other of the patterns drawn here. So probably did many Carolingian and Anglo-Saxon merchant ships.

The starting point must be the Gokstad and Oseberg ships, the most perfectly preserved of them all (Plates 24, 25). The Oseberg ship was, from the completeness and intricacy of her ornament, a queen's barge for sheltered waters, and not a workaday boat, warship or merchant ship. She tells us at once that within the general pattern there were variants for special purposes.

The displacements are approximations since the exact waterlines can never be known. The Gokstad ship was 76 ft (23 m) long, displaced 32 tons and was propelled by 32 oars with, almost certainly, one man normally to each oar, a total of about 10 h.p. or 0.31 h.p. per ton. This is only a third of the power per ton available to drive the Nydam ship and shows that although the two vessels may look very similar to those unfamiliar with ship design, they were very different. The Gokstad ship would not have gone very fast under oars alone and it is obvious that she was not a rowing ship with auxiliary sail but a sailing ship with auxiliary oars.*

She was also the first ship we know of in the north to have been

---

* A member of the Royal National Life-boat Institution who worked on the old pulling lifeboats quoted 4.5 tons laden weight for a 10-oar boat—0.7 h.p. per ton. He told the author they could not make headway against the wind in a heavy sea and were sometimes carried along the shore on carriages and launched upwind of the wreck. For long offshore rescues they used sails.

Table 1. Clinker-built ships and boats AD 400–1000

Name	Date	Length ft (m)	Beam ft (m)	Mid-depth ft (m)	Length/Beam ratio	Tons displacement	Oars	Sail	Planks per side	Plank timber	Keel or flat	No. of frames	Frame timber	Fastening Plank to frame	Fastening Plank to plank	Where found	Remarks
Nydam	400	73.8 (22.84)	10.7 (3.26)	3.3 (1)	7.0:1	8.6	30	No	5	Oak	F	19	Oak	L	R	Schleswig	1 ton ballast; each plank continuous bow to stern. Oars 10–12 ft (3–3.7 m)
Ashby Dell	400	54 (16.5)		6 (1.8)			14	No		Fir or pine				L	L	Suffolk, Eng.	Sternpost morticed, cleats treenailed to planks
Sutton Hoo	600	89 (27)	14 (4.27)	4.5 (1.37)	6.3:1	21	40	?	9		F	26		T	R	"	Mast step may have been removed.
Sutton Hoo	600	22.5 (6.9)	6 (1.8)	3 (0.9)	3.9:1		16/18	No	5/6		F				R	"	
Barset	8th	42.7 (13)	8.8 (2.6)		4.9:1				6	Pine	F		Pine		R, L, T	Norway	Lower strakes riveted, upper sewn and treenailed
Ladby	9th	67.5 (20.6)	9.5 (2.9)	3.9 (1.2)	7.1:1		30	Y	7		K	20			R	Denmark	Replica sailed well
Tune	850	65.5 (20)	13.1 (4)		5.0:1		22	Y	10	Oak	K		Oak	L	R, T	S. Norway	Plank ¾ in. (2 cm) thick
Oseberg	800	70.5 (21.5)	17 (5.1)	6.9 (2.1)	4.2:1		30	Y	12	Oak	K	17	Oak	L	R	"	Mast and oars of pine
Gokstad	850	76 (23.1)	17 (5.2)	6.2 (1.9)	4.5:1	32	32	Y	16	Oak	K	16	Oak	L	R	"	Oars 17.5–19.2 ft (5.3–5.9 m)
Gokstad	850	32 (9.75)	6.1 (1.86)		5.2:1		6	No	4	Oak	K	9	Oak	T	R	"	
Skuldelev 1	1000	54 (16.5)	14.8 (4.5)	6.6 (2)	3.6:1	19.5		Y	12	Pine	K	14	Oak	T	R	Denmark	Merchant ship
Skuldelev 2	1000	92 (28)	14.8 (4.5)	5.2 (1.6)	6.2:1		40/52	Y		Oak	K	37/39	Oak	T	R	"	Warship
Skuldelev 3	1000	44 (13.3)	10.8 (3.3)	3.6 (1.1)	4.1:1	9.4	4	Y	8	Oak	K	11	Oak	T	R	"	Coaster, 7 oar ports, 4 worn
Skuldelev 5	1000	59 (18)	8.5 (2.6)	3.9 (1.2)	6.9:1	5.3	24	Y	7	Ash / Oak	K	16	Oak	T	R	"	Warship. 3 upper planks ash
Skuldelev 6	1000	39 (12)	8.2 (2.5)		4.8:1			Y	7	Pine	K		Alder / Pine	R, T	R	"	Ferry or fishing boat
Graveney	870	46 (14)	9.8 (3)	3 (0.9)	4.7:1	10		Y	10 or 11	Oak	F	13?	Oak	T	R	Kent, Eng.	Knobbed treenails
Utrecht	745/965	54 (16.5)	13 (4)	4 (1.2)	4.2:1	23	2	Y	3	Oak	F	38	Oak	T	T	Holland	Willow treenails, swim ends, heavy rubbing strakes

L = Lashing.   R = Rivet.   T = Treenail.   Y = Yes

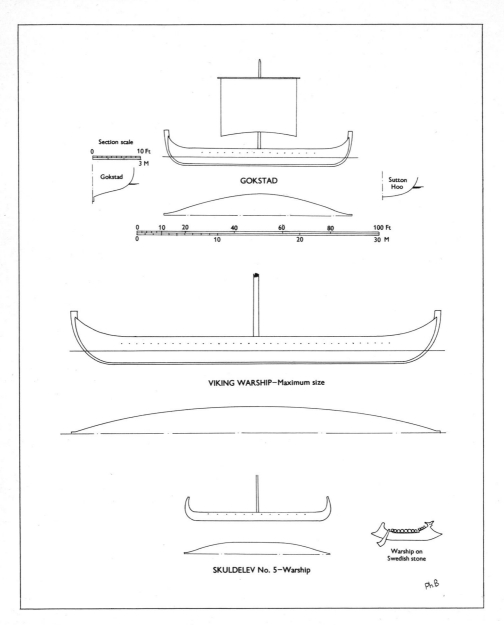

Section scale

0   10 Ft

3 M

Gokstad

GOKSTAD

Sutton Hoo

0   10   20   40   60   80   100 Ft

0   10   20   30 M

VIKING WARSHIP—Maximum size

Warship on Swedish stone

SKULDELEV No. 5—Warship

Ph.B

designed by a 'naval architect' though nobody ever called him that at the time. The term is used here to describe a man with such a knowledge of sailing ship design that he could combine a deep keel for lateral resistance with a broad beam for stability, yet at the same time restrict the displacement to the minimum required to float the ship and her load at the most advantageous waterline.

13 Ships of 9th–11th centuries AD

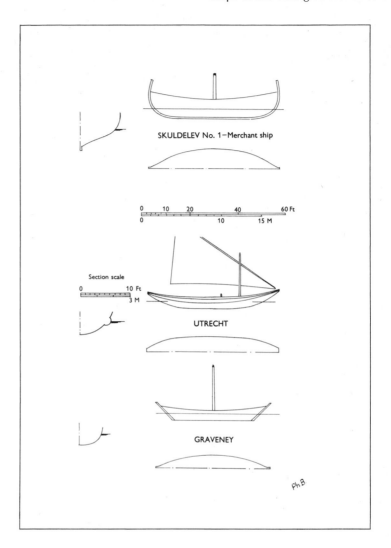

SKULDELEV No. 1–Merchant ship

0 10 20 40 60 Ft
0 10 15 M

Section scale
0 10 Ft
3 M

UTRECHT

GRAVENEY

Ph.B

If the Gokstad ship had had a convex midsection like the Nydam and Sutton Hoo ships she would have needed a lot of extra ballast to load her down to her marks. The S curve of her midsection, formed by the deep keel, hollow garboards and the high turn of the bilge, is the hallmark of her designer's skill. You will find this feature in a fast French frigate of the Napoleonic wars or in an extreme form in a modern ocean racing yacht. As far as northern Europe is concerned the idea was developed in Scandinavia in the 8th century.

The Skuldelev knarr in spite of being a cargo ship exhibits this feature even more clearly, showing that within the limits of her sailplan she was a fast sailer with much finer lines than a medieval cog (as far as we know), or the average 18th century merchantman.

Ships up to Gokstad size were probably owned by adventurous individuals or several banded together, and used for summer raiding across the open sea. There were smaller raiding ships, though a glance at the 59 ft (18 m) Skuldelev warship shows that if size goes much smaller the displacement and carrying capacity falls away at a remarkable rate. If much larger, it is difficult to find large enough timber for the method of construction used. The keel of the Gokstad ship was a single piece of oak over 60 ft (18 m) long, almost the largest size obtainable.

Nevertheless much larger ships were built. Haakon Shetelig in *The Viking Ships* lists sixteen ships of 30 to 35 thwarts or 'rooms', and measurements given in the *Flateyjarbok* give the length of a 40 thwart ship as 17.0 ft (52 m). These dimensions must be accepted with reserve. It is difficult to imagine an undecked ship 170 ft (52 m) long being strong and rigid enough for a seaway, and some ships seem to have been built with much less space between the oarsmen. In the 'levy' ships built by order to standard measurements, 20 thwarts were said to have been crammed into 50 ft (15 m), with only 2.6 ft (79 cm) between the oars instead of just over 3 ft (1 m) in the Gokstad ship. Six ships of 30 to 35 'rooms' were built between 995 AD and 1062 AD; the others came too late to be included here.

Fig. 13 shows a ship of 152 ft (46 m) with 37 rooms and 74 oars. This ship is conjectural, and on the same proportions as the Gokstad

24 Model of Gokstad ship AD 850. (Crown copyright Science Museum, London)

25 Model of Oseberg ship AD 800. (National Maritime Museum, Greenwich)

ship would have had a displacement of 256 tons and a sail area of 6400 sq. ft (595 m²). A 'modern' trading schooner would set this area as six sails on three masts. There is no evidence whatever of Viking ships having more than one mast or one sail, and the largest sail that could have been handled with the simple gear of the time was probably about 2000 sq. ft (186 m²), the size of the foretopsail of the tea clipper *Fiery Cross*. But big ships are usually much more slender than small ones, and the Skuldelev No. 2 longship which is 92 ft (28 m) long compared to the 76 ft (23 m) of the Gokstad ship has a length/beam ratio of 6.2 against the smaller ship's 4.5. If the big Viking ships were seven beams long with depth in proportion, the displacement of our 152 ft (46 m) ship would have been only 64 tons and her sail area 1600 sq. ft (149 m²), a manageable size.

Her 74 oarsmen would have developed 22 h.p. or 0.34 h.p. per ton, a little better than the Gokstad ship. The Saga tells us about three ships built in 1206 that '...had two rows of oar holes between the well-rooms...24 oars in the lower bank and 48 in the upper.

The oars in the upper bank were 36 ft [11 m] long'. This suggests that there were yet larger or heavier ships than that in Fig. 13.

The keel of the *Long Serpent* was said to have been 129 ft (39 m). There are all sorts of unlikely details given for these great ships, such as that the freeboard was 18 ft 5 in. (5.6 m) in one case and that in another the ship worked so much that four chests of spare rivets were carried. The *Mariasuden* (*Ship of Mary*) was cut in half in 1184 and lengthened by 22 ft (6.7 m). Our conjectural ship has a freeboard of only 7 ft (2 m) and it can scarcely have been more. With fair certainty we can say that the fleets of Guthrum, Cnut and Harald Hardradi contained many ships like this, some perhaps rowed by two men to each oar or else double banked in some other way. When we read in the *Anglo-Saxon Chronicle* that Alfred built ships twice as long as the Danish ones we can be sure they were only twice the length of the small raiders and not much more than 100 ft (30 m) overall.

Fig. 13 also shows the smaller warship from Skuldelev now in the Viking Ship Museum at Roskilde, Denmark. The Sagas state that ships of 20–24 oars were used on rivers because they were easier to lift out and carry around the shallows and rapids. These ships were sometimes known as karfis, and the karfi was always spoken of not as having a certain number of thwarts or rooms like a long-ship but as having a total of so many oars. Since the term karfi comes from the Byzantine word for the ships of the Rus, it is possible that this was the type of light craft used to navigate the rapids on the Russian rivers. Whether the Skuldelev ship was actually a karfi is not known. She seems a little on the small side, being slimmer than the Gokstad ship and displacing only 5.3 tons, leaving very little room for cargo after the weight of her oarsmen (2 tons) is deducted. The effect of size is also shown in a much higher power/weight ratio than the Gokstad ship—1.36 h.p. per ton—very useful on a fast-flowing river.

A number of very successful replicas of Viking ships have been built. One based on the Gokstad ship crossed the Atlantic in 1893 and another crossed the North Sea in 1947. More recently some Danish Scouts built a replica of the Ladby ship 68 ft (20.6 m) long, which they called the *Imme Gram*. This ship sailed well and although she was much narrower than the Gokstad ship, 9.5 ft (2.9 m) instead of 17 ft (5.2 m), several horses were transported aboard her to prove that it could be done.

Figure 13 shows next the larger merchant ship from Skuldelev, now in the Roskilde Museum and nearly restored. We tend to assume that knarrs were deep full-bodied merchant ships of much greater carrying capacity than the warships, but the displacement of this one is 19.5 tons and she is considerably the larger of the two knarrs at Roskilde. It is possible she could safely float a little deeper and carry a few tons more. There may of course have been much larger knarrs. In the small knarr of 9.4 tons there are seven oar-ports, five forward and two aft, but only four have been used. The total auxiliary power to work the ship into and out of harbour was between 0.1 and 0.2 h.p. per ton; in the large knarr it was much less. The last chapter told of Gunnbjorn Ulfsson's ship being blown to-wards the skerries at Angmagssalik: he was lucky the wind changed, for his few oars were insufficient to work him clear against a strong wind.

The accommodation profile shows considerable areas of raised deck forward but an open cargo hold (Plate 26). The confident assertion that knarrs were more seaworthy than longships is not borne out. They may have had slightly higher sides and taken less water aboard, but if they shipped a big one there was only a small crew with wholly inadequate bailing scoops. Fully loaded it would have been very difficult to bail at all.

The warship pictured next to Skuldelev No. 5 in Fig. 13 and based on a carving poses an unsolved problem for no ship like it has ever been found. Why did they make her that shape? It is hardly likely that there would be a ram at each end of the ship, so we seem to have something like the decorative ram-like bows of some Roman merchant ships. The break in the sheerline is vaguely similar to that shown on some of the ships in the Bayeux Tapestry and the star-board quarter rudder seems to be of typical Viking shape. Provided she is not just a badly memorised reproduction of a Byzantine ship

26 Large merchant ship from Skuldelev, Denmark AD 1000. (National Maritime Museum, Green-wich)

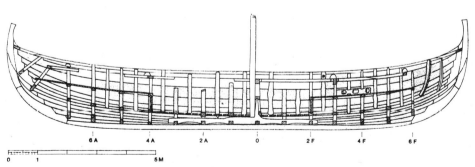

6 A   4 A   2 A   0   2 F   4 F   6 F

0   1   5 M

Wreck 1. Preliminary reconstruction of longitudinal section. 1 : 100.

that the artist saw in his travels, the most we can say is that there must have been a whole class of Scandinavian ships about which we know almost nothing.

The Utrecht boat of 745–965 AD shows that there were some boats quite different from the general pattern (Fig. 13, Plate 28). Viewed from the bow she is remarkably like some traditional Dutch workboats of recent times which are unlike anything else in Europe. It almost seems as though the local types developed in the 1st millennium AD carried right through into the 19th century; Viking influence can be seen in the small boats of the Orkneys and Shetlands today.

The Utrecht boat was found near the site of the great Frisian port of Dorestad, which seagoing ships approached either via the Rhine and the Lek or the rivers from the north. Her displacement was 23 tons (the estimate of the Central Museum, Utrecht). The bottom plank is 47 ft (14.3 m) long and 6 ft 4 in. (1.93 m) wide amidships! It is 4 in. (10 cm) thick and its transverse midsection is the arc of a circle. The bending of very heavy timber has always been a speciality of Dutch shipwrights, and this could have been a very wide plank bent to shape or a hollowed portion of a smaller tree spread out. Or it may have been an enormous baulk of timber hollowed to shape with adzes. The vessel is so far unique in having bilge strakes made from a 4 ft (1.2 m) diameter tree trunk split lengthwise. Each piece is 62 ft (18.9 m) long, bent to the shape of the waterline. There is one normal plank between the bilge strake and the bottom plank which it overlaps clinker fashion, and one strake above the bilge strake. There were 38 heavy frames joining

27 Utrecht ship. (Central Museum, Utrecht)

the bottom plank to the bilge strakes. Treenails were originally the only fastenings but some iron nails were added later.

The gunwale strakes contain a pattern of holes which suggest that the ship was decked, and the museum's reconstruction has a large hatchway in the after part of the 'deck'. A small step in the eleventh floor timber from the bow indicates either a mast or samson post. The museum model has a long lateen yard such as was used by the Romans in the Mediterranean but is not known to have been used in the north before the 16th century. There is one pair of tholes just abaft the 'mast' and a *port*-side quarter rudder.

28 Utrecht ship reconstruction. (Central Museum, Utrecht)

Eighth or 10th century sailors would undoubtedly have been prepared to take her to sea, but she was more likely used on inland waters, like the 19th century tjalks of similar shape which sailed on the Zuider Zee. The power under oars (1 h.p. for 20 tons) was not enough to work her off an open beach in wind and sea; we are probably correct if we visualise her with a small square sail, drifting along river and canal when wind, current or tide would serve and towed from the bank when they would not. Under these conditions she might have carried hay or other light cargo piled high above her gunwale like the old Thames barges.

The Graveney boat (late 9th century) found on the saltings near Whitstable in north Kent is another example of a boat that was different. She was clinker-built with a flat keel plank, a convex mid-section, and eleven planks each side (only eight planks on each side were found). But the stem and sternposts steeved up at about 30° from the horizontal, or rather more if the keel was rockered. Only one post was found and this is considered to be the sternpost in spite of the painter still fastened to it. The rest of the ship was sym-metrical, and if the bow and stern were also alike she would have been similar to the ship shown on the Dover seal of 1284.

It is difficult to make any very accurate estimates of her displacement but it was probably about 8 tons. We do not know if she was decked. There seems to have been a mast step amidships and she must have been a sailing ship for at only 0.5 h.p. per ton it would have taken sixteen men to row her, a totally uneconomic crew. Towards the end of her life the mast step disappeared and the slots in the frames were filled in with packing pieces.

The planks were fastened to the frames by treenails with domed heads larger than the shanks. These were driven in from the outside and the inner ends were held tight by wedges. The planks, made up of sections 10–13 ft (3–4 m) long, were fastened to each other by round-section nails riveted over roves as on the Nydam, Sutton Hoo, Gokstad and Oseberg ships.

The Graveney boat may have been foreign but the chances are against it. She was found in an area of heavy Viking raids but these did not necessarily interfere greatly with the comings and goings of native merchant ships. One would expect the last voyage of a trader to be a round one if only to get the crew home and avoid port dues. After all most of the ribs that stick out of the mud today are those of barges and smacks that finally sank at their home moorings.

The Anglo-Saxons are supposed to have called the Vikings 'Aescmen' or 'Ashmen' because of the ash planking of their ships. But of all the ships listed in Table 1 only the small warship from Skuldelev has ash strakes and then only the top three of about ten on each side. It is much more likely that the Vikings were named after their 'ash blonde' hair. Every plank and frame in every other ship was either oak, fir or pine. Masts and oars were pine where it was obtainable.

In the Gokstad ship the deck was made up of unfastened boards, portable for bailing or stowing loot and stores. In the Oseberg ship the deck boards were nailed down. We can be almost certain that the big ships had continuous decks, which must have enormously strengthened them against hogging and sagging. Whether they would have been made watertight we do not know.

It used to be thought that the men rowed standing in the larger ships as there are no thwarts or fittings for them in the Gokstad, Oseberg or Tune ships. But the slant of the oars is wrong, and the modern view is that each oarsman sat on his seachest. The term 'half-room chest' occurs in the sagas.

Viking ships have been described both as very seaworthy and very unseaworthy. Seaworthiness ultimately depends on stopping a ship filling with water when, unless it has buoyancy apparatus, it will sink. In modern vessels this is achieved by almost complete decking with the few openings closed by tight hatches. Seaworthiness also depends on strength and full stability, so that if the wind blows the ship onto her beam ends, her shape, ballast and watertightness ensure that she comes back upright and undamaged. Neither the Viking longship nor the Viking merchant ship fulfilled any of these essentials, but well handled they could face *most normal* conditions of sea and wind with confidence. Neither type could face abnormal winds and confused breaking seas. Sumburgh Roost, the Pentland Firth, Portland and Alderney Races could be deathtraps for them. (Earl Hakon, a follower of Cnut, was drowned in the Pentland Firth in 1049.) Within the limits of undecked boats, and only within those limits, the Viking ships were very good indeed.

A lot has been written about the dragon figureheads. In fact very little is known about them. There are two stemposts in the British Museum, one about AD 600 and the other of AD 800, which end in very mild-looking fish or snake heads. The Oseberg ship has a scroll terminating in a small snake head like the bow ornaments on the Gotland stones. The Ile de Groix ship had a scroll stern ornament and the Ladby ship seems to have had some quite simple bow decoration. Most of the finely carved animal heads from Viking times formed parts of beds, chairs and carts.

However, it was said that the dragon head was unshipped when approaching a foreign shore so as not to alarm the inhabitants. This suggests that the victims did not regard every rakish ship under oar and sail as a Viking ship and that the Picts, Scots, Frisians or Irish might have regarded such a ship as one of their own. In other words 'Viking type' ships might have been common, and localities that had not suffered the scourge may not have been able to tell the superior Scandinavian ships from the local types. After all, apart from the subtlety of underwater shape and the finer points of rigging the Gokstad ship was a pretty obvious solution to the current requirements. Notker's *Charlemagne* says that some Viking raiders in the Mediterranean were mistaken for merchant ships until the Emperor recognised them. It seems the layman was no better at ship recognition then than he is now.

The vessels in Table 1 unfortunately do not represent a random sample from the whole of Europe. Due to the pagan practice of ship burial the pattern is heavily weighted towards the Viking side of Europe. There were other Viking ship burials in Scotland, Orkney, Ireland, the Isle of Man and Ile de Groix, but too little was recovered from them to be of much use.

On the evidence preserved, merchant ships in northern and eastern Europe were clinker-built and not much above 50 ft (15 m) and 20 tons laden displacement. Some had deep keels and some flat bottoms. All had one sail, and the difficulty of handling larger sails for small crews with primitive gear restricted the size of the ships. Undeveloped tidal harbours put a limit on draught. There may have been oared merchant ships on difficult sailing waters and the great rivers, which were small enough for portage. As with the tea clippers, high freight rates paid for expensive crews. Rimbert's *Vita Anskari* describes a voyage from Cologne to Hedeby in a craft with two cabins. King Harald of Denmark was travelling north in company and left his open longship for the warmth and dryness of the Frisian ship.

It is probable that carvel-built ships in a non-Viking tradition survived or flourished in western Gaul and Celtic Britain. The old Latin terms *scapha* and *barca* were used in the documents of the Carolingian empire; and under the Romans and before carvel ships and barges were built all along the coasts and rivers of France. With this tradition in mind it is not safe to assume that William the Conqueror's fleet, built mainly between the Seine mouth and the Cherbourg peninsula, consisted entirely of clinker-built ships. They were built in an area occupied by the finest shipbuilders and sailors in western Gaul for 800 years before the Vikings settled, and there is at least a possibility that some of William's ships were built to the older local tradition.

This had been reinforced in Spain when the Arabs moved in at the end of the 8th century, sailing out of the Straits of Gibraltar and operating at least as far north and east as the Gironde in carvel-built Mediterranean-style ships. The Romans maintained a fleet of galleys in the Gironde and the Visigoths took it over until at least AD 475; Charlemagne kept a squadron there to deal with Moslem raiders from Spain. In the 14th century the Black Prince operated galleys in the same area, when converted merchant ships were used for naval operations in the English Channel. Southwest Europe seems to have been a place where the warships were Mediterranean-type carvel-built galleys following a tradition that was Phoenician, Roman and Arab.

The broad flat centre plank without external keel in the Nydam, Sutton Hoo, Utrecht and Graveney ships may have been due to the localities in which they sailed, where there were mud or sand bottoms or shingle beaches on which they were required to sit upright. The ships from further north operated, in their home waters, from deep-water fjords. The Blackfriars Roman ship and possibly the Bruges boat (of which very little was found) had similar flat plank keels and also worked in muddy estuaries. But the evidence is too scanty for us to more than hint at the possibility.

The Gokstad and Skuldelev longships, like all Viking war vessels that can reasonably be called ships, had oar ports just large enough to take the oar loom, one or two slots being cut to allow the passage of the blade. Each port could be closed by an internal shutter. The knarr also had ports. Is it just possible that a longship badly swamped under sail could have opened her after ports to use as suction bailers as in a modern racing dinghy?

The smaller Viking boats, the 20 or 30 footers, were delightful; they were almost the same shape as the old Thames skiffs, wherries and randans—forward one might almost say they were exactly the same shape. Three boats, 32 ft (9.75 m), 26 ft (8 m) and 21 ft (6.5 m) long, were found with the Gokstad ship. The 26 ft boat was made of only three planks a side. Whereas a modern dinghy of half her length would have 1 in. (2.5 cm) by $\frac{1}{2}$ in. (1.25 cm) bent timbers every 6 in. (15 cm), the Viking boat had just four grown frames which probably served as the moulds round which the planks were bent and were continuous from gunwale to gunwale.

Although the Bayeux Tapestry shows boats being towed, the Viking raiders must have carried their boats at sea. They were anything but lifeboats and would have been as easily swamped as the Thames passenger wherries were when the Victorian steamers began to rush up and down the tideway. There must have been times when a raider needed to get fifty men ashore quickly while the ship herself stayed afloat, and there must have been times when they wanted to sail away quickly. It has been assumed too lightly that early mariners always hauled their ships up the beaches: they would have preferred deep water. Imagine a crew badly defeated somewhere near Southend, struggling back to the shore with wounded to find their 30-ton ship two hundred yards above the low tide mark. The smaller ships like the Skuldelev could probably have been carried like the Sheringham crab boats of the last century by thrusting the oars through the ports.

The mast of the Gokstad ship was a solid pine stick nearly 12 in. (30 cm) in diameter and estimated by Shetelig to have been 43 ft (13 m) high. An old rule stated that the mast height should equal the ship's girth amidships. A W Brogger gives the length of the yard 33–36 ft (10–11 m) and the sail area as 750 sq. ft (70 m²). This is only 25 sq. ft (2.3 m²) per ton so the performance in light winds was not very good; by comparison a racing dinghy carries 250 sq. ft (23 m²) per ton and a cruising yacht 100 sq. ft (9 m²) per ton plus a spinnaker of nearly twice the area of the plain sail. In light airs it was probably quicker to row, and gave the crew something to do. In force 5 winds the Gokstad ship would have been marvellous; in force 2 she would have broken a yachtsman's heart. As mentioned above the very big ships must have had a sail of nearly 2000 sq. ft (186 m²).

There is a reference in the Vinland Saga to shortening sail though exactly how this was done is not known. There is no evidence of a bonnet laced to the foot of the sail as on the medieval cogs. The illustrations on the Gotland stones seem to indicate reefing pendants. There is also a maze of criss-cross ropes descending from the foot of the sail which may have been a means of keeping the sail flat on the wind. The makeup of the sail is also obscure. The Gotland stones (Plate 29) show a diagonal pattern but the sails in

29 Gotland Stone.
(Crown copyright,
Science Museum,
London)

the Bayeux Tapestry have vertical cloths. This was the practice until quite recently and resulted in the stress being applied down the cloth seams where there was multiple thickness. The diagonal lines were probably pure decoration. There is also mention of a tacking pole to extend the tack of the square sail when sailing close to the wind but exact details are not known.

In the Gokstad ship the mast had shrouds and a forestay and the sail was controlled by sheets to the clews. There is doubt about braces to the yardarms, and these are not shown in the Bayeux tapestry. The shrouds were fastened to loops passing through holes in the gunwales. Slack in the rigging must have been taken up by shortening the loops. The mast was seated on a heavy step bridging four frames and braced both laterally and longitudinally several feet higher up by a very heavy tabernacle, the after bracing strut being portable to allow the mast to lower aft for rowing or when beached. It is not clear where the halyard was belayed or the precise purpose of the solid blocks (without sheaves) found in the ship. Purchases of several parts would be used nowadays to control a sail of this size. In the longships there were always plenty of men to tail onto a halyard or sheet but a knarr usually had a crew of only four or five. The handling of the sails in the larger ships must have presented such a problem as in itself to have set a limit to their size.

All the ships and boats in Table 1 were clinker built. The Barset, Tune, Gokstad and Oseberg ships still had their lower strakes lashed to the frames via pierced cleats standing up from the inner faces of the planks like those of the Nydam ship. It has been suggested that this was in deliberate preference to nailing, to obtain a more flexible hull. It is more likely it was an archaic survival from the days of very wide planks or even from the days when nails were unknown. Flexibility of this degree would seem to be more a nuisance than an asset. However such eminent authorities as Arne Emil Christensen Jr and the late Uffa Fox do not agree. On the Skuldelev knarrs all the strakes were nailed or treenailed to the frames, but these were broader, deeper ships of much more rigid shape.

The usual method of fastening the planks to one another was with iron nails clenched over roves in the modern manner. But the Barset boat had her upper planks sewn together and in the Ashby Dell boat of AD 400 and the Utrecht and other ships treenails or pegs were used even though they were only 2 in. (5 cm) long. To adze out a plank from a great baulk of timber leaving lugs at frequent intervals was an incredibly slow business even for fine craftsmen, and as soon as shipwrights discovered a way of sawing out a plank and nailing it to the ribs they must have heaved a sigh of relief. In one case (Ashby Dell) the lugs were nailed onto the plank, which does suggest that the lashings were considered of special importance.

In the Nydam, Sutton Hoo, Gokstad and Oseberg ships the plank ends were taken into the rabbets in the stem and sternpost in the modern manner. On all five Skuldelev ships the upper six planks on each side stopped about 2 ft short of the face of the stem and stern. Each end of the ship was V-shaped in plan combining post and short simulated clench-laid planks in one intricately carved piece of wood about 10 ft long down the cutwater and about 2 ft from the stem or stern face to the end of each 'plank'. The V-shaped groove was about 8 in. deep and the 'plank' ends were stepped.

This was a tour de force of craftsmanship when there were plenty of expert woodcarvers with unlimited fine timber to carve. There are other examples from Scotland and Greenland. It was a refinement of the method used to form the ends of the Als boat over 1000 years earlier. Like the cleats and lashings of the lower planks of the Gokstad ship, one suspects that it was an age-old idea which because it worked was retained into an age when much simpler methods were available (see Plate 26, page 209).

All these ships were underpowered and this gave them a special grace. You can see this in reverse if you examine craft driven by the big outboard motors of today—blunt ends, immersed transoms, bad trim and general ugliness. With only small sails and muscle power every line, section and buttock had to be easy and fair.

None of these ships was a mere cargo box, and because they had fine ends and no closed deck they could not be overloaded but must always be light and buoyant to lift to the seas and not to wallow with green water sweeping over. The enormous thickness of wood in some of the ships did not necessarily make them heavy since most of the weight was low down and served as ballast. Timber was so plentiful it could be used without stint.

A tour round the coasts of northern Europe in the 11th century AD would have discovered carvel-built galleys and cargo ships; deep keeled clinker-built warships, knarrs and vessels of state; flat keeled clinker-built warships and seagoing traders. There would have been local types with flat bottoms and round-clinker, carvel and reverse clinker, with pointed bows, scow bows and spoon bows including fishing boats for working off beaches, some with wet wells; ships with permanent cabins and pilgrim ships with temporary divisions to give privacy below; cattle ferries and passenger ferries.

On present evidence we hardly dare to suggest more than one mast, and talk of lateen sails or spritsails with caution. The 11th century traveller might have found his ships lashed together, nailed together or pegged together, and nothing much would have surprised him, except perhaps the sailors' total relaxation in harbour and endless, sleepless effort in crisis.

19 Sea Power—The Last Invasions

William crossed the cold Channel
And reddened the bright swords

Norway's warrior sea-king
Has been enticed westwards
To fill England's graveyards

King Harald's Saga

Harold of England died at Hastings on 14 October 1066 after a day-long battle between 15,000 men; the climax of a campaign that started in January with the death of the king men called the Confessor. By the most moderate estimates 1200 ships were involved, belonging to four separate fleets. These fleets manoeuvred over 200,000 square miles of sea and sailed 3000 miles carrying 30,000 men. We can only guess at the distances covered by the courier vessels carrying messages between Tostig of Northumberland, Hardradi of Norway, Malcolm of Scotland, Swein of Denmark and Baldwin of Flanders. In the prologue and epilogue to the campaign five other fleets sailed the seas, 600 more ships and 20,000 more men.

The tragedy took fourteen years to reach its climax and nine years to die away, and we can study the comings and goings of the ships from landfall to landfall and harbour to harbour; their design and building, their fitting out and navigation, wrecking or safe ending. The whole is set before us in coloured thread, epic poetry and monkish prose.

In 1042 Edward (the Confessor) sailed home from exile in Normandy. He left behind him the memory of an English prince who had accepted Norman hospitality and become king of England, a richer country than Normandy and one cursed with many claimants to its throne.

During 1049–51 Edward paid off his fleet of fourteen ships, relying instead on obtaining ships and crews when required from the seaports of Sandwich, Dover, Fordwich and Romsey. For a navy of long-service professionals which had existed ever since 1012 he substituted an occasional levy of hastily gathered ships with crews who would only serve for limited periods.

In 1051 William of Normandy received, or thought he received, a promise or half promise of the English throne. One English chronicler says he came to England. But whatever Edward promised in 1051 he had second thoughts in 1054, when he recalled the

Aetheling from Germany where he had been taken from the wrath of Cnut in 1017. The prince took three years to travel to London via Cologne and the Rhine, and Harold was sent to Flanders in 1056 to bring him across the Channel. In 1057 he arrived and died.

In 1052 Earl Godwine of Wessex sailed back from banishment in Flanders, siezed the Isle of Wight, joined his son Harold who had brought more men and ships from Ireland, and sailed for London. How Edward must have longed for the fleet he had disbanded. He gathered a few ships and brought them to the capital. Godwine and Harold sailed up-Channel and into the Thames, gathering ships and men at every port along the route. With masts lowered the ships were rowed up on the flood through the arches of London Bridge to surround Edward's fleet on the north bank. Godwine won his pardon by threat of force alone and lived seven months to enjoy it.

Harold became Earl of Wessex, and Tostig Godwinsson Earl of Northumberland. Only the old earldom of Mercia was not under Godwine rule. In 1062 Harold sailed from Bristol to a brilliant campaign against Gruffydd of Wales whose capital and port was Rhuddlan on the river Clwyd. In a few months he was back in London with Gruffydd's ship's figurehead among his trophies.

As the moment of high drama approached Harold was 44 years old, 'a little man…but he stood proudly in his stirrups' as Hardradi said of him before Stamford Bridge. His sea experience included the Irish Sea, the Bristol Channel, Lands End and the whole sweep of the coast to London. In 1064 it seems that the King sent him to Normandy to negotiate with William.

Harold's route was south or SSE of the Isle of Wight depending on whether he was going to the ducal capital at Rouen or intended to anchor in one of the little rivers near Bayeux. According to the Bayeux Tapestry Harold rode down from London to Bosham, lifted up his tunic, and hawk on wrist, waded out to his ship. The tide must have been nearly full, ready to carry them out of Chichester harbour on the ebb. Roman merchant ships discharged ballast at Fishborne and the whole area is sheltered by the Wight and Selsey Bill which then extended further out to sea. Man has probably not much changed the pattern of saltings, sand and salt water by the little sea walls he has built, and we may safely picture Harold's ship being rowed out between East Head and Sandy Point. Whether it was one of those days when the light turns the sand to deep purple or whether his mind was on the scenery we shall never know.

Generally speaking it is no use pretending that the ladies who worked the Bayeux Tapestry had an eye for a ship; sometimes the same one is differently shown in different places. Harold leaves

Bosham in a vessel which looks like all the others, flat-sheered with conventional ornaments and no beauty of line at all. But the ship in which he comes back is the most beautiful in all the ship pictures of the period, and when we redraw her, making the wavy lines in hull and mast firm and straight, she becomes even better. This is the only known ship of the time which is not equal-ended; the bow overhang far exceeds that of the stern and the tight curve aft gives a coiled spring effect to the whole ship (Fig. 14).

In works like the Bayeux Tapestry the designs were first drawn on the canvas by some scholar, usually a monk, but someone else must have stepped in here who had a real feeling for ships. Harold was the premier earl on a high diplomatic mission for his king and the ship was probably built by the best shipbuilder in the kingdom. She may have been 100 ft (30 m) long with a crew of sixty.

But Harold never reached a Norman haven: the wind backed towards the south and drove him up Channel until his ship came

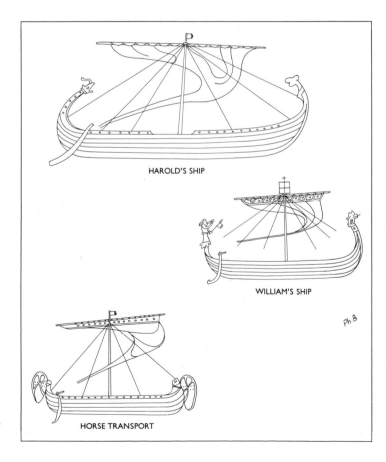

HAROLD'S SHIP

WILLIAM'S SHIP

Ph. B

HORSE TRANSPORT

14 Bayeux Tapestry ships

to harbour in the Baie de la Somme. The tapestry shows them sounding their way in among the sandbanks while the anchor is made ready. Then the mast is unshipped ready for drawing up on the beach. It was Guy of Ponthieu's territory, and like a Cornish longshoreman of later times he tried to make the most of it and hold Harold for ransom. But William rescued him and got another promise or half promise of the English throne.

In October 1065 Tostig was driven out of Northumberland and sailed from the Humber to Bruges in the country of his father-in-law Baldwin of Flanders, whose other son-in-law was William of Normandy. On 5 January 1066 Edward the Confessor died and commended his kingdom to Harold.

William immediately began to organise an invasion and Tostig to gather a fleet to raid the coasts of England; 800 miles to the northeast Harald Hardradi, King of Norway, was also levying ships to invade England. He had a vague claim through Cnut. Tostig, willing to use either of them for his own ends, arranged to rendezvous with Hardradi between the Humber and the Northern Isles. All that summer messages must have crossed the North Sea in swift ships as the King and the Duke struggled to make their fleets ready before the autumn storms. We can imagine a letter from Tostig carried by some high-born theyn from Bruges to Trondheim, a letter in the stilted and obscure prose of the time. In a month Tostig would have got his answer and neither man would be sure what the other meant.

Harald Hardradi had been forcing Norwegians to obey his orders for 20 years, and if they had to plunder or fight to do so under his command. Exiled at 15, he had spent several years in Russia before joining the Varangian guard and raiding far and wide in the Mediterranean. In 1038 he had led them across the Straits of Messina to Sicily, fighting side by side with Norman knights in Byzantine service. In the Varangian revolt of 1042, according to the saga, he stole two galleys and carried off the Empress's niece. Their way was barred by a chain which they charged at full speed; men ran aft to lift the bows and forward again to slide the ships over, breaking the back of one of them. Harald was a Christian who had fought his way to Jerusalem to clear the route for pilgrims. He had bathed in the Jordan and given generously at the shrines of the Holy Land. He founded the town of Oslo as a base for attacking Denmark and raided in the Limfjord with a squadron of light ships, using their shallow draft to evade the more powerful Danish forces. When they were finally trapped his men dragged the ships across dry land into the North Sea and escaped.

The battle of Nissa in 1062 was fought between the fleets of

Harald of Norway and Swein of Denmark. Harald's flagship was called the '*busse*' and had recently been built at Nidaros near Trondheim. She had 70 oars and was as long as the *Long Serpent* whose keel measured 129 ft (39 m), but broader. Her real name is unknown. With the *busse* and over 200 ships Harald sailed from Trondheim into Oslo fjord where the fleet was scattered by a storm until

> *Fighting troops are lying*
> *In every creek and skerry;*
> *Shield protected warships*
> *Shelter in lee of the land.*

There were 150 Norwegian ships and 300 Danish in the battle, which was just off the Swedish coast opposite Aalborg in Denmark. The saga says that the great ships in the centre of each fleet were roped together and rowed forward to meet the enemy. Fighting started in late afternoon and lasted all night. An unroped Norwegian squadron worked round the fringe of the battle. The roping was intended to keep the half-hearted in the fight, and when defeat came many Danes jumped overboard and swam to the free ships, leaving more than seventy empty ships to Hardradi. In 1065 Tostig sailed to Denmark to get Swein's help but the king, smarting from his defeat, said simply that he 'intended to be guided by his limitations'.

Such was the career of Harald Hardradi, who was now preparing to challenge Harold of England or William of Normandy for the English crown. Both invaders had the utmost difficulty in getting their fleets ready in time. William had laid his plans in February 1066 and started building at the end of the winter on the very coast between the Seine and the Cherbourg peninsula where the Allies landed in 1944. It was sheltered from westerly gales and far enough from England to make day raiding difficult. This was important for towards the end of that summer there were 600 ships assembled there.

Lt. Col. Lemmon, DSO in *The Field of Hastings* estimates the fighting strength of the Norman army as 8000; 3000 cavalry, 4000 infantry and 1000 archers. An ammunition wagon is shown in the tapestry and there are references in the chronicles to portable forts brought over in the ships. William set up his tent on the battlefield, and the tents of the period were elaborate affairs that needed a lot of shipping space.

The most difficult part of the operation was carrying the 3000 horses, and we can scarcely envisage more than eight of the big battle stallions per ship, each with his rider and groom: they would have needed 375 ships. Fifty infantry and archers were probably crammed into a ship, needing 100 ships altogether. There remain the garrison troops not present at the battle, camp followers, ammunition (30,000 arrows) and wagons to carry it, portable forges, tents, food and fodder for the horses. The tapestry shows casks of wine being loaded.

Fodder was the bulkiest item. A horse eats an enormous amount of hay and supplying cavalry with hay was always a bigger problem than supplying motor transport with fuel. The cab horses of London used to be supplied by endless numbers of Thames barges with hay piled up to ten feet above the gunwales. William's cavalry could commandeer fodder but they had to have a few days' supply in case they found the hay and grain burned by Harold's men—3000 bales would have been a minimum, or 30 ship loads.

Two thousand garrison troops and camp followers would have needed another 40 ships, stores for 10,000 men and the ships' crews might have filled 20 more. A few more would have carried the tents, arrows and weapons. About 600 transports should have been sufficient but there were probably warships, pinnaces and perhaps towed landing craft or small boats as well. A contemporary chronicler, William of Jumièges, writes that there were 3000 ships which must surely be an overestimate. William of Poitiers infers over a thousand.

The majority must have been built between the Cotentin peninsula and the Seine close to where the Veneti had developed 50 ft (15 m) flat-bottomed merchant ships by 60 BC, and the transports of 1066 may have developed from them, perhaps being carvel built. The tapestry does not show whether the ships were clinker or carvel; they all have multicoloured strakes but there is nothing to show whether they overlapped. The Normans' Viking ancestry was spread very thin and the older ideas may have triumphed just as did the old language. And just as Caesar had to mobilise the whole shipbuilding resources of the Channel shore and hinterland to build his invasion fleet, so probably did William. He may have had Frisian ships from his father-in-law's territory in Flanders, Viking types from the regions where they were normally built, ships in the old style of western Gaul, and barges from the big rivers.

The tapestry shows an important building detail: a stout post with some sort of sheave block hanging stands in the water and newly built ships are connected to it by ropes as if they were launched by hauling them into the water. Some ships are shown without oars, some with a continuous row of oar ports in the top strake, and some with an interrupted upper strake extending from the bow to a few feet before the mast and from some way abaft the mast to the sternpost. Harold's ship is shown like this. It may have been a convention to show a Saxon ship but it is just as likely to have been a real difference. In the early pictures Harold's ship tows a small boat although normally these were carried on board. William's ship the *Mora*, which was the gift of his wife and may have been Flemish, has a lantern at the masthead. She was one of the few named ships of the time and her figurehead was said to be of a boy pointing ahead. The tapestry shows him at the stern and it may be that someone sketched him in at the wrong end. The *Mora* has no oar ports, while some ships carrying horses do have them. They all have a single mast amidships, a square sail and a starboard rudder. Many of the ships were built by William's subjects at their own expense. The Abbot of St Ouen is said to have provided 20 ships, William fitz Osbern 65, and Odo, Bishop of Bayeux and William's half-brother 100. Some of William's ships have enormous shields hanging over bow and stern. C H Gibbs Smith suggests this may have been anti-ramming protection, though they are more likely to have been to guard against accidental damage when the fleet was getting under way. But further evidence is needed, for shields hang over the stern of Harold's ship as well.

While William was straining every nerve to get his fleet ready for midsummer, and he was quite capable of chopping off a man's hand if he did not work fast enough, Tostig was raiding England. In May his ships were seen off the Isle of Wight. Most of his crews were Flemings so he was probably based on Bruges. He raided along the Sussex coast and occupied Sandwich. Here he was joined by another exiled Northumbrian called Copsi who had sailed from Orkney with seventeen ships. Hardradi, who ruled the Northern Isles, must have given permission and it is a sign that he and Tostig were working together. Harold was too late to stop Tostig seizing the shipping in Sandwich harbour and recruiting or impressing their crews. He sailed away with 60 ships, raided in the Burnham River near the old Roman fort of Brancaster on the north Norfolk coast, and sailed into the Humber. He disembarked on the south bank, where he was badly beaten by the Lincolnshire militia.

Yorkshire stood firm for Harold and the Sandwich men sailed back to Kent. Tostig was left with twelve small ships which he took to Scotland, where the King allowed him to stay all summer building up his fleet. Gigantic forces were massing against Harold. William was recruiting from all the neighbouring territories including Brittany with its magnificent sailors. Flanders was giving shelter and aid to Harold's enemies. The King of Norway was on the move, and the King of Scotland was aiding and abetting both Tostig and Hardradi. The Pope had given William a banner.

Yet Harold, like the hero in some great epic tragedy, almost beat them all. William's invasion was not an act of strategic genius but a reckless gamble that did not deserve to succeed. There is good reason to think that his first plan was to sail across to the Isle of Wight where in May or June Harold took command of the English fleet which must have consisted of at least 100 ships. They must have carried nearly as many Englishmen as fought at Stamford Bridge or Hastings. Harold's ships almost certainly lay in Brading Haven and his lookouts were on St Catherine's Hill and St Boniface Down whence from nearly 800 ft they could have seen 30 miles. On a clear day with the invasion fleet moving at 3 knots Harold would have had 10 hours in which to get his ships to sea. He would have started moving on sight of a beacon fire, but delayed putting to sea until a messenger spurring some shaggy pony brought him fuller information.

There would have been none too much time at certain states of the tide, and the tactical situation would have been totally changed if for reasons of weather and tide William had rounded the Island westabout. However if he had come from the east, bearing in mind that Selsey Bill then extended further out to sea, Harold's victory would have been certain. As William's deep-laden ships came straggling in, the English longships could have attacked them at will, and burning brands would have started the stallions plunging and screaming and set the hay barges on fire; ships that tried to escape eastwards would have been trapped on the Owers rocks. Sea battles of this period never took place on the open sea: it involved too much rowing, and we know from watching modern boatraces that crews row themselves to exhaustion in 20 minutes at full speed.

Whatever William's original intentions he could do nothing against the persistent northeasterly winds and on 12 September he ordered the fleet to St Valery. There had been a considerable westerly shift of wind or his ships would never have got there; the course from the Dives to miss the headland of Le Havre is 020° T and they could not sail within 70° of the wind. The minimum distance to clear the sandbanks of the Seine estuary and get round the point is 23 miles and the flood tide sets in towards the mouth of the Seine at between $\frac{1}{2}$ and $1\frac{1}{2}$ knots. They could not have made St Valery non-stop for they only had 4 or 5 hours before the tide turned: they must have anchored between Cap d'Antifer and Fécamp and sailed on next day, just reaching St Valery-sur-Somme before the tide ran against them again. They were on a lee shore the whole way and might have had to coast on a night tide. Some ships were driven ashore and wrecked, luckier ones must have waited for high tide to kedge off the mudflats. Ships were lost and men died and deserted; only William's ruthless leadership kept the expedition together.

The chroniclers were all pro-Norman but there is no reason to doubt their stories of William's agony at St Valery, praying for a southerly wind and watching the weather vane on the Church for fourteen long days, at last bringing the saint's body out of the church in an attempt to change his luck, and on 27 September it did. A southerly wind only a few days earlier would have delivered William's fleet into Harold's hands; a week or two later and the sailing season would have been over. It came just after Harold could hold his fleet together no longer and had despatched what was left of it to the Thames. The winds were strong and many ships were lost on the way.

In ordering his fleet to the Thames on or just after 8 September Harold must have realised that the same wind was probably bearing Hardradi and Tostig towards England. The Thames was between the threat from the north and that from the south. It turned out to be too far from either, but Harold could not know where Hardradi would strike (later Viking invasions were towards the Thames) and there was a chance that William might be driven still further east. Francis Drake would have made a counter strike across the Channel, but Drake was not king of a realm that needed his personal presence to hold it together. As autumn wore on with its 12 hours' darkness and promise of worsening weather, Harold had yielded to pressures and laid up his fleet. It had been afloat for more than the statutory period of the levy and there was nothing he could do about it.

Hardradi did not leave Norway until September. His fleet numbered 300 ships or more and included some that had fought at Nissa and others he had had built at Nidaros during the summer. They sailed on a north or northwest wind and the great *busse* was probably in the van. Part of the fleet went via Shetland and the remainder direct to Orkney. On the way across to Bressay Sound Hardradi's squadron fell in with a lone knarr belonging to a man called 'Corpse' Lodin, a sort of marine undertaker who searched the shores of the northern seas for bodies to bring back for Christian burial. King Harald summoned him aboard the *busse* and was told of ill omens that threatened his campaign. By secret agreement Lodin joined the expedition to bury the dead. The story comes from the 11th century and is confirmed by another account which states that Lodin had brought back corpses of princely rank from Greenland on the command of Saint Olav.

The fleet did not stay long in Bressay Sound and the inhabitants must have been glad to see it go, for the crews outnumbered the population. The Sound, five miles by one, must have seemed full of ships. They anchored next in Scapa Flow and Hardradi left his queen and daughters in Orkney. There must surely have been private quarters aboard the *busse* for the women. With recruits from Scotland he rendezvoused with Tostig off the Northumberland coast, burned Scarborough, and sailed into the Humber and up the Ouse to Riccall. He had brought 9000 men 800 miles and put them ashore ten miles from York, the northern capital of England and of Tostig's earldom. It was about 18 September. The fleet had sailed 800 miles in little more than ten days at sea.

Only a detailed topographical map can show the daring of this deep penetration into the Yorkshire countryside. Riccall is 20 miles above Goole up the winding river Ouse, and Goole itself is 50 miles from the open sea. The river is only fifty yards wide where the ships were moored, and if they lay in line ahead with lines bow and stern they would have occupied six miles of river. The few English ships in the area had retreated before the Danish fleet and were now at Tadcaster on the Wharfe where Harold of England and his army joined them on 24 September.

York was an 'overseas port' in the 14th century and the Domesday Survey of 1086 classified the Ouse as a navigable river. A print of 1730, before the great age of river improvement, shows small full-rigged ships at York. Today the river is embanked almost the whole way above Goole, but no one can say with certainty what it was like in 1066. Square-sailed ships could hardly have sailed up it, and the knarrs which must have formed a significant part of Hardradi's fleet could not have been rowed up like the longships. They were almost certainly bow-hauled unless the wind was exceptionally favourable. The lower reaches of the river were of course tidal; the banks were probably low and the river liable to flood over thousands of acres, but generations of boatmen must have laid down faggots, hurdles and bundles of rushes to get a firm towpath. The saga tells us that the weather was exceptionally fine and warm and this may have been the key factor, tempting both Hardradi and William to embark on hazardous sea crossings at the very end of the sailing season, and making it easier for Hardradi to move his fleet so far inland. At Stamford Bridge the Norwegians were in a carefree mood and some of their armour had been left behind in the ships.

Fifteen miles to the northeast of Riccall, at Stamford Bridge, Harold caught them unprepared with half their force guarding the ships. Tostig and Hardradi died in the rout. By his terrific march of 150 miles in five or six days Harold had demonstrated once again that a good army moving on interior routes along the remnants of the Roman roads could counter a landing from a Viking fleet. The simple sailing ships of the time, too expensive to maintain in being for long, could not guarantee the realm in the face of contrary winds. Harold's holding force in the north had been beaten but it had weakened the invaders before he got there. This and the need to guard his ships had led to the downfall of the greatest Viking of his time. It was 25 September, so late in the season that Harold must have thought there was a chance William would not invade that year. But he had left lookouts on the southern hills and they watched the Norman fleet approach on 28 September; they brought the news to Harold on 1 October.

Only 24 ships of the great fleet were needed to take the Viking remnant home under Hardradi's son Olaf. We can picture the ordered seamanship as crew after crew slipped moorings, turned their ships round and rowed downriver hoisting sails while in the Humber to catch the southerly wind that had brought William to Pevensey. Olaf had given his promise never to invade England again.

Two hundred and fifty miles to the south the Norman army had embarked the moment the wind backed south. The Baie de la Somme dries out completely and 600 ships were on the mud or drawn up in long rows along the shore. They could hardly have floated for more than two hours either side of high tide, and there were 3000 valuable high-spirited battle stallions to be loaded in four hours if they were put aboard from quays while the ships were afloat. If a start had been made on the previous tide the loading would have had to be carried out in the dark and the horses cooped up in the ships for 15 hours or so before sailing. Men-at-arms, camp followers, ammunition, stores and fodder may have been in the ships for days, but the horses must have been put aboard in those last frantic four hours.

Everything must have been ready; wharves, stagings, hards and ramps, so that 100 ships could load at one time and slip away to their allotted moorings to await the signal to sail. William must have had a remarkable beachmaster. Think of twenty racehorses jibbing at a starting gate and then consider this achievement. Imagine the stink and sound of frightened horses, and the curses and caresses of their grooms hour after hour as the sea crept up over the mud and then crept away again while every moment was vital. While it would seem to have been much easier to bring all the transports inshore and load them on the mud this would have been much more difficult than appears from the Bayeux Tapestry where the horses are pictured being jumped over the gunwales. Even on ships as small as the Roskilde knarr ramps would have been needed. The horses would have been aboard longer before sailing.

Sunset was just before 6 p.m. and it was nearly dark when William hoisted a lantern to the *Mora*'s masthead and gave the order to sail. The wind was light and the night was clear. Not one ship of the 600 had any means of holding course but by the stars and the set of the wind. An overcast sky or a shift of wind would have brought disaster, but soon it blew up strong and true on the port quarter.

Beachy Head is 60 miles northwest of St Valery. William intended to make the shortest crossing he could from territory under his control, but it is a region of baffling tides. The ships were heavily laden and carried small working sails and no light canvas. From the time taken for the crossing, only 12 hours, we can be sure the wind was force 5 or 6 all night, enough to make most landsmen sick. It was an astonishingly fast passage.

When the *Mora* anchored off Beachy Head just before dawn (6 a.m.) it must have been nearly low tide for she entered Pevensey Haven at 9 a.m. and could hardly have sailed in before half flood. The wind had fallen light, for the *Mora* waited in the mist for the rest of the fleet to come up. Was William lucky that the soldier's wind had failed just before he drove on to the English cliffs, or had his navigator picked up the bottom line with his lead?

A man was sent to the masthead while the Duke broached a cask of wine, at least appearing confident that all those ships would find him in the mist without disaster. For a while the man saw nothing, then the late September sun broke through the morning mist and he saw a forest of masts approaching. The tide had turned and took them to Pevensey Bay and all the ships are supposed to have sailed through the narrow entrance on that tide. In fact they must have taken two or three. William had achieved complete tactical surprise by his night crossing, and good luck on top of good judgement gave him perfect conditions for landing.

As always we know about the commander-in-chief and his knights and bishops. The man we most want to know about is the 'fleet navigator' but he, like the sailing masters of the ships, is un-known. It was a wonderful feat to get that great fleet of deep-laden ships across in good order. Good luck alone could hardly have accomplished it, but bad luck and bad management could have spread those hundreds of ships over hundreds of square miles of sea.

Today we can hardly understand the awful ambition that led a man who had absolute power over a fertile dukedom to hazard all and sail overseas with virtually his whole fighting force. There was no overpopulation in Normandy nor was he a landless younger son. But William was a vassal of the king of France and he could only exist as a king. And if any of his captains that evening at St Valery had refused to go, he would have done to them as he had done to others: flayed them alive. Some call it strength of purpose and some call it megalomania.

Pevensey Haven was a great lagoon to the east of the ruins of the Roman castle. Some remnants of the Roman port facilities may still have existed when William disembarked, but there were marshes north and east and the fleet seems to have sailed on to Hastings for the main landing. Harold arrived back in London on 6 October and was on the battlefield by the evening of the 13th; 24 hours later he lay dead by the hoar apple tree.

England had not seen the last of invasion. In 1069 the Danes, free at last of threats from Norway, made a landfall off the coast of Kent with 250 ships and sailed north to the Humber probing the defences of Dover, Sandwich, Ipswich and Norwich on the way and finding them all firmly held. Profiting from Hardradi's downfall they landed nearer the sea and, joined by a Saxon army, defeated the Norman garrison at York. But when they heard that William was on his way north they retreated to their ships and entrenched themselves on Axholme Island in the midst of the rivers and fens to the south of the Humber. William defeated another Saxon army and the Danes re-occupied York. William then laid waste all the country round and forced them back to their ships.

In 1070 Swein himself arrived, but some of his crews joined Hereward on the Isle of Ely and William's ships arrived to close the exits to the sea. By summer Swein and William had made peace and the Danes sailed away leaving Hereward to fight on his own. Hereward fought long and well in the watery maze round Ely just as Alfred had fought well at Athelney. Both campaigns were essentially amphibious and probably made use of crude plank-built punts like the Somerset peat punt in the National Maritime Museum. In 1072 William's fleet sailed up the east coast to Scotland in support of the army and Malcolm did homage to him on the banks of the Tay.

In the years between, William sailed back and forth to Normandy, ever on the move and always fighting somewhere. The last Danish invasion came in 1075 when another Cnut led 200 ships to the northern shores. But the last Saxon rebels were broken and the castles of Northumberland stood firm. In 1085 the same Cnut in alliance with the King of Norway and the Count of Flanders planned what must have seemed to William to be the greatest threat yet, with so many ships and men able to sail from bases so near to England. He did not plan to meet it at sea but moved all his supplies away from the southern coasts and recruited a great force of foreign mercenaries to fight on the beaches or as near them as possible. His experience was so vast that we should be very unwise to criticise his strategy. The invasion fleet assembled in the Limfjord too late to sail that year, and the following summer the murder of Cnut brought the threat to an end.

The Viking age was over for England; Norway and Denmark no longer seem to be bothered by overpopulation. Both sides of the Channel were firmly held and Normans were soon to build their castles in Wales and Ireland. Christianity put an end to slavery and denied the Scandinavians one reason for raiding. The Church decreed that one man have only one wife and reduced the number of landless young men of noble birth.

The discovery of the Holy Sepulchre in 333 caused a growing stream of men and women to visit the holy places. By the 10th century the number was enough to make extra demands on shipping and by the 11th pilgrims from all the northern nations made the journeys to Santiago de Compostella in northwest Spain, Monte Gargano and Rome, and the Holy Land itself. Scandinavians often went out by sea via Gibraltar and the Mediterranean and back along the Russian rivers to the Baltic. The monks of Cluny had hostels on many routes, some especially for Norsemen.

Some pilgrim parties numbered thousands, and while those that started by sea from Britain and Scandinavia must have been much smaller, bands of fifty at least must have boarded ships for Boulogne or Quentavic, Bordeaux or Corunna. They were men and women of all ages and social status, sick and well. On the longer voyages some must have been given covered accommodation and the wealthiest separate cabins.

Men from all over the north went on the First Crusade. Edgar Aetheling, scion of Alfred's line, hurried out from Scotland in 1097 and turned up at St Symeon in command of an English manned imperial fleet loaded with siege engines. In 1107 a Norwegian fleet under royal command sailed from Bergen in Norway to Acre in Palestine where the timely appearance of a Venetian squadron saved it from defeat by a Fatimid fleet.

Though men still fought they also thought of higher things and the following century saw the slow development, not of the slender ships of war, but the round ships; the cogs, nefs and busses, carrying cargoes of stockfish, wine, wool and building stone on their lawful occasions. Where the 10th century knarrs had filled their holds with slaves, the ships of the succeeding centuries carried the building materials for the great cathedrals.

20 Navigation, Pilotage and Seamanship

I beseech the immaculate Master of Monks
To steer my journeys
May the Lord of the lofty heavens
Hold his strong hand over me

HAFGERDINGA LAY

Man only learned to fix his position on the open sea three centuries ago, when he discovered how to find his longitude by lunar observation and lengthy mathematics. He was still without an accurate clock. He learned to measure latitude at sea perhaps a thousand years earlier.

We do not know how the Neolithic and Bronze Age peoples of Europe found their way across the sea, but we know something about the methods used by the Neolithic sailors of the Pacific whose navigators formed a very special aristocracy of the sea. Polynesian navigators were trained for up to ten years with the aid of models and standing stones until they could memorise all the stars that marked thirty or more points around the horizon. They learned the positions of hundreds of stars, for during a night's sail they steered on a succession of stars which when they touched the horizon as they rose and set formed leading marks. In cross-currents or when making leeway the Polynesian navigator 'aimed off' by steering on yet another sequence of stars.

There is little evidence that they took latitude sights as we understand them. They had no basic theoretical knowledge but they had discovered over the years that each island was associated with a star which at its zenith passed directly or almost directly over it (i.e. the declination of the star equalled the latitude of the island). These stars they also knew by heart. The proa or double canoe was sailed north or south until the navigator lying on his back judged the island's star to be overhead, then he turned the boat east or west to run down the latitude to the landfall. There was still a margin of error and the final course was corrected by the smell of the land, the set of the swell, the reflection of the island on the cloud above, or the flight of birds. The nights in the central Pacific are long and clear; there is little twilight and the sea is too deep for sound-

---

The only miles quoted in this book are nautical miles but the adjective has been retained in this chapter to stress the link between arc and distance. One minute of latitude equals 2027 yards or one nautical mile.

ings. Whether Polynesian navigation was wholly indigenous or originated in the lands from which their ancestors came is uncertain.

No doubt the Bronze Age peoples of northern Europe had an equal knowledge of the stars. Professor Thom has shown that the hundreds of stone circles, crosses and lines in Britain and Brittany were laid out by practical Pythagorean geometry and many of the stones were positioned to foretell or record the movements of the sun, moon and bright stars. The unit of measurement used in the planning of the monuments seems to have been the distance between the fingertips of the architect when he stood with arms outstretched, the 'megalithic fathom'. It is tempting to regard monuments like Stonehenge in England, Calanish in the Hebrides, or Carnac in Brittany as 2nd millennium navigational academies or standing nautical almanacs but it is unlikely, although they were erected by seafaring peoples and many are close to the sea. The European megaliths must have functioned primarily as calendars showing farmers the times of sowing and harvest, and priests and chiefs the dates of public functions, not as nautical almanacs.* The Polynesian standing stones or 'stones of voyaging' pointed the courses to distant islands. The night before he sailed a navigator could refresh his memory by watching his leading stars cut the horizon in line with the stones. If any of the European monoliths were placed for the same reason they have not yet been identified. Professor Thom's surveys show that many of the 'circles' are really ellipses or egg-shapes, which suggests that they were not intended as sidereal compasses.

The longest Bronze Age passages were probably Brittany to the Scillies, 100 nautical miles, and Shetland to Norway, 190 nautical miles, but we do not know for certain that either took place. The majority of crossings were short enough to be made in daylight, and in northern summers days are long and nights short. But between Shetland and Norway boats would have had to spend two nights at sea and it would have helped vastly to steer on a star.

The sun must have been the normal guide to direction and the stars would only have been used on calm clear nights. At night or when 'lost' by day the sea was generally shallow enough for the navigator to feel the bottom with his lead—Neolithic peoples fished in 100 fathoms and could therefore sound to equal depth. In medieval times the memories of the men who sailed the Bay of Biscay, the Channel and the North Sea were filled not so much with

* A good example is contained in Abbot Ceolfrid's letter to the king of the Picts in AD 710 telling him how to calculate the date of Easter from astronomical observation. (Bede, *History of the English Church and People*.)

the risings and settings of the stars as with soundings and the com-
position of the seabed, mile by mile around the coasts of northern
Europe.

From the 4th century BC at the latest the scientists of the Mediterranean world began to lay the basis of astronomical navigation.
Pytheas of Massilia (Marseilles), who lived in the time (330 BC) of
Alexander the Great, obtained the lengths of mid-day shadows
cast by gnomons at Massilia and Constantinople and concluded
that they were on the same latitude. He set up his experiment at
Massilia under ideal conditions. The lengths of his gnomon and its
shadow at noon have come down to us at second or third hand and
indicate that he was within 15 minutes of the actual latitude or 15
nautical miles. Whoever made the measurements at Constantinople was less successful: difference between the latitudes of the
two places is 2° 17' or 137 nautical miles. Since they had no
accurate figures for the sun's declination the experiment could
only be carried out twice a year, at the equinoxes. Pytheas also
observed the sun in Iceland or Norway, and finding that it did not
set in mid-summer decided that he was a long way north of
Massilia.

Eratosthenes (276–196 BC) established several other parallels of
latitude. Hipparchus made a star catalogue about 160 BC and
measured longitude by comparing the times of an eclipse of the
moon at various places and working out the longitude from the
difference. Columbus was the first man to find longitude by this
method in the New World and his error was 18° in latitude 10° N
or about 1000 nautical miles.

Hipparchus or someone else about the same date invented the
astrolabe for measuring the sun's altitude, but the seaman's astrolabe was not introduced until the 13th century AD at the earliest
and probably not until 1484. In its shipboard form it was a heavy
metal ring of up to 9 in. (23 cm) in diameter with a sighting arm
pivoted in the centre. One navigator held the astrolabe by the
shackle on top, allowing it to hang plumb. Another adjusted the
alidade or arm until the sunbeam shining through the hole in its
outer end appeared as a spot of light on the graduated ring. Pole
Star sights were taken by sighting directly through the holes.

There is no evidence that the Egyptians, Phoenicians, Greeks or
Romans took latitude sights *at sea* though Pytheas undoubtedly
made careful observations at his ports of call. Greek scientists
deduced that the earth was round from horizon observations and
attempted to calculate its diameter. Renaissance scientists 2000
years later were a long way out and so probably were the Greeks.

The maps of Ptolemy and Plato, supreme intellects of their day, were little more than crude sketches based on hearsay and useless for navigation.

The Arabs seem to have been the only western people who practised stellar navigation during our period. Their navigational treatises were in the form of poems to make it easier to memorise the immense amount of data. They contain Pole Star altitudes for places on the coasts of the Red Sea and the Indian Ocean, 'compass' bearings, sailing dates and distances. The poems we have date from the 15th century, but G R Tibbetts has shown that the tradition dates back to 1000 AD or possibly before. Ibn Majid's longest poem of the late 15th century AD contains 1082 verses.

The oldest instrument certainly known to have been used for latitude observation at sea is the Arab *kamal*, probably used in the Indian Ocean and the Red Sea before the 10th century AD but not known to European navigators before the Portuguese reached Indian waters in 1497. It is still in use on Arab dhows and is a rectangular board with a cord to its centre point. Knots in the length of the cord correspond to the latitudes of the ports of call. The observer holds the selected knot to his eye, holds the board in front of him at the full stretch of the string, and aligns the star with the top edge and the horizon with the bottom edge. The depth of the board is four *isba*, the width of four fingers, and 224 *isba* were considered to equal 360°. The Arabs used the rising and setting points of stars to indicate direction before the 10th century AD.

The quadrant used by the Portuguese navigators who sailed down the west coast of Africa in the 15th century AD relied on a plumbline instead of the horizon and could only be used in a dead calm sea. Two observers were needed, one sighting the Pole Star while the other watched the plumbline; the error due to eye position alone could be $1\frac{1}{2}°$ and the two men had to correlate their readings. The quadrant was not used in earlier times but shows the errors possible with crude instruments. The Pole Star was used by the Portuguese and the Arabs because it needs no correction for declination; also because direct observation of the sun results in temporary blindness, and early smoked glass introduced other errors.

It is difficult to believe that any form of latitude observation was used on short voyages made much before the 10th century AD. Crude star observations are only useful on long north–south voyages like those of the Polynesians from Hawaii to New Zealand (3600 miles) and the Arabs in the Red Sea (1200 miles).

Some of the Roman administrators who came with Julius Caesar would have been in touch with all the astronomical knowledge of the Mediterranean world (the booklet on the Roman villa at Brading, Isle of Wight suggests that the astronomer pictured on the mosaic floor is Hipparchus). But from the point of view of practical navigation it would not have amounted to much. The Mediterranean is narrow from north to south and long east to west and it is most unlikely that latitude observations were taken there. The scientists of the Roman world with all the experience of the Greeks, Babylonians and Egyptians behind them could take fairly accurate readings with simple instruments on land, but these experiments could not be repeated at sea. They could read and express themselves accurately and fluently, do arithmetic and geometry, and had made progress in more advanced mathematics, but they still used Roman numerals. The Babylonians are said to have divided the circle into 360 parts but there is no evidence that anyone had yet expressed latitude in degrees. Indeed the Romans, like Pytheas before and the Vikings afterwards, described latitude in terms of hours of daylight. Eratosthenes expressed 23° 51′ as $\frac{11}{166}$ of a circle.

The Saxon emigrants were farmer-sailors and would have known the principal stars well enough to steer by them and keep time. They would have observed the sun's declination but been unable to quantify it even if they had so desired. The science of navigation would have made no progress through them for they did not need it. In this and earlier migrations man's knowledge of geography rested on the evidence of his eyes and the memories of those few who had sailed before and come back, or who had talked to others who had. His ships were so unseaworthy, his crew and passengers so precious, and their physical endurance on the open sea without shelter so limited, he could not risk bad weather, cold, wind or fog.

Professional fishermen from Neolithic times onward may have gone far offshore, unlike the migrants who kept close to land and sought the short sea crossings. But the fishermen and their forebears had fished the same locality for centuries and their boats were not overloaded with families and animals. They would have known where the land lay and felt their way over the seabed by lead line when the guiding stars were hidden.

They alone, confident in their boats and their seamanship, could have risked being caught out in bad weather, but the chances they took were great and many would have been lost. The ability of simple men to forecast weather is strictly limited as they can have only a few hours' warning of change. The possibility that seamen had an instinct that we no longer have is not borne out by the facts. Warrington Smythe in *Mast and Sail in Europe and Asia* recorded that when a seamen's society presented the Danish fishermen with barometers in the 19th century the casualty rate dropped dramatically.

Man rarely sails completely into the unknown. The American and Russian astronauts did not leave earth's gravity until they were sure they could maintain an exact course from lift-off until final landing. Columbus thought he knew where he was going and believed his globes and charts were correct.

But the Irish monks were in a class by themselves. Somewhere off the Celtic shipping lanes they expected to find a 'river of Eden' or an 'earthly paradise' and by prayer and abstinence they hoped divine guidance would lead them to it. In their search for solitude and grace they probed the northern seas, commending their souls to God and venturing further and further into the unknown. They could mostly read and write but it is doubtful if any of them had any technical knowledge that gave a lead over other explorers. But as the years rolled on, in spite of the garbled accounts of Saint Brendan's voyages, the stories the monks brought back to their brethren formed the basis for someone else to venture further. Their stories would have come under the critical scrutiny of educated men like Adamnan, Abbot of Iona; men who had travelled widely. The monastic libraries may have become storehouses of practical geography and perhaps the Vikings benefited by them. But whatever knowledge the wandering saints passed on, the secret of their discoveries is to be found not in their knowledge of astronomy but in the psychology of martyrdom.

Before talking about Viking navigation we must pause to consider two great aids to course-keeping at sea, the rudder and the sail. The rudder enables one to sit or stand in relative comfort to steer on a star, and the athwartship tiller used by many early peoples enabled the helmsman to face aft and steer on a back bearing if necessary. The so-called steering oars of the Saxons and Vikings are really quarter rudders, quite as efficient as our central ones. We do not know when the quarter rudder was adopted in the north for no hint of anything pre-Roman or Saxon has been found. It must have come at least as early as the fully rigged sail which may have been around 500 BC. And it was probably invented in the north, for although the Mediterranean peoples used rudders in 2000 BC they used *twin* quarter rudders which as far as we know were never put on non-Roman ships in the north. The true steering oar seen on the carvings of Celtic boats calls for more effort and is difficult to use when facing aft. The quarter rudder turned by a tiller was an enormous improvement.

With a constant wind a helmsman can steer a sailing boat by sheeting the sail at the proper angle and holding a course to keep a clean flow of air around it. None of the ancient sailing ships could sail closer than 70° to the wind, but when it was abeam or abaft and blowing steadily from the same point they could be steered in the right direction without the aid of compass or stars.

Nobody, Viking, Roman, Greek or Phoenician, used the magnetic compass, but Odysseus (1000 BC) steered on the Pleiades, Arcturus and Orion and kept the Bear (or Dipper) on his left hand side when sailing east. Scholars may have shown the north-seeking qualities of a piece of magnetised iron floated in a bowl of water; they may have even demonstrated it on a boat in harbour in the stillness of evening. But it would not have worked in a small ship in a smart breeze when the crew had to brace themselves against being thrown about and the sea went 'thump, thump, thump' against the bottom. Only in flat calm and fog would it have been of any use. If there had been any light in the sky at all the navigator would have deduced the sun's approximate position and steered by that. And the terrific magnetic variation in the northwest Atlantic was to trouble much later navigators.

The Vikings almost certainly used a light-gathering crystal to show them the direction of the sun when the sky was overcast, and modern Faroese fishermen turned a knifeblade point down on the thumbnail to find the sun's direction by the diminishing shadow. The navigators of Transport Command of the Royal Air Force were instructed to check the magnetic compass against the sun compass every hour. If the Vikings ever used a floating needle in a ship they would have had to be very careful lest a sword, an axe, a mail shirt, or the enormous iron nails of the ship itself caused it to swing.

The Norwegians began to settle in Iceland in 870 AD. It seemes very likely that whatever navigational methods they used were developed not during their early raiding and trading in the narrow seas but when they adventured north and west. Not only did the voyages lengthen out to 350 miles east–west across open sea and 1000 and 700 miles north–south along the coasts of Norway and Greenland respectively, but they entered a region beyond the softness of more southern seas where exposure killed and ship-wreck starved.

When the Norwegians were settling in Iceland the Swedes were in touch with the learning of Byzantium and were trading with the Arabs, who had oceanic navigational techniques.

The Norse Vikings are said to have measured latitude by a shadow board with a gnomon which could be raised or lowered according to the sun's declination. The board was floated in a bowl of water to give an artificial horizon. Professor Samuel Eliot Morrison says they had declination tables but this is an oversimplification. Modern tables give the sun's altitude every two hours for every day of the year, the change every 24 hours being between 22 minutes in March and 2 seconds on mid-summer day, i.e. between 22 nautical miles and zero. The Norse had nothing like this; they did not know what a degree of latitude was and could not conceive the division of a right angle into 5400 parts. At the most, they could have had five or six notches on the gnomon giving approximate changes in declination between March when the sailing season started and mid-summer, the gnomon being raised notch by notch at about fortnightly intervals and correspondingly lowered between 21 June and September when the ships were laid up.

The errors must have accumulated in such a frightening way that only a very few, very careful and gifted captains would have used the instrument. A 1° error is equivalent to 60 nautical miles, and there was observation error, declination error, instrument error, and error due to water slopping about in the bowl. They might have added up to 200 nautical miles north or south of the actual position.

If they used it at all it is much more likely that captains took the 'shadow board' ashore when coasting along Greenland or Norway, on the day when they knew from experience that the declination notch was correct. This way they might have cut the error to perhaps $\frac{1}{2}°$ or 30 nautical miles. There is no mention in the sagas of any instrument for taking latitudes at sea, and the latitudes of places on the coast of America were only expressed as so many hours of day and night.

It is doubtful if the Vikings took star shots at sea though we cannot rule out the possibility. Polaris shots would have presented considerable difficulties to them, although to us its angle above the horizon is constant and it neither rises nor sets. But in northern latitudes where summer daylight lasts nearly 24 hours Polaris is only seen in spring and autumn, and in the 11th century it was 7° off the Pole (in Bronze Age times 12°). Unless difficult corrections were applied it could be observed only once in 24 hours.

It may be argued that 16th century mariners practised astro-navigation with crude measuring devices, so why not the Vikings. The later captains sailed much greater distances and aimed at continents and not small islands. The back-staff and cross-staff were considerably better than anything the Vikings possessed; and the Renaissance captains usually sailed in lower latitudes.

Even in the 19th century there were hundreds of small ship skippers who voyaged far and wide on dead reckoning only and did not know how to take sights. The Vikings were probably the same, and although a very very few may have been able to navigate to the limits of the knowledge of the time most would have used simpler methods. Few of them could write and so they must have kept account of course and distance by some sort of traverse board—'a round boord full of holes like a compasse—upon which by the moving of a little sticke, they keep account how…they steare'—as Captain John Smith described one in 1627. The Viking traverse board would have been cruder still because the compass rose was unknown to them.

Speed reckoning cannot have presented much of a problem for their ships were all much of a kind and their performance only varied between narrow limits. The best short measure of time if they needed one was the seaman's pulse-beat. The hour glass was a much later invention, which came to be used with a knotted log line, but it does not seem to have been very accurate. To quote Captain John Smith again, 'Some use a log line and minute glasse to know what way she makes, but…it is not worth the labour to trie it.'

Perhaps the final word on Norse methods is a paragraph in the *Hauksbok* which describes a position reached in a voyage up the west coast of Greenland in 1267:

> Albeit the sun shone both by night and by day, being no higher in the south than that a man lying across a six-oarer with his head against the side had the shadow of the gunwale nearest the sun upon his face, though at midnight the sun stood as high as at home in the settlement when in the northwest.

That expedition possibly reached 76° N. Anyone who had made such a marvellous voyage would have fixed his 'farthest north' by a better means than that if he had had one.

Information about courses and winds was given to the early captain in the form of sailing directions, the periplus of the ancient Mediterranean and the rutter (route-er) of the medieval north. The number of people who could read in pre-Roman Britain could probably have been counted on the fingers of two hands and in Viking times it was still a rare accomplishment. We can picture the landbound merchant or his educated slave reading the periplus or rutter to the captain who memorised the distances, landfalls, winds and currents.

Medieval sailing directions gave soundings up to 100 fathoms and described the seabed as fair grey sand, white sand, clear sand, black ooze, clay ground, etc. The hand lead with a 6 lbs (2.7 kg) weight and 20 fathoms of line could be cast when the ship was moving. The old-fashioned deep sea lead had 100 fathoms of line with a 28 lbs (12.7 kg) weight and the ship had to be stopped when it was used. There are illustrations of both lead and sounding pole being used in the period of this book.

The longest voyage made by the Vikings was a regular direct crossing from Hernoe near Bergen in Norway to Greenland—1500 nautical miles. The sailing directions were as follows:

Sail west passing Shetland just in sight to port.
Continue west passing the southernmost mountains of Faroes half below the horizon.
Continue west keeping south of Iceland 'so that the seabirds and whales can be seen' [i.e. skirt the Iceland fishing grounds, which teemed with whales and seabirds in medieval times].
Continue west until sighting Hvitserk [high land in south Greenland].
Turn southwest towards Cape Farewell.

This voyage was almost due west along the 61st parallel, but there is no mention of sun sights whatever.

Even if the early navigator had been able to find his position accurately he would not have been able to plot it and lay off a new course: he had no chart. A chart is a representation of the world's surface properly projected from a globe onto flat paper or parchment and therefore correct to scale in latitude and longitude. The first true chart was Mercator's Chart of the World of 1569. Unless the basis of the chart is correct any course drawn on it, although apparently leading to the destination, will be incorrect.

We take charts for granted today, but the accurate network of parallels and meridians with each degree interval subdivided was one of the major achievements of the 16th century and nothing like it was known to the Vikings or their predecessors. The so-called Polynesian charts were only memory aids. They look like ornamental table mats made of sticks and shells and are not to scale nor geographical in layout. Properly interpreted, and there is probably no-one still alive who can do it, the number of shells and the slant of the straws, etc. enabled the man who made the 'map' to remember the islands and the winds and currents. The Bering Strait Eskimos scratched similar information on bone and ivory.

In bad weather early ships probably ran before the wind under a bare pole. They could not have clawed up to windward under reduced sail, and with loose boulders as ballast they would have preferred to keep the wind off the beam. Viking ships were symmetrical fore and aft about a central mast and therefore neutral in yaw. They must have steered beautifully (the tiller of the Gokstad ship is only 40 in. (1 m) long) and perhaps a scrap of canvas was lashed up forward to hold them downwind. These were the vessels and sailing conditions in which America was discovered. After days of anxious running and rolling, the ballast moving and grinding in the bilge, land showed up ahead.

The altitude of the land astern and the landfall ahead made all the difference. Coming from Norway or the Faroes to Iceland ships steered to sight Vatnajokull (7000 ft). Sailing from Iceland to Greenland Eirik the Red kept Snaefelsness (4744 ft) in sight astern for as long as he could. Altitude and the frequent mirage conditions of northern latitudes enormously increased the sighting distances, and modern sailors confirm old records that Iceland and Greenland could sometimes be seen at the same time from the middle of the Denmark Strait.

The *Landnamabok* records that a man called Floki carried ravens. These are non-migratory birds, large enough and black enough to be watched to 5000 ft and able to see nearly 80 nautical miles from that altitude. R G Bowden, who drew the maps in this book, suggests that ravens have the further advantage of being easy to feed. On his first day out from the Faroes, Floki released a raven when he was well out of sight of land. It flew back the way he had come. Next day another raven climbed high into the sky but seeing no land returned to the ship. On the third day a raven flew off to westward and Floki followed its direction until they sighted Iceland. Noah of course used birds and similar stories are found in Roman and Buddhist literature (5th century BC). There is every possibility that the Irish monks followed geese migrating to Iceland in the spring and returning in the autumn. Leif Eiriksson recognised the approach of land by the sighting of land birds. This sort of sea lore—birds, the loom of the land, clouds over the peaks—checked and re-checked, was immortalised by the late Harold Gatty in the *Raft Book* written during World War II to help sailors and airmen adrift in the Pacific.

It is difficult for us to realise how coarse the early peoples steered. They divided the azimuth circle either by applying the directions of the eight winds, or by adding to the points N, S, E and W the points of mid-summer and mid-winter sunset and sunrise and imaginary similar points east and west of N and S. This divided the circle into twelve unequal parts.

A Viking standing on the coast of Norway would have divided the horizon into N, S, E, W and then subdivided into out-north, out-south, land-north, land-south, meaning NW, SW, NE and SE, terms already used by the Anglo Saxons. This made eight points only, and when they talked of steering north they meant any direction within $22\frac{1}{2}°$ either side of north.

Map 7 shows the North Atlantic winds and currents in May 1970. In the Viking age they were probably much the same. Little sailing took place before May or after September, and the same general pattern persists throughout the summer though there are detail differences from month to month. The diagram on the map shows the only winds which a square-rigged vessel of the era could use.

To sail due west, for example, all winds blowing from 340° westwards to 200° were useless. The modern yacht able to sail to within 45° of the wind would tack, but tacking in a ship unable to sail with the wind more than 20° before the beam is a wearisome business and the Viking would either have waited for a favourable wind or sailed on the nearest practical course, trusting to a later wind shift to take him towards his destination. The wind roses show that in the eastern Atlantic outward bound there is a good chance of this happening. From the Faroes to the normal landfall in Iceland, for about 50 per cent of the time the winds are favourable and blow at force 4. The course is 313°. If a captain insisted on sailing on a west wind his best track would be 340°, i.e. 27° to the north of his ideal course, which after two days' sailing at 5 knots would have put him 119 nautical miles off course. To avoid this, at some point he would have had to turn southwest on to 200° and after ten hours or so turned back on to his original course to fetch his landfall. The essential thing to remember is that he had no chart on which to lay off his tracks!

In addition to all his other mental filing, the northern mariner had to memorise the known tidal data for the chief ports in his area. In medieval times there were neat little tide-roses to help him. Tides were thought to be 45 minutes later each day; 45 minutes is $\frac{1}{32}$ part of 24 hours and was drawn as a segment of a rose showing 32 bearings of the moon. 'Moon NE/SW Dover' meant high tide was 3 hours after the *new* moon had crossed the meridian at Dover, i.e. northeast; and the next high tide was 12 hours later, i.e. south-west. These were spring tides.

But no tide-roses are known from Viking, Saxon or Roman times when the horizon circle was only divided into 8 or 12 parts, and the pre-medieval tidal data must have been considerably less refined, as well as sparser. And even the medieval shipman was only given the date and time of the *new* moon. He had to keep his own calendar and correct for other dates, adding or subtracting 45 minutes for every day after or before the new moon date. He was a long, long way from our world of exact measurement, without the poorest sort of watch or clock, and the 45 minutes is an average figure for a period which varies widely. There is an Anglo Saxon pocket sundial in existence but it is only calibrated for the times of church services, and it had of course to be orientated N–S in use.

Unfettered natural selection may have produced men of higher ability than ourselves whose senses, unblunted by technological aids, were keener. But they could not do the impossible. They could measure neither time nor distance accurately so could never have been certain whether they were running at 7 knots or 6. They could not determine longitude and therefore their most careful shipboard star sights, if they made them at all, could only have put them in a position rectangle that covered an error of 100 miles from north to south and an unknown distance from east to west. Therefore they sailed the shortest possible distances between land masses and to be at sea a week was a long voyage; even then they did not intend to be out of sight of land or the indication of land more than 48 hours.

Throughout this period the good longshoreman was superior *on his own coast* to the best far-ranging skipper. Even the modern yachtsman finds this however carefully he studies his pilot books and charts. But whereas the yachtsman rarely takes a pilot, the foreign-going Roman, Saxon or Viking would have done so as often as he could find one by force or fair dealing. The most elaborate mnemonics in the most retentive mind could not provide all the information, and his ship was so underpowered that he had to work his tides with the utmost care.

Ships wrecked or missing must have been dreadfully frequent. The proportion of youth, recklessness and unbridled temper was much higher when the world was younger. There were no master's certificates nor the most elementary checks on seaworthiness. The hothead and the happy-go-lucky sailed without weather forecasts or barometers.

'Where is my wandering boy tonight?' was not only a Victorian lament. From the Ice Age to the Crusades there were also mothers and wives who gazed out over angry seas with dread in their hearts.

Dockyards and Craftsmen

King Harald...had a ship built at Eyrar. Its
prow had a dragon's head and its stern had a
dragon's tail, and the bows were inlaid with
gold. It had 35 pairs of rowing benches...The
king had all the fittings made with the utmost care

King Harald's Saga

All these ships needed harbours, but in the whole sweep of the north European coast hardly any fixtures remain. Honor Frost has described the ancient harbours of Tyre and Sidon. Tyre means rock, and in 1000 BC it was a rocky island joined to the mainland by a causeway removed in time of war. There were harbours on both sides of the island, the western one built of 9 ton blocks of stone. It could be closed and defended. At Sidon cisterns cut in the rock wall were filled by heavy sea swell above the level of the harbour water. Guillotine sluices released it to wash the silt out of the harbour.

Caesar's description of the Veneti strongholds in Brittany would have fitted Tyre. 'Most of the...strongholds were so situated on the ends of spits...it was impossible to approach them by land when the tide rushed in...' The tide range in Brittany is enormous and the Romans found they could not reach them by ship at low tide. Sometimes they went to the enormous labour of building causeways. Some of the remaining Iron Age camps of Brittany fit his description. But there is no reason to expect elaborate harbour works like those of Tyre or Sidon. Ships loaded and unloaded on whichever side of an island gave a lee. In bad weather they would have been drawn up on shore or run to shelter in whichever of Brittany's great natural harbours lay to leeward.

Strabo's description of the tin trade in Cornwall at a place which sounds like St Michael's Mount suggests another pre-Roman port of Tyrian characteristics at the opposite end of the trade route to the Breton strongholds. From the 11th century AD Mont St Michel and St Michael's Mount were associated Benedictine monasteries.

The other sort of harbour was situated as far inland as the tide would go, unlike today when as ships get larger and larger ports get nearer the sea until finally enormous engineering works create new harbours in the open sea. York is a perfect example of an early inland harbour; Canterbury, Rouen, Bruges and Dorestad were others.

There was possibly a third type of harbour, an island further off-shore where by agreement cargoes were transferred to local ships from foreign ships that were part pirate, part trader. This may have happened off the northern coast of Minoan Crete.

Nowadays we take harbours for granted, but this has not always been so. At Carradale on the Mull of Kintyre there is a snug little harbour that looks as though it has been there for centuries. But it was built in 1962 and you can still buy postcards showing a dozen 40 ton fishing boats hauled out on the rocky shore.

The Roman naval beaching point at Caer Gybi stands at the inner end of Holyhead harbour. Its frontage along the beach is about 70 yards and the fort is about 70 by 40 yards. The walls ran down over the beach enclosing the foreshore as was done also at Engers and elsewhere on the Rhine. Ten biremes or triremes could have been beached at Caer Gybi in reasonable safety from Irish raiders who had landed at some hidden cove.

There is very little left of Roman naval works, but by the very size and nature of their fleets we can recreate Roman dockyards at say Boulogne, Dover or Rouen without straining credulity. Actual *dockyard* sites are not known except perhaps Lydney on the river Severn, which is known only from a reference to the commander of the dockyard there.

In Nelson's time a Royal Dockyard had an enclosing wall, superintendent's house, offices for clerks and draughtsmen, covered boat store and building berths, timber stocks, rope walk, blacksmith's shop, sail loft, oar-making machinery. There are no exact plans of earlier dockyards but the installations must have been the same. English dockyards in the 16th century covered about eight acres to support a fleet of the same tonnage as the Classis Britannica; that of 14th century Venice was about the same acreage for the same size fleet; and the headquarters of the galleys of Saint John at Malta enclosed two or three acres for far fewer ships.

Roman warship design was not just a rule-of-thumb business. Archimedes had discovered the law of displacement around 200 BC and the Romans were never too proud to learn from foreigners. Their public buildings were designed by professional architects who used drawings.* Furthermore Roman dockyards were called upon to build all sorts of special ships: catamarans with multiple artillery, transports, landing craft, imperial barges, yachts. Suetonius even tells us about a collapsing ship designed for a political murder.

* The architects of the Gothic cathedrals used full mould loft techniques for setting out the features of their buildings. The plaster 'tracing floor' of Wells Cathedral (1175–92) can still be seen. (The author's grandfather, a master shipwright, used to draw his lines on the plaster wall of an attic bedroom.) The largest Viking ship could probably have been built without drawings; whether it was is another matter.

The Classis Britannica used more or less standard galleys which if they needed drying out in the Mediterranean needed it just as much in the Channel, where they probably required repair and refit even more frequently. One wonders how much the galleys leaked when they were put back into the water. Was the elaborate mortice and tenon system of locking the planks together partly designed to prevent the seams opening? If so, what happened to the strain locked up in the hull when the wood shrank?

Since nothing resembling a stone or brick ship-house has been found outside the Mediterranean we must assume not that there were no covered berths but that they were wood framed with perhaps open sides. As the Classis Britannica had tiles stamped CLBR the roofs of its ship-houses and other dockyard buildings were generally tiled. When the Romans withdrew they probably burned the ship-shelters or left them to be plundered for building material. Certainly there cannot have been anything of the permanence and architectural magnificence of the galley bases at Athens or Carthage. Just sloping ramps in the tidal mud, a capstan per ship, a roof and perhaps a bed of brushwood for the galley to rest on. The Graveney boat was hauled out on just such a mattress in the 10th century but she was only a small merchant vessel: perhaps they hoped to sell her better by keeping the buyer's feet clean.

Tackles and windlasses are very ancient, certainly early Bronze Age and probably Neolithic. People who moved 25 ton stones and raised them vertical obviously knew ways of obtaining mechanical advantage. The Ferriby windlass, if we are right in considering the single fork of wood as part of one, is nearly contemporary with Stonehenge.

Only a tiny fraction of Roman organisation is left and what we have from Saxon, Carolingian, Viking and Norman times is almost nil. But the Stone Age peoples of the Pacific stored their war canoes in houses for just the same reason as the peoples of the classical Mediterranean, and there are a few remains of Viking slipways and boathouses including a slipway on Birsay in Orkney. Private boathouses are mentioned in the Saga of Grettir the Strong. The organisation of the barracks at Aggersborg, Trelleborg, Fyrkat and Odense (chapter 16) was so massive, regular and permanent as to suggest people with an almost Roman passion for orderliness and discipline (the unit of measurement was the Roman foot). It is easier to imagine Danish ship-houses than to reject the possibility. When we consider their losses of ships in battle added to those lost at sea, wrecked, stranded and strained beyond repair, some sort of Scandinavian royal dockyard system seems a certainty.

The four Danish barrack camps mentioned were all so close to river or fjord as to suggest adjacent facilities for ship storage and repair. Johannes Brøndsted in *The Vikings* says 'Trelleborg was manifestly a military and naval base…presumed that vessels were towed up the river to the camp and that each of the ship-shaped houses provided quarters for a ship's crew.'

Considering the shipbuilding and barge-building capacity of the pre-Roman peoples of the north, the tremendous Roman and Viking organisation, and remembering that Carolingian and Saxon kings also built similar fleets, we can try to assess the timber, stores, tools and tackle needed and think about the craftsmen who put it all together. There must have been considerable stocks of timber. Roman, Saxon and Viking ships were put together with far too much skill and feeling for structural integrity for the builders to have dreamed of using green timber.

Early shipbuilders used timber of a quality unknown today. The Brigg dugout was carved from a 5 ft (1.5 m) diameter oak which grew to 50 ft (15 m) before the first branches left the main stem. The limewood planks of the Als boat were 25 ft (7.6 m) long by 2 ft (0.6 m) wide. The strakes of the Nydam ship were 80 ft (24 m) long by a foot (0.3 m) broad. And the early shipwrights not only searched for simple straight or curved timber; the builders of the large war-ship from Skuldelev in Denmark sought for and found a 35 ft (14 m) oak trunk with a branch at right angles half way up perfectly situated for conversion into a keelson with integral mast step. It was common practice.

We are away from the Mediterranean world of acacia, cypress and cedar of Lebanon. The normal northern shipbuilding timber was oak. Brigg, Ferriby, Veneti, Blackfriars, New Guys House, County Hall, Nydam, Oseberg, Gokstad, Tune, Skuldelev 2, 3 and 5, Graveney and Utrecht ships were all built of oak. After oak came pine: 2nd Nydam boat, Barset boat, planking of Skuldelev knarr, planking and frames of Skuldelev 6. There remain a few ash planks and some frames of alder. The keelson of Skuldelev 6 was birch and there were odds and ends of lime and birch on one or two boats. Treenails were usually willow, wedged with pine, oak or willow. Spars and oars were pine.

No Roman warships have been found, but it is almost certain those in northern Europe were framed in oak and planked with oak or pine. These were the timbers we should have found stacked in the dockyards of the Classis Britannica and the building sites of Charlemagne, Alfred, Edgar, Cnut, Hardradi and William the Conqueror. The stocks would have been nothing like the quantities in the naval dockyards of Nelson's time. The biggest Roman dockyard in the north might have had about the same amount of timber seasoning as big yacht builders like Fife or Camper & Nicholson in the 1930s.

The principal tool used to make the lugged planks of the Ferriby, Als, Nydam, Oseberg and Gokstad ships was the adze. It also put the hollows in the thwarts of the Als boat just as it dubbed out the hollows in domestic chair seats up to a century ago.

Although there are two-handed bronze saws of 1400 BC in Heraklion museum it is difficult to say if iron pit-saws were used to convert trees into planks before the 12th century AD. The thin tempered blade rusts easily and was extremely difficult for a rural smith to make. We do not know how the Romans made planks during their periods of high speed shipbuilding, but Ausonius mentions water mills for sawing stone.

The saw was not used in the conversion of the timber for the Skuldelev ships. The run of the grain in the oak planks shows they were radially split from the log, up to 32 planks from a tree, each one extending from the centre to the sapwood ring. The pine planks were split across the log, two only from each one. The finished planks show plane marks but not adze marks. They were slightly thicker down the centreline and tapered towards the edges where they were clench-nailed against their fellows. This is a fine example of the exquisite design sense of the northern shipbuilders which shaped every piece of timber in their ships.

Contemporary pictures suggest the trees were converted in the forest and show splitting with wedges. The long-handled tools depicted in the Bayeux Tapestry and described as adzes have the blade in line with the shaft and one is being used like an axe to trim the edge of a plank. The adze was extensively used but it is not so much in evidence as we might expect.

There were about 4000 nails in the big Skuldelev warship, the clench nails being 2 in. (5 cm) long to fasten planks about 1 in. (2.5 cm) thick down the centreline and $\frac{1}{2}$–$\frac{3}{4}$ in. (1.5–2 cm) thick along their edges. When Cnut or Hardradi or Ethelred ordered a levy of a hundred ships the clerk of the ships or whatever his title was had to arrange for the hand forging of half a million nails, half a million roves and the shaping of a hundred thousand treenails, to fasten together twenty or thirty thousand large pieces of carefully shaped timber weighing 5000 tons.

Instead of clench nails the Romans had to make tenons and dowels on the same scale to join very accurately shaped thicker planks edge to edge. They also needed tens of thousands of iron nails up to 2 ft (0.6 m) long to drive through an equal number of pegs in the ribs and planks. Production problems on a similar scale faced the Veneti in Brittany and the river barge builders of northern Europe when they built the transports for their Roman masters.

Celt, Roman, Saxon, Carolingian, Viking and Norman had to drill hundreds of holes $\frac{1}{2}$–2 in. (1.5–5 cm) in diameter and up to 6 in. (15 cm) deep. From at least Roman times onwards they did this with iron shell augers which until the specialisation of toolmaking in the 19th century were made for boatbuilders by local blacksmiths.

Ropewalks undoubtedly existed wherever ships were built. Egyptians, Romans, Anglo-Saxons and Vikings used laid up ropes and the Romans set up their shrouds with lanyards and deadeyes. The raw material of the ropes is less easy to determine. Tollund man was strangled with a two-strand leather rope 2000 years ago and Anglo-Saxon sources say the best ships' ropes were made from walrus hide.

Grass or bass ropes were often used as mooring lines until the invention of synthetic fibres. Uffa Fox watched Breton fishermen making ropes. One end of a handful of rushes was fastened to a twister and a man walked backwards with the free end feeding in fresh rushes from a bundle while his mate turned the handle. Soon they had made a twisted strand 30 fathoms long and then they twisted two together to make a rope. Something like this was done wherever ancient ships were rigged. Roman ships normally carried rope anchor cables since Caesar particularly mentions the Veneti anchor chains. But Honor Frost records that chains were sometimes used to moor warships in the Mediterranean to resist the knives of underwater swimmers. (The sentries were armed with tridents.) The Bayeux Tapestry shows rope cables.

Veneti, Anglo Saxon, Viking and some Roman anchors were of a rather inefficient-looking iron 'fisherman' type. Most Roman anchors, however, were wood, iron fluked and weighted with lead. A Roman anchor stone has been found off the south coast of England. Ancient ships must have carried many anchors to make up for their low holding power.

Of the rope and sailmaking fibres, hemp was grown in Italy and east-central Europe, jute in Greece, esparto grass in eastern Spain. Flax grew in Ulster, Yorkshire, Brittany, northern Spain and the Pas de Calais. Cotton came from Turkey, Egypt and Moorish Spain. Ancient peoples produced excellent materials from unlikely sources. The Natural History Museum in London exhibits a root which a Mesolithic people soaked, pounded, shredded, teased, spun and laid up into an admirable twine. The Ferriby boats were caulked with a rope of hair moss, Gokstad and Skuldelev ships with a tarred rope of animal hair, and the carvel-built Blackfriars ship with crushed hazel withies.

Northern sails were probably made of wool or flax though some cotton may have been used. Wool was available everywhere but the fibres are too soft. Even with the utmost skill in spinning and weaving, and strengthening the seams by doubling and over-lapping, woollen sails must have been too heavy to take up a flow curve in light airs and too weak to hold their shape on the wind in a blow. Flax was the ideal sailcloth material to the end of the sailing era.

In the 19th century Britain naval sailcloth was made up into cloths where the flax grew and sewn up into sails inside or outside the Royal Dockyards. The sail loft, a smooth flat floor large enough to take the largest sail flat and roofed against wind and rain, must have been essential in any period. The quick production of hundreds of sails needed good working conditions. The Bayeux Tapestry and other sources show elaborately decorated sails and we think of hundreds of devoted women stitching or weaving the designs. But these showy sails must have been restricted to 'royal' ships and the designs were probably cut out of fabric and stitched on, or just painted on.

The galleys of the Classis Britannica needed 20,000 oars and 500 200 lbs (91 kg) anchors; the fleets of Cnut, Hardradi or William the Conqueror 25,000 oars and 1000 anchors. These are only approximate figures but the scale is right. Five hundred ships needed at least 20,000 tons of timber, which meant 20,000 trees or more. Such a fleet would have carried 1000 small boats. But a warship needs much more than its hull, sails and oars—it needs flags, missiles, weapons, boarding nets, paint, fittings, furniture and all this the dockyards had to supply.

Roman craftsmen were probably slaves including foremen and possibly even up to superintendent level; they were probably housed inside the dockyards with their families.

The finest craftsmen were the ship decorators. Roman ships appear on bas-reliefs as highly decorated; the ram head was a heavy bronze casting probably more for decoration than use. (Note that it was on the waterline where it increased the sailing length of the ship and was partially supported.)

The men who carved the designs on the Oseberg ship for a Norwegian queen are supreme in shipbuilding history and several are distinguished by their different styles on this one ship. They can scarcely have worked in the open and this reinforces the possibility of covered slips in the Viking period. Almost as good were the craftsmen who carved the stems and sterns of the Skuldelev ships (chapter 18) and the Roman slave craftsmen who made the mortice and tenon joints in the mating faces of their carvel-laid planks.

Stone Age peoples can do it too, like the Gilbert Islanders of the Pacific who obtained perfect flatness between two sections of keel by rubbing soot on one face and noting where it marked the other— the classic method of Maudslay, the pioneer of machine tools.

Examples have been given of the speed of ancient shipbuilding— 220 Roman ships in 90 days, 600 ships built in about 180 days by William the Conqueror—the rate is about equal, 70 to 100 ships per month, 3 or more a day! These are not rare exceptions and are not likely to be exaggerations.

Mass production is the movement of the work from one assembly group to the next and is generally considered to have been invented in American railway works where trucks started as a pair of wheels and moved on railway lines from worker to worker to become complete wagons. In Dante's time visitors reported a similar system in the Arsenal dockyard at Venice. Hulls were towed past one store-house after another while cranes dropped in spars, oars, ammuni-tion, etc. This was two centuries after the last events described in this book, but the launching of three ships a day for two or three months whether by Romans, Vikings or Normans is so astounding as to give us visions of similar fitting-out methods. There is no evidence for it, but these high-speed building programmes are so much more like Henry J Kaiser of Liberty Ship fame than Julius Caesar that we are left wondering how they did it.

Bibliography

Adlard Coles, K and A N Black	North Biscay Pilot, 1970
Admiralty	Channel Pilot
	Irish Coast Pilot
	North Sea Pilot
	Yangtze Kiang Pilot
	Routeing Chart—North Atlantic
	Standard charts
Adney, E T and Chapelle, H I	The Bark Canoes and Skin Boats of N America, 1964
Aitchison, Leslie	A History of Metals, 1960
Anderson, R C	Oared Fighting Ships, 1962
Anson, Peter F	Fishermen and Fishing Ways, 1932
Antiquity	Medieval Skin Boat, Paul Johnstone, 1962
	Bantry Boat, Paul Johnstone, 1964
	Neolithic Explanations, Humphrey Case, 1969
	First British Navy, C E Dove, 1971
	Graveney Boat, Angela Care Evans and Valerie H Fenwick, 1971
	Bronze Age Sea Trial, Paul Johnstone, 1972
	Camouflage in the first British Navy, L Tavender, 1972
	Iron Age Camps in Northwestern France, R E M Wheeler, 1939
Atkinson, R J C	Stonehenge and Avebury, 1959
Barraclough, Geoffrey (Ed.)	Eastern and Western Europe in the Middle Ages, 1970
Basch, Lucien	'Ancient Wrecks and the Archaeology of Ships', 1972 (International Journal of Nautical Archaeology)
Belloc, Hilaire	The Old Road, 1911
	William the Conqueror, 1933
Birley, Anthony	Septimus Severus, 1971
Blair, Peter Hunter	Roman Britain and Early England, 1963
Brandon, R J	South Biscay Pilot, 1971
Brogger, A W and Haakon Shetelig	The Viking Ships, 1951
Brøndsted, Johannes	The Vikings, 1960

Brown, R Allen	The Normans and the Norman Conquest, 1969
Bruce-Mitford, Rupert	The Sutton Hoo Ship Burial, 1972
Buchan, John	Julius Caesar, 1932
Calvert, Roger	Inland Waterways of Europe, 1963
Cameron, Ian	Lodestone and Evening Star, 1965
Campbell, Marion	Mid-Argyll, 1970
Chadwick, Nora	The Celts, 1970
Chapelle, H I	American Sailing Craft, 1936
Childe, V Gordon	Skara Brae, 1933
Christensen, Arne Emil jr	The Viking Ships, 1970
Clark, Grahame	Prehistoric Europe, the Economic Basis, 1952
Clark, Grahame and Stuart Piggott	Prehistoric Societies, 1965
Clark, Roy	Black-sailed Traders: The Keels and Wherries of Norfolk and Suffolk, 1961
Cole, Sonia	The Neolithic Revolution, 1959
Collingwood, R G	Archaeology in Roman Britain, 1969
Cotter, Charles H	A History of Nautical Astronomy, 1968
Cotterell, Leonard	The Great Invasion, 1958
	The Saxon Shore Forts, 1964
Coull, James R	The Fisheries of Europe, 1972
Craster, O E	Ancient Monuments of Anglesey, 1953
Cunliffe, Barry	Fishbourne, 1971
	Cradle of England, 1972
Cutting, Charles L	Fish Saving, 1955
Delmar-Morgan, Edward	Normandy Harbours and Pilotage, 1969
De Paor, Maire and Liam	Early Christian Ireland, 1958
Dillon, Myles and Nora Chadwick	The Celtic Realms, 1967
Douglas, David C	The Norman Achievement, 1972
Duckham, B F	Navigable Rivers of Yorkshire, 1964
Dudley, H E	The History and Antiquities of the Scunthorpe and Frodingham District, 1931
Duff, Wilson	'Thoughts on the Nootka Canoe' (Provincial Museum British Columbia, Report for 1964)
Dyer, James	Southern England: An Archaeological Guide, 1973
East Riding Antiquarian Society	Transactions, 1910 (Brigg boat)
Emery, W B	Archaic Egypt, 1961
Everyman Classic	The Saga of Grettir the Strong
Fox, Uffa	Sailing, Seamanship and Yacht Construction, 1934
Frost, Honor	Under the Mediterranean, 1963
Glob, P V	The Bog People, 1969
Gogarty, Oliver St John	I Follow St Patrick, 1938
Graham, Donald	The House of Islay, 1967
Grant, Michael	Julius Caesar, 1969
Green, Charles	Sutton Hoo, 1963

Greenhill, Basil   Boats and Boatmen of Pakistan, 1971
Grimble, Rosemary   Migrations, Myth and Magic from the
                                      Gilbert Islands, 1972
Hadfield, Charles   The Canal Age, 1968
Hagen, Anders   The Viking Ship Finds, 1968
                                  Norway, 1967
Hamilton, J R C   Jarlshof, 1953
Harvey, John   The Master Builder, 1971
Hawkins, Gerald S   Stonehenge Decoded, 1966
Heaps, Leo   The Log of the Centurion, 1974
Henderson, Isabel   The Picts, 1967
Hodges, Henry   Technology in the Ancient World, 1970
Hornell, James   Water Transport, 1946
                                  British Coracles and Irish Curraghs, 1938
Hornell, James and   Canoes of Oceania, 1936
  A C Haddon
Hutchinson, R W   Prehistoric Crete, 1962
Ingolstadt, Herga   Land in the North, 1965
Jankuhn, Herbert   Nydam und Thorsberg, 1964
Kitto, H D F   The Greeks, 1951
Klindt-Jensen, Ole   Denmark before the Vikings, 1957
Knight, E F   Small Boat Sailing, 1901
Kuhn, Herbert   The Rock Pictures of Europe, 1966
Laird Clowes, G S   Sailing Ships, Vols 1 and 2, 1932
                                  British Fishing and Coastal Craft, 1937
Landstrom, Bjorn   Sailing Ships, 1969
Lasko, Peter   The Kingdom of the Franks, 1971
Lemmon, Charles H   The Field of Hastings, 1956
Leslie, R C   Waterbiography, ca 1870
Levy, C R   The Gate of Horn, 1948
Lewis, David   We the Navigators, 1973
Lewis, Archibald R   The Northern Seas, 1958
Liversidge, Joan   Britain in the Roman Empire, 1968
Lloyd, Alan   The Year of the Conqueror, 1966
Loyn, H R   Anglo-Saxon England and the Norman
                                      Conquest, 1962
Manley, Gordon   Climate and the British Scene, 1952
March, Edgar J   Inshore Craft of Great Britain, 1970
Marsden, P R V   A Roman Ship from Blackfriars, London,
                                      1964
Marstrander, Sverre   Ostfolds Jordbruksristninger: Skjeberg, 1963
Merrifield, Ralph   Roman London, 1969
Mongait, A L   Archaeology in the USSR, 1955
Monkhouse, F J   A Regional Geography of Western Europe,
                                      1959
Morley, George   The North Sea, 1968
Morrison, J S   Greek Oared Ships 900–322 BC, 1968
Morrison, Samuel Eliot   The European Discovery of America—
                                      Northern Voyages, 1971
National Maritime Museum   Maritime Monographs and Reports No. 1:
                                      Aspects of the History of Wooden
                                      Shipbuilding, 1972
Nature   Vol. 234   Weather, Vikings and Polynesians

Olsen, Olaf and Ole Crumlin-Pedersen — Vol. 233   Earliest cargo / The Skuldelev Ships, 1967

Ordnance Survey Maps (including facsimiles of first edition) — Ancient Britain, 1964 / Britain in the Dark Ages, 1971

Penguin Classics — Two Lives of Charlemagne / Beowulf / Laxdaela Saga / The Vinland Sagas / Njal's Saga / King Harald's Saga / The Agricola and Germania, Tacitus / The Annals of Imperial Rome, Tacitus / The Histories, Tacitus / The Twelve Caesars, Suetonius / A History of the English Church and People, Venerable Bede / The Conquest of Gaul, Julius Caesar / Lives of the Saints

Philipsen, J P — 'The Utrecht Ship' (Mariner's Mirror, 1965)

Phillips-Birt, Douglas — Waters of the Wight, 1965 / Fore and Aft Sailing Craft, 1962 / The Naval Architecture of Small Craft, 1957

Piggott, Stuart — Ancient Europe, 1965

Pirenne, Henri — Mohammed and Charlemagne, 1939

Powell, T G E — Prehistoric Art, 1966

Raftery, Joseph — Prehistoric Ireland, 1951

Ramskou, Thorkild — Prehistoric Denmark, Copenhagen, 1966

Rantzen, M J — English Channel Tides, 1969

Reed's Nautical Almanac

Richmond, I A — Roman Britain, 1963

Rigold, S E — Portchester Castle, 1969

Runciman, Steven — A History of the Crusades, 1971

Scott, J M — Gino Watkins, 1935

Sherwin, Keith — Man-powered Flight, 1971

Small, Alan — Excavations in Unst, 1965

Smith, C T — A Historical Geography of Western Europe before 1800, 1967

Smith, John Captain — A Sea Grammar, 1627 (1970 edition)

Souter, William Clark — The Story of our Kayak and Some Others, 1933

Steers, J A — The Sea Coast, 1953

Stenton, Sir Frank — Anglo-Saxon England, 1971 / The Bayeux Tapestry, 1957

Taylor, E G R — The Haven-finding Art, 1971

Thom, A — Megalithic Monuments in Britain, 1968

Thomas, Charles — Britain and Ireland in Early Christian Times, 1971

Tibbets, G R — 'Stellar Navigation in the Medieval Indian Ocean', 1972 (Journal of The Institute of Navigation, USA)

Transactions of Institution of Naval Architects — Speed/length ratios, 1953

Trueman, A E — Geology and Scenery in England and Wales, 1971

Tylecote, R F — Metallurgy in Archaeology, 1962

Voss, Captain — The Venturesome Voyages of Captain Voss, 1901

Wainwright, F T (ed) — The Northern Isles, 1962

Warmington, B H — Carthage, 1960

Warrington-Smythe, H — Mast and Sail in Europe and Asia, 1906

Webster, Graham and Donald R Dudley — The Roman Conquest of Britain, 1965

Whitelock, Dorothy — The Beginnings of English Society, 1952

Whitelock, Dorothy (ed) — Anglo-Saxon Chronicle

Wilson, David — The Vikings and their Origins, 1970

Winbolt, S E — Britain BC, 1943

Worcester, G R G — Sail and Sweep in China, 1966

Wright, E V and D M Churchill — 'The Boats from North Ferriby, Yorkshire, England', 1965 (Proceedings of the Prehistoric Society)

Index

Index to Persons

Index to Places